A Front Row Seat
The Impeachment of
Rod Blagojevich

The cards I was dealt and lessons learned

By Roger Eddy

SonofIllinois—Hutsonville, IL
ISBN: 978-1-7349992-1-1
Title: *A Front Row Seat: The Impeachment of Rod Blagojevich*
Author: Roger Eddy
Digital distribution | 2020
Paperback | 2020
Hardcover | 2020

First Edition - 2020

Published in the United States by New Book Authors Publishing

Dedication

This book is dedicated to my wife, Becca.

Throughout our forty years of marriage, she has sustained me every step of the way. Through all of the campaigns, long hours performing two jobs and the often crazy schedule during my ten years in the General Assembly, she has been the constant. Could not have done it without her love and support

Table of Contents

Chapter One
The World Was Watching

There he was, the man it seemed as though the entire world was watching. As he strolled towards the witness table in room 114 of the Illinois State Capitol, from my elevated view, I studied his demeanor. Quite a crowd had gathered for the long-anticipated appearance of this witness who would provide critical insight and testimony.

On January 8, 2009, not unlike all of the other mornings that we met as the Special Investigative Committee, security was tight. It was especially rigid getting into the Capitol and security was even tighter in the corridors that led to the hearing room. However, unlike the previous days, the place was packed and teemed with cameras, television crews, and onlookers. It was easily the largest crowd that had gathered so far to hear testimony regarding the work of our committee.

This Special Investigative Committee included twenty-one republicans and democrats from the Illinois House of Representatives and had been assembled to determine whether there was enough evidence to recommend to the full House that the Governor of Illinois, Rod Blagojevich, should be IMPEACHED.

Other previous testimony was important to the work of our committee, but this man found himself in the middle of a huge controversy. After all, he had been named to the Senate seat as the replacement for President-elect Barack Obama that was at the epicenter of one of the most scurrilous charges against the accused governor.

This date marked exactly one month since the second term sitting Governor of Illinois had been arrested at his home by the FBI. Their investigation of his wrongdoings had begun five years earlier, prior to his 2006 re-election over three-term Illinois State Treasurer Judy Topinka.

Topinka had attempted to make the 2006 election about the ethics of her opponent, Blagojevich. Ironically, negative ads about Topinka that tied her to fellow convicted Republican, and former Illinois Governor George Ryan, took their toll. Fueled by millions of campaign dollars, Blagojevich garnered 49.8% of the vote. It was not a majority, but a plurality that put Blagojevich into his second term. Topinka managed just 39.3% of the vote and a third-party candidate, Rich Whitney from the Green Party, received an impressive 10.4% of the vote. The negative ads about both major party candidates had pushed many voters to choose the 'alternative' candidate.

The federal investigation of Blagojevich included evidence obtained from hidden microphones planted in the Blagojevich campaign office as well as hundreds of hours of phone taps. *Operation Board Games* was the name given to the federal investigation that, in the end, provided enough evidence to eventually unseat a sitting governor and send him to federal prison for fourteen years. The governor was given the code name, "Elvis", during the investigation due to his often referred to love for the famous entertainer.

At 6 a.m. on December 8th, 2008, federal agents phoned the landline at the governor's Chicago residence. Some of the agents were waiting across the street, and others were already right outside of his door. The call informed Blagojevich that the FBI had a federal warrant for his arrest and that he had five minutes to open the door and come out or agents would come in. Because the governor had two minor children asleep in the home, major disruption could be avoided if he would simply step outside. Blagojevich loudly inquired of the agents, "Was this a joke?" But this was not a joke, and minutes later, as he stepped outside, federal agents cuffed him, read him his rights and informed him that he would be coming with them to the Chicago Federal Courthouse.

One month later, here we were. The man selected by Rod Blagojevich to replace Barack Obama as United States Senator from Illinois, Roland Burris, had entered the hearing room to a bevy of flashing cameras, microphones and reporters. And there I was.....in the front row! I couldn't help but consider the importance of this moment. This was the first time in the nearly two hundred year history of Illinois that a governor was the subject of Impeachment hearings. In fact, in the history of the entire United States, Impeachments like this had been extremely rare.

Illinois has become infamous for their Governors being imprisoned after holding office. As we were in the midst of this investigation, Blagojevich's predecessor, George Ryan was still sitting in prison, serving out his five year sentence for federal corruption. Two other Illinois governors had also been sentenced to and served prison time. Otto Kerner was governor from 1961-1968 but resigned from the office to become a judge. He was later convicted of bribery related to his time

2

as Illinois governor and was sentenced to three years in prison. Dan Walker, Illinois Governor from 1973-1977 plead guilty to bank fraud committed after leaving office. He spent about a year and a half in federal prison. It appeared as though Blagojevich may join the disgraced ranks and be the fourth Illinois governor to serve time in prison.

As Roland Burris was sworn in and seated himself at the witness table to provide testimony, the cameras moved in and C-SPAN covered the testimony live, I sat there and wondered to myself, "How in the world did I end up in the front row?"

(Roland Burris sworn in before House Impeachment Committee- Eddy photo)

Chapter Two
Shuffling the Deck

The year was 2001, sometime in mid to late October; around six weeks after four U.S. domestic airplanes had been hijacked by nineteen hijackers. Two of the planes were crashed into the World Trade Center Towers, the twin towers in New York City, a third plane crashed into the Pentagon in Washington, DC. A fourth plane was commandeered by heroic passengers and crashed purposely into a rural area of Pennsylvania, and with the immortal words, "Let's roll," potentially thousands of additional lives were saved. George W. Bush had been elected President a year or so earlier, in November of 2000. The United States was rallying to respond to the attack of September 11th and patriotism was at a fever pitch. Back in January of 2001, Apple introduced iTunes (followed soon by iPod), and Microsoft Windows XP came along later that year. It was the year of anthrax attacks, the death of Dale Earnhart during a practice lap at Daytona and the year the, "Shoe Bomber", Richard Reid, attempted to blow up a plane by hiding a bomb in his sneaker. Wikipedia made its' debut, and folks went to watch *Ocean's Eleven*, *Shrek* and *A Beautiful Mind* at the box office. *Friends, Survivor, ER, The West Wing* and *King of the Hill* became popular on television.

Like hundreds of other days at Hutsonville CUSD # 1, this particular morning started quietly with familiar routines unfolding. Students were stepping off of school busses and dutifully marching toward the two buildings that are the daytime domicile of about four hundred kids ranging from grades prekindergarten through twelfth in this rural community nestled along the Wabash River in east-central Illinois. Routines are good for kids of all ages. Students not riding the yellow buses either drove to school or were dropped off by parents at appointed areas. All students knew exactly where they were supposed to go once they landed on school grounds and I watched them as they made their way to the designated stations. I was not the only eyes on the students as they moved about. There were dozens of aides, teachers and others keeping an eye on the morning routine. Of course, this all made me happy to watch. As the superintendent of this school district, I was always interested in watching the daily routines unfold with proper supervision and without a hitch. Yep, routine it was and routine I liked. However, as I soon found out, this day was going to be anything but routine.

I walked towards my office as the students continued to meet their day. As always, I grabbed a fresh cup of coffee, and said good morning to my secretary Lori Crumrin. Some years later, she and all others in this position, became known as Administrative Assistants. No matter what her title was, she was definitely much more than a title. If the title was an accurate one, it would be, 'glue'. Lori and her counterparts are the ones that truly hold things together in a school system.

As always, I could count on Lori for a smile, a greeting and reminders of any meetings scheduled for the day, reports that were due or messages that needed to be returned. This day, there was nothing pressing so I sat at my desk and began to work on the calculations necessary to prepare the annual property tax levy. This was one of several routine items that were included on the November Board of Education meeting agenda. While it was routine, it was a tricky calculation due to the way education is funded in Illinois. It required a series of guesswork as to the assessed fair market value of various property classifications to determine the amount to levy to establish a tax rate by the fund and an overall rate to fund district operations. Hutsonville is a rural community and one of several small villages, along with West Union, York, Old York and Annapolis, which make up the district. The district is about 15 miles long and 12 miles wide.

Most of the total property value is farmland, although little of the farmland is considered valuable compared to the rich farmland of central Illinois. None the less, the farmland value calculation was important for the levy process. From that point, more guesswork and estimations are necessary to complete the tentative levy to present it during a public meeting before the November Board meeting. Never mind the full explanation of the levy process, rest assured that while it is tricky and involves some guesswork it is not, as they say, rocket science.

I gathered information to calculate the levy for a couple of hours and then heard the phone ring. A moment later, Lori asked if I had time to chat with Steve McGahey and Bev Turkal.

Steve was a local business owner in nearby Robinson and Bev was a retired school superintendent. Bev just couldn't stay retired. Some people flunk retirement. She served as an interim school superintendent after her retirement, also became the manager of the local country club (Quail Creek), and later the President of our local Community College (Lincoln Trail). I knew Bev well and considered her a friend and colleague, someone I bounced questions off of during my early years of being a superintendent. She was a mentor. I did not know Steve well, just knew of him. But, of course I would meet with them. In fact, they could come over that morning. I was ready to take a break from the tax levy.

I began to wonder what they could want. After a few moments, I speculated they wanted to discuss the idea of consolidating the four county school districts into one district.

For years, many people thought consolidation, "Had to happen." Enrollments numbers in the four school districts (all K-12 unit districts) were declining, special education and vocational education programs were already shared and many people thought consolidation would streamline costs and result in more money for classrooms rather than administration, plus property taxes might be lowered. I was actively involved with a group called *The Committee of Ten* that was meeting to determine if just two of the four county school districts, Palestine and Hutsonville, should combine. Our two school districts had cooped football for many years and many thought it was time to see if at least these two could combine into one district.

I was reminded of the irony that I was working on the property tax levy at the exact time Steve and Bev were coming to visit me. I had now convinced myself that they wanted to talk about how important consolidation was to the entire county. That had to be it. Steve was active in the Chamber of Commerce and Bev was considered the education expert in the county and they were coming to discuss how important consolidation was to the future of Crawford County.

For as many that were pro-consolidation though, there were at least as many who were not. Small school districts wanted to remain independent and the truth is that the hardest thing to kill is a school mascot. Years of tradition and love for the alma mater had trumped earlier efforts to combine the four districts. The Tigers of Hutsonville, the Pioneers of Palestine and the Panthers of Oblong were not going to be combined to become a large county school without a fight, especially combining with the Maroons of Robinson. To most community members, Robinson (the largest of the four) would be seen as simply trying to take over the other schools and they would fight any takeover tooth and nail. Some people thought that perhaps two of the districts (Hutsonville and Palestine) had a better chance of combining alone along the eastern side of the county.

Almost everyone believed that Oblong would never agree to consolidation with Robinson. My Board of Education seemed committed to keeping a high school in Hutsonville as long as they could offer quality education, and stay in good shape financially while keeping property taxes relatively stable. As I imagined how difficult any effort at combining any of these four school districts would be, Lori tapped on the door and announced that Steve and Bev had arrived.

Steve shook my hand and Bev gave me a familiar hug and sat down. As she sat down, Bev declared that she would bet that I could never guess why they were in my office. When she said that, my earlier thoughts that the meeting must be about consolidation were wiped away. I had to quickly admit that if they were not going to try to discuss consolidating schools then I had no idea why they were there. No sir, this was not going to be a routine morning after all.

Steve asked me how closely I followed politics. My answer was simple. While I had been a History Teacher and taught Government courses, I had not been involved in or paid much attention to politics. When he asked me if I were a registered Republican or Democrat, I told him that I guess I was neither. I wasn't even sure what he meant by registered. I had voted for people I considered good people on both sides of the political aisle over the years. He wanted to know if I had been watching the redistricting of the "map" and noticed that Crawford County was going to be in a new legislative district which did not have an incumbent State Representative. I had to admit that I had not known that. I did know who our current State Representative was (Dale Righter) but admitted that I assumed that Dale would continue to reside in the new District and run for office once again as our Representative. Steve was doing a great job of informing me about the new legislative map and that this was now an open seat. I still had no idea why they were in my office except, I suppose, to provide me with this civics lesson?

Bev knew me pretty well and could tell by the confused look on my face that I was having a hard time trying to figure out why they were in my office. She looked at me and said, "Roger, you don't understand why we are here, do you?" I admitted that I initially believed they were there to discuss a county-wide school consolidation and to try to convince me

7

that we should drop the idea of just a two school consolidation and support the consolidation of the entire county.

The confusing part was they wanted me to know about the county getting a new State Representative. I admitted I had no real clue as to what they wanted. After laughing off the notion that they were there to get me to support county-wide consolidation, she said it, "Well, we are here representing some other businessmen, and along with them, we think you should run for State Representative in this newly formed legislative district."

Say what?!

Chapter Three
Arranging the Cards

I was dumbfounded at the suggestion that I run for State Representative. The thought of running for a state office had never, nor would have never entered my mind before this visit.

Nonetheless, what seemed preposterous initially began to seem like a possibility, or maybe even a good idea somewhere in my subconscious. As a former History and Government Teacher, I certainly revered the institutions which make up our government. I taught my students the value of civic involvement. The contributions of notable historical figures left me in awe of the brilliance that led to this unique experiment in government we call the United States.

The history and struggles of this great experiment leading us to become the greatest nation on earth are something that I have always respected about our American heritage. From the Revolution against Great Britain, the Continental Congress and Articles of Confederation, and all of the brilliant compromises that resulted in The United States Constitution, this great Nation has not only endured, but it has led the world. For over two hundred years of changing times and challenges this form of government has met every challenge. A Civil War did not end the Republic and foreign threats were turned away in two World Wars. Yet, here I was, contemplating whether or not I would attempt to become an elected representative *of the people* within that great structure.

The sacrifices of millions of soldiers also formed my love for this great nation.

My father, Harold Eddy Jr., was a Marine and proud veteran of the Korean War. He taught me at a young age to respect and hold my freedom dear and to realize that freedom was not free. He taught me to respect those who had fought, sacrificed and died to secure it. As a youngster, each Memorial Day and Veteran's Day dad would get my brother and me out of bed, before daybreak, so we could place hundreds of American flags at the final resting places of veterans. These people, from our small communities, were laid to rest at several cemeteries scattered throughout the countryside of the villages of my rural northern Illinois childhood home. I distinctly remember reading some of the headstones of those who had died and it struck me that some of those who had sacrificed their lives were teenagers, killed in action to secure the opportunities that now lay ahead of me. Dad made sure that these veterans were not only remembered but revered. Although many of the lessons I learned from him involved things other than patriotism and love of country, these early memories came back to me. As I contemplated the idea of serving in office, I thought about my upbringing and felt a nudge towards running for office.

There was also my father-in-law, James Brooks. He enlisted in the Marine Corp as a North Dakota teenager to fight in World War II. He experienced combat at the most intense levels as part of the infamous Island Hopping campaign in Japan. Later, his deal with God, as he dug into a foxhole at the front lines, brought him to the ministry. "Get me out of here alive and my life is yours." I still cherish the many hours I spent with Jim talking about the war, his deep love for America and his great desire for the U.S. to thrive. He was somewhat hesitant to discuss much about his contributions to WWII as a soldier, as many of this greatest generation are. He recalled other horrific memories of combat with tears at the corner of his eyes. To him, he saw the *real heroes* lose their lives and he considered himself fortunate.

How fortunate I was to have two former soldiers who loved this nation as influencers in my life.

During college, at both Joliet Junior College and Northern Illinois University, I was fortunate enough to have professors who brought to life the rich and colorful story of this country. Unknown to those great teachers, they steered me in the direction of teaching History.

What an incredible and unlikely story it was that shaped our nation. It seemed that most of the real sacrifices had been made and I was a benefactor of those sacrifices and those brilliant enough to form the foundations of the United States. It is the responsibility of each new generation to maintain the greatness established by those preceding them.

I was active in professional organizations and had previously provided testimony before the Illinois House and Senate. There was no question I had strong opinions about the direction in which public policy should go in Illinois, especially regarding public education. On several occasions I had contacted our own State Representative voicing my opinion about a variety of legislative proposals.

For example, the education funding formula in Illinois at that time resulted in a terribly inequitable education for many children. The quality of one's education depended largely on their zip code. Per pupil spending in Illinois varied from as much as $25K per student to less than $5K per student at that time. I knew that this formula had to change and a more equitable funding formula was needed. Potentially, with a seat in the legislature, perhaps I could help advance a change.

Maybe this **was** something that I was supposed to do? My dad and father-in-law were both still alive at the time so I asked for their input. Not to my surprise, both of them were very much in favor of the idea. My dad did warn me about the dirty, negative side of politics and asked me if I was prepared to experience the potential ugliness of politics. The truth is that I wasn't sure what that meant at the time. How bad could it be? I have since come to find out how ugly politics can become.

Of course, there were many doubts in my mind as well. Except for Student Council Representative in high school, a seat on the Illinois High School Association Board, and being elected as one of the Directors of the Illinois Principal's Association a few years earlier, the only other position I ever had was as a Hutsonville Village Trustee. The Village Trustee position had been a decade earlier. But Bev Turkal's words continued to replay in my head: "We are here representing some other local businessmen, and along with them, we think you should run for State Representative in this newly formed legislative district."

My initial response to Steve and Bev was that I was an educator. Fresh out of college, I did obtain an insurance license and sold insurance door to door in the summer. I continued to sell insurance part-time in my early years of teaching. And, I, like most, had a variety of other jobs including making pizzas at a pizza place called Suzie's. But by now, I had been a teacher, coach, high school principal and superintendent for almost twenty years. During those summers, I would paint and perform yard work for extra money. Education was the world I had known and the world that I felt comfortable in and enjoyed. The work was challenging and very rewarding.

My wife Becca and I had five great children. Becca was an Early Childhood teacher and we both loved our work. Our five children all attended Hutsonville schools with our oldest in his junior year. I was

11

as *comfortable* as an educator. I knew what I was doing and the school was doing great. Our school district test scores were considered very good, and Hutsonville had been designated as an Illinois Blue Ribbon School District by the State Board of Education. Financially, despite a funding formula that provided very little equitable support, things were stable for CUSD # 1. Besides, the school district had recently been awarded a school construction grant from the State of Illinois to build a new high school. Pending the passage of local referendum that would provide for twenty-five percent of the cost, the state would pay seventy-five percent of the amount needed for this once in a lifetime multi-million dollar project.

In addition, I was in the middle of that effort to determine if the two small school districts of Hutsonville and Palestine, on the east side of Crawford County, should combine through consolidation and form one district. It was hard to imagine doing anything else with my career other than being involved in education and being a dad to five very active and growing kids.

Despite all of this, when Bev asked me if I would think about it before I said no, I agreed to let it roll around in my head for a few days and get back to her. After all, it was flattering to be asked and part of me liked the idea of providing a voice for education as a member of the legislature. I always advised young people to keep an open mind about their future and to never say no when you might say yes. I promised her that I would sincerely think about the idea. I knew one thing was for sure, this was too big of a decision to say yes or no to without talking it over with Becca and our family. I understood it was a decision that would define our future.

After Steve and Bev left, Lori came into my office with a couple of routine messages.

I wasn't sure I should say anything to her about the conversation with Steve and Bev. I was so distracted; she knew something was on my mind. I had to tell her about the conversation that had just occurred.

Just as I was finishing filling Lori in, one of our local school board members came into the district office. Fred Clatfelter had been a long time board member at Hutsonville and one of the main reasons I returned to Hutsonville to become superintendent. I began my career at Hutsonville as a teacher and coach and a few years later became a high school principal there. When a job closer to where I grew up in Northern

Illinois came open, I left to become the principal of a larger high school closer to where I grew up.

I was the principal at Watseka High School for five years. The five years at Watseka are filled with great memories. Together with a terrific staff, wonderful supportive parents and great students, we established a culture of *Warrior Pride.*

The superintendent at Watseka was a guy named Martin Getty. Marty was the superintendent at nearby Palestine in Crawford County prior to leaving there and eventually became the Superintendent at Watseka. Marty was a terrific mentor and became one of my best friends. Soon after he retired, Marty passed away much too young of cancer.

During the five years I was away from Hutsonville, Fred stayed in contact with me. In those five years, the superintendent who had been at Hutsonville for over fifteen years, retired. His name was Gary Matteson. Gary was the superintendent when I was initially hired at Hutsonville. After Gary's retirement, Hutsonville went through two Superintendents in four years, both seizing opportunities in bigger districts. When the position opened up a third time, Fred contacted me. At that time, I was completing my endorsement and certification that would allow me to be a superintendent. Fred urged me to apply and was my biggest fan during the hiring process.

Fred was a very active and committed board member and often stopped by to see how things were going. He was also very politically active in local party politics. Fred served on the Board of Directors of the Illinois Association of School Boards for several years. When Fred came and casually asked how things were going. Lori, known to come to the point replied, "Oh nothing much, Roger is going to be a State Representative." At that point, I strongly disputed Lori's comment. I told Fred about the conversation that occurred earlier with Steve and Bev. I insisted that it was a crazy idea and I wanted to stay in education, I enjoyed what I was doing and didn't want to give up my role as superintendent to become a legislator. Case closed.

Or, was it?

To my surprise, Fred liked the possibility of me running for State Representative. He told me that I should think about it and that it would be a chance to highlight education in the legislature and perhaps work on some important funding changes for rural schools. I was concerned about many things at that point. I insisted that I would not give up my work in education to become a State Representative; I wanted to remain at

Hutsonville as Superintendent and finish the things I had started there. Fred agreed and thought I could do both.

The seed had been planted for sure. But, I needed to talk with other board members and, most importantly, I needed to talk with Becca and my family before I called Bev back.

Our life was full. Becca was an Early Childhood program director and teacher. We were blessed with five very active children. Life was great. The staff at Hutsonville was fantastic, and my Board of Education allowed me to manage the district without a hint of micro-management. The board established policies, held various committee meetings and worked hard to develop budgets that made the best use of limited resources. They performed the way a board is supposed to. I could not imagine a better place to raise my kids. Much of the reason we had returned to Hutsonville was to raise our family in that small town, rural environment.

The evening of the visit with Bev and Steve, Becca and I were at the residence of my brother in law and his family. During idle chit chat, I recounted the visit earlier that day about the possibility of my running for State Representative. The response was as expected to an idea that had come out of the clear blue. There were lots of questions. I explained what had been explained to me including some of the details. This was a newly formed district and our current State Representative no longer would reside within the new district. There was not an incumbent of any kind residing within the district. My brother-in-law, John Brooks knew more about the map and legislative district than I did.

After listening to the account of my morning meeting, the main question from John was whether or not I would be prepared to leave my current job and run for State Rep. In a blink I said, "No way." If I had any thoughts of running for the legislature, it would only be if I could continue my work in education. This discussion went on for several minutes with no definitive resolution. What shifted in my mind was that this idea was worthy of more thought and should not be quickly dismissed. We left for home with our minds swirling.

It is funny how things like this tend to disrupt sleep and make the mind race. That night, I don't think either Becca or I slept soundly. There was so much to think about all of a sudden. How would this work? Most importantly, how could I do both jobs? Was it possible to be a school superintendent and State Representative at the same time? Would I enjoy the role, what would I miss? What exciting new challenges could be in store? There were way too many thoughts, way too many questions for our minds rest to sleep well. At some point during the restless sleep, Becca woke up, woke me up and said, "I think you should do it."

Sometimes, a single day can make such a huge difference in the course of a lifetime. I knew this was one of those days

Chapter Four
A Pair of Jacks

Jack Chamblin and Jack Morris were two very politically connected businessmen from Robinson, Illinois. Robinson is the county seat of Crawford County and located just about 200 miles south of Chicago. With a population of around 7,000 as of the 2010 census, while Robinson is the largest populated town in Crawford County; it is by no definition a big town. Notably, it is home to Marathon Oil Refinery which provides over 600 very good-paying jobs for area residents. It was also the place that Heath Candy bars were invented and current NBA player, Meyers Leonard, attended high school. In addition, it is the hometown and birthplace of author James Jones. He wrote the famous novels, *From Here to Eternity* and *The Red Thin Line.* A local Country Club and Resort, Quail Creek, is widely known and was once a stop on the PGA Tour in the 1960s.

Both Chamblin and Morris were well known in the county and the region for their forays into politics. They operated through a political action committee (PAC) known as CRAW-PAC. This organization had previously supported candidates for office, including several previous Illinois Governors. It was my understanding, from Bev and Steve, that these two men were primarily responsible for the visit to my office. During a recent meeting, it seems that Bev, Steve and the pair of Jacks were discussing the new Illinois legislative maps which had been approved by the Illinois General Assembly.

Every ten years, after the census is taken, new legislative districts are established as per the U.S. and Illinois Constitution. CRAW-PAC, led by Chamblin and Morris, had an eye on selecting and supporting someone from Crawford County to run for the House of Representatives. In their mind, the new map boundaries created a great opportunity. In previous elections, the group had attempted to have an individual elected from Crawford County and fell short.

The newly drawn 109th legislative district did not have an incumbent State Representative living within these new boundaries. That fact would make it easier for a new person to be elected since an incumbent would hold a clear advantage. The former State Representative for this area, Chuck Hartke, resided outside the boundaries of the new 109th legislative district. Hartke was a Democrat and had served in the Illinois House for a long time. He would have been very difficult to defeat. The Jacks had already supported a candidate who had lost to Hartke, but this time there was no such concern. No incumbent in the new district meant a lot.

The four primary CRAW-PAC decision-makers met in the office of Jack Chamblin's Bradford Supply Company and discussed potential candidates. They were intent on supporting someone from Crawford County in this new district. The 109th legislative district included all or parts of eight counties in southeastern Illinois. The counties included all of Crawford, Clark Cumberland and Lawrence, most of Edgar County, plus portions of Effingham, Wabash and Shelby.

I was not at the meeting but understood that several names were brought up and dismissed for various reasons. Jack Morris mentioned that he had recently heard me speak at a meeting that took place at our local community college, Lincoln Trail College. I honestly do not remember which meeting that was but years later, Jack Morris told me the meeting regarded technology, the Internet, and the potential effect that technology could have on our rural area. In any event, the speech impressed him and from that single encounter, my name was brought up by Jack Morris at the first meeting.

Of course, Bev knew me from our work in education and Steve McGahey also knew me as Superintendent of the Hutsonville School District and the pending consolidation discussions with Palestine School District. Steve, who owned a business in Robinson, was a long-time resident of the Palestine school district. He was very active in and supportive of education issues both in Palestine and in the county. Whatever the combination of reasons was, the four settled on my name as a potential candidate. Steve and Bev were dispatched to meet with me to determine if I had any interest.

I decided to call Bev back a few days after the initial meeting and informed her that, surprisingly, although I was not ready to say I wanted to run, I was interested in further discussion. Bev was excited and suggested that the next step would be a meeting with the influential Pair of Jacks.

The meeting with Chamblin, Morris, Steve, and Bev took place in the same office that was used by the four for the initial discussion of whom should run. Jack Chamblin's office was in the back of a large building in Robinson near Marathon Petroleum Company. His lucrative and quite successful business, Bradford Supply Company, serviced the oil industry in the region. I met Steve and Bev in the reception area and after a few minutes, we were escorted to the very back of the building to the office of Jack Chamblin.

When I walked in, the room was thick with cigar smoke. A stocky blue-eyed man stood up to greet me. Chamblin was a former football player at the University of Illinois and it was obvious that he was a former athlete. Also in that room was a man I had never met before. We were at the same meeting at the community college. His name was Jack Morris. I knew Morris was the son of Mary Heath Morris and was connected to the famous Heath family. I also knew that he ran a very successful investment company called Heath Investment Capital. So, there they were, in the back corner of a smoky office, my pair of Jacks. Talk about being introduced to politics in the proverbial smoke-filled room!

I can't remember the entire conversation. I do remember my initial impressions of these two men who would soon become a very important part of my future, and therefore, the future of my family. They both struck me as highly successful and intelligent men. Jack Chamblin was very obviously a man who minced no words and came to the point. He was a decision-maker and someone you would want on your side if there was a looming battle. He was a tough guy, no question. Chamblin had contacts everywhere and was mainly responsible for helping bring a state prison to Robinson. Several governors had visited Chamblin's Hilltop Ranch. I came to respect him very quickly as he seemed to command respect, and I quickly understood why some people were intimidated by him.

Jack Morris was well-read and politically astute and connected. He was the one that had studied the new map and determined the type of person that CRAW-PAC should support. He knew the history, demographics and political leaning of the new legislative district. It was obvious that Jack Morris had a keen understanding of what lay ahead. His knowledge of Illinois political history, especially of the GOP is second to none. He later became a valued mentor and advisor during the

18

time I was in office. We spoke often and his instincts were always spot on.

I must admit, I was impressed. The discussion that day was more of an interview during which the Jacks, plus Steve and Bev, could assess whether or not Jack Morris's keen intuition, in this case, was accurate. There were numerous questions. I suspected that they had discussed they were going to ask and which of the four would ask which question. Was I the right guy to support this office or had Morris been wrong. I felt like the meeting went well and that both of the Jacks indeed believed that I could be the right candidate. When the topic of my current position as superintendent came up, I made sure they both knew that if I ran, I wanted to continue to work in education. The meeting ended with nothing determined for sure. It was, as stated, more of an interview, but one that I thought had gone well. They stayed after I left to continue the discussion. This was serious business.

There was more to be done before there was a definite answer as to whether or not I would be a candidate. Apparently though, I had passed the initial interview phase. Within a week or so, Chamblin and Morris had arranged for me to meet with some of their powerful Republican friends.

First, we went to the University of Illinois to meet with former Illinois Governor Jim Edgar. Edgar was a Fellow at the University of Illinois. I was a bit nervous when at that meeting. I had met Edgar years earlier when, as Governor, he visited Watseka High School while I was Principal there. When I reminded him of that tour, he kindly said he remembered that day. I am not so sure he did but for all I know, he might have. It made me feel good though that he said he did and he might have. He mentioned a few times that he counts heavily on the advice of his friends when making decisions about supporting candidates. It was very clear that Morris and Chamblin were his friends. That's about all I remember about that meeting in his office in Champaign. Jim Edgar was an icon in Illinois and I was just in awe of sitting in his office and discussing the possibility of running for office. Again, it seemed like a sort of continuation of the interview process and a chance for Morris and Chamblin to get feedback from someone they trusted.

The next meeting was to be held in Springfield at the State Capitol. Lee Daniels was the Minority Leader of the Illinois House of Representatives and someone that the Jacks thought I should meet. Daniels had first been elected in 1983 and his first election was in a newly drawn district. For a couple of years, from 1995-97, he was the Speaker of the Illinois House. The GOP had won a majority of house seats and Daniels was elected Leader by the House GOP Members. But that was short-lived. Michael Madigan once again became Speaker in 1997 when the Dems reclaimed the Illinois House. Madigan was a product of Chicago ward politics and had been a State Representative for decades (much more on Madigan later). Lee Daniels has been the only other Speaker of the Illinois House besides Madigan in the past nearly forty years. Daniels was an attorney by trade and a graduate of the John Marshall Law School. Well respected and successful, Daniels is currently a Fellow and senior advisor to the President of Elmhurst College.

So, we traveled together to the Capitol to meet with Daniels and were ushered through a maze of hallways back to a waiting area and then eventually summoned into a large, beautifully appointed office. When we entered, we sat and waited for the arrival of Leader Daniels. When he arrived, there was no mistaking that winning political smile and his perfect political demeanor. I had seen him on television several times. In-person, he was a handsome, professional-looking, well dressed and well-spoken man. It was not lost on me that he knew the two men who had escorted me to the meeting. Both Jacks were recognized by Daniels and they exchanged pleasantries before I was then introduced as the person they would like to see as a State Representative in the next General Assembly.

What followed was a couple of open-ended questions from Daniels. First, he wanted to know my background. Had I been involved in party politics? The answer was no. Had I been elected to other positions? Other than the Hutsonville Village Board, the answer was also no. Well then, what was my background? I told him about my professional and personal life.

He listened very intently; his eyes seemed to burn a hole in me. The only other question he then asked was, why? Why do you want to do this? What I did not reveal at that point was that I was not sure yet that I did want to run. What I told him was that I thought I could serve the people of the region well, with patriotism and a great desire to serve the public. I also added that I thought it would be good to have a practicing educator in the General Assembly. It became very apparent that we had a limited amount of time reserved with the Leader.

While he listened well, his time was valuable and it was soon time for him to greet another visitor. He told the two Jacks that he valued their opinions and that if they thought I was the person that should be supported, he would agree to help as much as he could for now. Since it was likely a contested primary, the assistance could not be official until after the Primary Election. With that, the meeting was over. We all shook hands and the three of us headed out of the Capitol to our car and back to Crawford County. The Jacks were extremely pleased with the meeting; it had gone well and surpassed their expectations.

These many years later, I just remember how in awe I was of Leader Daniels office. Nothing in the process so far had intimidated me. Although I can't describe the feeling I had while sitting in that office as intimidation, the feeling was one I will never forget. Perhaps the reality of what was happening was setting in.

I already met with State Representative Dale Righter who had been State Representative in part of the area that became a portion of the newly formed 109th District. He had decided to run for State Senate in the new 55th Senate District and not State Rep in the 110th Legislative District. Both the 109th and 110th Legislative Districts were encompassed by the new 55th Senate district. Dale was a lawyer and seemed like a perfect fit for public office. He was bright and articulate and had already made a great impression in Springfield as a State Representative. Our meeting went well and we got along great. He made no promises to publically support me in the primary election despite a little bit of pressure from the Jacks. He politely explained to me that it was just not something that normally happened in primaries. Understandably, he did not know me very well, and there was certainly no guarantee that I would win the primary if I chose to run. That could have put him in a difficult situation should someone else win. He would make himself available to answer questions though if I chose to run.

Another meeting took place in the office of Congressman Tim Johnson, also in Champaign. Bev Turkal and Steve McGahey accompanied me to that meeting. Johnson represented parts of the current legislative district as Congressman and he was running for re-election to Congress in the newly drawn Congressional District that included parts of the newly drawn 109th. The meeting went fine, although it was not nearly as memorable as the Edgar or Daniels meeting. He was rushed for sure and, as I recall, seemed to dissuade me from running.

On the ride home, Steve and Bev agreed that the meeting was not very productive. Johnson repeated the line about the primary and indicated that he would not be publically supporting any candidate during a primary. At one point in the meeting, he mentioned the need to have a fundraiser in Crawford County for his Congressional bid.

The time for meetings was over. The interviews had all gone well, but despite the lackluster feeling about the Johnson meeting, it was soon time to make a final determination. This was major decision could drastically change our lives.

Chapter Five
Ante Up

I had been dealt a pair of Jacks. It was soon time to make a final decision if I was going to draw to them or toss in the hand. The decision was delayed partially due to a lawsuit involving the proposed new legislative maps.

The gerrymandered map had been challenged in court with the final outcome of that litigation in limbo until late December of 2001 when the Illinois Supreme Court finally rendered a decision. Gerrymandering is the practice of drawing political boundaries in a clear attempt to favor one party over the other. Many believed this map was a clear case of gerrymandering created by the Democrat-controlled House. Legislative action took place back on May 31st of 2001 establishing the boundaries of the map, but leaders of the GOP took the proposed map to the court. Led by GOP State Representative Mark Beaubien as lead plaintiff, and supported by other GOP members of the General Assembly Rosemary Mulligan, Patricia Linder, Anne Zickes, Rick Winkel, and joined by Illinois Attorney General Jim Ryan, the Constitutionality of the proposed map was challenged in Court. The various legislative districts in the map were supposed to be compact and contiguous, among other criteria. This map did not appear to be either, at least according to the Republican Party.

This delay, in turn, caused delays across Illinois as far as formal announcements for office. In my case, for example, if the Court decided the Map needed to be redrawn, the possibility existed that an incumbent could be moved into the 109th Legislative District. That in turn, could eventually affect my decision. The same was true for all other lines and regions of the Illinois legislative map.

During that delay, I continued to schedule meetings. I was advised of the importance of meeting the leaders of the nine county's Republican Central Committees. Each of these Central Committees has a chair and precinct committeemen and women. Most of these committees met monthly to discuss issues related to their local party. I was provided a list of Chairmen, made phone calls to introduce myself to each of them and scheduled their next meeting on my calendar. In the meantime, there were more meetings with the four CRAW-PAC representatives. The Jacks were still cautiously making plans as everyone understood we could not wait much longer.

With my family firmly behind me, there was one more critical support network that I needed to secure. I had been completely firm in my resolve that if I was going to run for this office I would not end my work as superintendent at Hutsonville, which meant that I must have the full support of the Board and my staff.

In separate conversations, I discussed the idea with my Grade School Principal Guy Rumler, my High School Principal Rich Reynolds, and Lori Crumrin. I explained to each of them that the only way this would work should I be elected, would be for the Board to hire an Interim Superintendent to be present during the days I would be absent from the district. The fact is, it truly was impossible to do both jobs. The bulk of the time that the Illinois House would meet is the springtime, during Session. Session normally started in January and lasted until the end of May, with the legislature meeting around 45-50 days. This meant I would be gone from the school district at least that many days. While they had to wonder who the Interim Superintendent might be, all were supportive of the plan.

The Board of Education was also supportive. We discussed details including the fact that I would work around 171 days a year instead of the 220-230 days that I was currently working. It would be on a per diem basis and my pay would be reduced accordingly. The reduced pay would be used to pay an interim during the days that person filled in. I would also need to work some weekend days and holidays to get the job done. I would do my best to be available for all Board Meetings and still be heavily involved in decision making and developing monthly Board Meeting agendas.

Fred Clatfelter was supportive and excited about me running from the time he visited my office that October day when the idea was communicated by Steve and Bev. But, I needed the full Board to also support the decision. It was discussed at length during open board meetings and the entire staff of teachers, aides and support personnel were invited to weigh in. The entire staff was supportive without a single naysayer. At the end of all deliberations, in which the pros and cons were openly debated, the entire board would support my decision if I decided to run.

Board President, Tina Callaway, was outstanding in leading a detailed discussion which weighed the pros and cons of the arrangement. At the end of the discussion and thereafter, she was one of my strongest and crucial supporters. She stood up to some public critics. The early criticism came mostly from county Democrats whose main concern was that I was a strong candidate. In the coming years, when other critics came along, Tina continued to support the Board's decision. In much later campaigns, the attacks even became personal towards her but Tina never backed down. I truly regret the fact that Tina and others eventually became targets of cowardly political attacks.

Along with the support of my family, the support of the Board was necessary for me to get in the race, and we were getting closer to checking all of the boxes.

In early December, even though the Supreme Court decision regarding the map would not take place until late December, I made my run official. When the Supreme Court ruling was announced in favor of the map originally passed by the General Assembly by Chief Justice Moses Harrison, an eight-year veteran from downstate Collinsville, the decision was not unanimous. Both Justices Rita Garmin and Robert Thomas dissented but the map was upheld. The action was final December 27th, 2001, but that was simply too long to wait, the calendar pressured a decision and an announcement much sooner than that.

Behind the scenes, a campaign committee had been formed and registered with the State Board of Elections. People for Eddy would become the name of the committee. We had choices such as Citizens for Eddy, Citizens to Elect Roger Eddy, or perhaps Friends of Roger Eddy. But, at the end of the discussion, I chose the name. I had always believed in government by the people and for the people. Since nobody else had a strong opinion, it would be People for Eddy. One decision made, with about a million decisions to go.

The chairperson of the Committee would be Marie Pappageorge. Marie was the President of the Crawford County Republican Women's group and later served as President of the State Republican Women's Association. Fred Clatfelter would serve as Vice-Chair and Tina Callaway along with Bernie Gray as co-Treasurers. Bernie was the long time Mayor of Hutsonville, and a well-respected conservative Republican. Adding his name as Treasurer of People for Eddy provided a

25

great deal of credibility as Bernie was well-known throughout the area. Tina Callaway, as mentioned, was President of the Hutsonville Board of Education and President of the Farmers and Merchants Bank in Hutsonville. She was an active member of the County Republican Central Committee, bright as they come and could easily navigate the paperwork and reporting required by the State Board of Elections. The additional work had to be a pain at times but Tina never complained.

Everything seemed to be falling into place. While not publically announced, I had made my mind up during late November, during Thanksgiving, while our family was in the metro-Atlanta area visiting with my in-laws. My father-in-law, the Reverend James Brooks, was completely supportive and enthusiastic about the potential of having his son-in-law as a State Representative. If I had any doubts about running, his enthusiasm and a chance to rest over the holiday and think about the opportunity cemented my decision. When I returned to Hutsonville after Thanksgiving, I let everyone in the inner circle know that I would indeed be a candidate.

The decision was top secret while we waited for any forthcoming ruling regarding the map. The only thing that would change the decision was if an incumbent were moved into a new version of the map.

In early December, the official announcement of my candidacy was made. Press releases were prepared and I announced my candidacy among dozens of friends, family and supporters. That day, the local newspaper was on hand along with the radio station. My hat was officially in the ring, no turning back.

Eddy's ready

Roger Eddy announced his intention Monday to run as a Republican for state representative in the new 109th district. This district will take in all of Crawford, Clark, Lawrence, and Cumberland counties and almost all of Edgar County, the northern half of Wabash County and parts of Shelby and Effingham counties. Eddy, Unit 1 superintendent, announced his candidacy at the Hutsonville Elementary School Media Center because "education has been a very large part of my life for the past 21 years." Education and school funding reform will be a key message. "In Illinois, we spend over $30,000 per year to support the cost of housing each inmate in our prison system and less than $10,000 to educate each child in our public schools. It costs much more to send someone to the state pen than to send them to Penn State," Eddy said.

(My campaign announcement to run for State Representative-
Lisa Ulrey, *Robinson Daily News*)

The process of gathering petition signatures also started, and Fred Clatfelter coordinated this effort. We wanted to gather around 1500 valid signatures from throughout the eight counties, about triple the number required. The signatures would be reviewed for accuracy and filed on the first day of filing. It was little known that I delivered the completed petitions to lawyers on staff of the House Republican Organization for final evaluation in preparation for filing. HRO staff also stood in line and filed the petitions for me on the first day of filing. This was part of the behind the scenes support I was getting from the State GOP infrastructure that had been arranged by the pair of Jacks.

Jack Chamblin personally took care of securing an office for People for Eddy on Main Street in Robinson. He tossed me the keys to the office after calling me out to his Hilltop Ranch one day. I remember after catching the keys and getting back in my car for the ride home that things seemed very official now; keys and an office!

Jack Morris recommended a managing secretary for the campaign office. Her name was Kathleen Rankin. Morris said he thought she would be perfect for the role, and he was right. Kathleen proved to be a valuable and trusted member of the team. She, along with Fred, assembled a large group of volunteers to work day and night during the campaign. Kathleen secured a post office box for the campaign and we started to send fundraising appeals to friends and family.

All of this took money. As the father of five children, and never having contemplated running for an office like this, I did not have the personal wealth to fund my own campaign. I was very fortunate that dozens of friends and family members supported the effort by sending donations to help us with everyday expenses. Earlier in the process, the CRAW-PAC group assured me that if I decided to run, they would make sure money would not be an issue. They were true to their word and overnight over ten thousand dollars was received by People for Eddy. While most of those funds came from CRAW-PAC, I was also appreciative of the smaller dollar donations that friends and family had made.

Everything was coming together nicely it seemed. I had the support of people I knew well and trusted, folks that had been a big part of my career and life. Without having a trusted core, the early days of the campaign would have been very difficult. The one thing that we needed though was someone with campaign experience who could help us establish a plan and run the campaign in a credible, professional manner. While the help from Lee Daniels and the House GOP operation was appreciated behind the scenes, day to day campaign operations needed an experienced hand.

During the time deciding if I was going to run, I met Jay Ping, a bright young lawyer from Paris, Illinois. Jay was trying to determine if he was going to run for the House seat when I first talked to him. After chatting with me, Jay indicated that he would likely not run for the office. He asked me a few questions about my stance on some issues important to him and offered his support of my candidacy rather than running himself. Little did I know at the time how vitally important it would be to have Jay on my side

While discussing my campaign with Jay, I discovered that he had been active in political campaigns before. He worked on a statewide campaign in Missouri and understood what was necessary to run a well-organized and informative campaign. He was bright and articulate, a great writer who understood the issues important to the voters of the district. After some coaxing, he agreed to be my campaign manager.

It is hard to pinpoint one single event that was the most important thing that happened during the initial campaign. After all, this entire scenario was so unlikely. Suffice it to say that many people supported me that I could cite as necessary for future success. Jay becoming my campaign manager was a key element. His prior expertise and steady hand brought a sense of professionalism and calm to the operation. Many times, Jay talked me off a cliff or two, or three.

The rest of December and early January were filled with meetings almost every day after my school day ended. My school day was from 7:00 AM until about 4:00 PM. I liked to be at school monitoring the radios while the buses were out on routes. I attended the County Central Committee meetings in every County in the 109th District. The district was made up of all or parts of eight counties in this rural area. The counties, as mentioned, including all of Clark, Crawford, Lawrence, Cumberland, as well as portions of Effingham, Shelby, Edgar and Wabash counties. The newly approved 109th stretched from Mt. Carmel in the south to Chrisman in the north, a distance of about 110 miles from north to south. In the center of the long district, the east to west distance was around 90 miles and extended from Illinois' eastern border at the Wabash River to Shelbyville. I found out very quickly that if I was going to travel from Mt. Carmel to Shelbyville I better pack a lunch. It was during one of those drives in January of 2002 I remember President George Bush describing an *axis of evil* that must be dealt with. It reminded me of the greater challenges our nation was facing.

The Republican Party County Central Committee meetings were new to me. I had not been actively involved in party politics. Even though I was interested in elections and always voted, I never had the time or inclination to get involved. At each of the gatherings, I announced my intention to run for State Representative.

My opponents were often in attendance at the same meetings as well. In all, there were three announced candidates. In addition to my announcement, Don Stephen and Jim Barnett announced their intention to run for the office. Both were very good candidates. Unlike me, Stephen had been active in party politics in Clark County. He was a farmer, owned a hunting business and was board member of the State Farm Bureau. Don was a Vietnam Veteran and was active in the VFW and had legitimate concerns regarding Agriculture and Veteran's issues. If I had not been running, Don was someone I could have supported.

Jim Barnett was a Methodist minister and counted on support from a large number of Methodist congregations scattered in communities throughout the region. He was well respected and was also from Crawford County. Eventually, the three candidates would become known as, "The Teacher, The Preacher, and The Farmer".

During these Central Committee meetings, after a brief introduction and discussion of my background, reasons for running and stances on issues, there were often questions. One of the most prevalent questions was how I was going to serve as a State Representative and continue as a school superintendent. This, of course, was an appropriate question. The only issue I had with the question was it was not asked of the other candidates. Don was a farmer and ran a business. He was not going to stop farming operations or shut down his hunting retreat. As far as I knew, Jim Barnett was going to continue in the ministry. I knew of dozens of lawyers in the Legislature that continued to practice law. Other members of the General Assembly were farmers, police officers and businessmen. Why was everyone concerned with my choice to continue in the career I had chosen? After all, wasn't this a citizen legislature as envisioned by our founders? People were elected locally to represent residents of a region in the State Legislature and then return to their homes to hear from the people who elected them and continue to experience life and careers. The questions only made me more determined to continue my work in education.

The announcement phase of the campaign was nearly complete by the end of the first week of January of 2002 and the real campaigning was about to begin. Between the mid-December announcement and the March 19th primary, there were approximately 12 weeks. A plan for each of those days and nights, including weekends, was hatched between Jay Ping, Fred Clatfelter, Steve McGahey and the Pair of Jacks. Of course, I had some input and the school calendar was a consideration along with the Hutsonville Tiger athletic schedule. Two of my daughters were on teams and I didn't want to miss their games. It was all a giant puzzle and from day to day things changed based on circumstances. Generally, I was excited by the challenge and I was being provided the financial resources necessary to run an effective campaign. Most importantly, I had trusted friends and talented people like Jay on board. During that time, I think I averaged about five hours of sleep a night.

The pair of Jacks I had been dealt with, along with the well-wishes and support I was receiving post-announcement made me feel good about the cards I was now holding. I had drawn well to the pair of Jacks. We just had to make sure we played the hand correctly.

Chapter Six
A Winning Hand

To describe the weeks between the first of January and March 19th of 2002 as a whirlwind would be a vast understatement. I understood that between working at school and running for State Representative would be busy, but I could not have imagined *how* busy. The size of the district made things even more difficult.

Driving to any of the more remote locations in the 109th meant lots of time behind the wheel of my car. The drive from Hutsonville to the southernmost point of Mt. Carmel was fifty minutes. To the north, Chrisman was an hour and when I ventured into Altamont, which was the farthest point in Effingham County, it was an hour and fifteen minutes. Most of the meetings I attended in Cumberland County were anywhere from forty-five minutes to an hour away. Shelbyville was the longest trip at almost an hour and a half. Thankfully, I had been provided the financial resources by campaign contributors to pay for most of my travel-related expenses.

I knew that the driving was necessary though, and so was a plan to make the most out of the evenings and weekends. Making sure I made the most out of the time spent in any particular location, meant that the number of meetings I scheduled there correlated with my amount of driving time. Per Jay's instruction, I could also be found introducing myself to the editors and reporters at every local newspaper in the 109th.

Except for a couple of school holidays, I was at my job during the day at Hutsonville and made sure that any campaign work did not interfere with my duties there. I kept an accurate calendar as to my days of work and my campaign life, which was necessary to do for several reasons. First of all, I owed it to the Board, staff and students to focus on my job during the school day. They had shown great trust in me by supporting my campaign, and I was going to honor that trust.

In addition, I knew people from other campaigns would be watching for errors. Everything, including phone calls, emails and my calendar was subject to the Freedom of Information Act (FOIA). This meant that I must wait until the end of the school day before I dealt with any calls or emails or left for any Central Committee meetings or campaign events. It was winter and darkness descended shortly after I left school. Any precinct walking would be limited so it was mostly done on weekends. I needed to meet people and walk precincts that contained heavily Republican voters. Jay Ping, with help from the State GOP, took care of preparing my walking schedule.

It was also important that I regularly visit those Central Committee monthly meetings. The precinct committeemen attending these meetings were the leaders of the respective counties GOP. It was especially important to get to know the Chairs. So, I continued to attend the meetings throughout January and February, and I discovered that it was fairly common practice that these Committees did not make endorsements of any specific candidates in a contested primary election.

Despite that, Don Stephen requested that the Clark County Central Committee in his home county endorse him. The request was denied based on their long-standing policy of non-committal if the Primary were contested. Don had been active in the Clark County Central Committee and expected the practice of not endorsing to be waived. When the Committee Chair, Gary Tingley, informed the three candidates of the decision not to endorse their home county candidate, I was encouraged. As a long-time political player, it was clear that Gary did not predetermine Don as the likely winner. Gary knew the other County Chairs in the 109th well and determined through discussions with them that there was no consensus that Don, or anyone else, was the favorite. If he had, they would certainly have endorsed him in his home territory. Of course, it also helped that the pair of Jacks I held showed up at a Clark County Central Committee meeting and informed the group that they were supporting Eddy and according to Jack Chamblin, "Eddy would have the dough."

Tingley knew the difference that kind of funding support would make in a Primary. CRAW-PAC was serious about providing funds and the proof was already on the State Board of Election website. Thousands of dollars had already been donated to People for Eddy for the other candidates and the world to see. There was a public website on which all donations were required to be reported.

None of the other County Committees made an endorsement either. Nobody wanted to take a chance on alienating the potential winner, and that was all fine with me. As a newcomer to this entire process, I was happy to be running on a level playing field.

The beat went on for weeks. I would leave school as soon as I could, drive to a meeting somewhere in the 109th to introduce myself and then get home late, all to start again the next day. During this time, Kathleen and Fred were also hard at work. Volunteers stuffed envelopes with mailers by day and night. Thousands of campaign brochures, written by Jay Ping, were sent to the most likely GOP voters. The mailing lists were purchased from various companies specializing in compiling such lists and were analyzed by Jay and the House Republican Organization. It was critical to get my information to the folks who always vote Republican in the Primary.

Between the printing and mailing expenses, money was a critical ingredient. The mail effort was constant and lasted throughout the campaign. Phone banks were also set up and volunteers would call likely voters asking for their support. Whenever it seemed like funds were getting tight, another infusion of dollars would come from CRAW-PAC and others. An education group called The ALLIANCE PAC provided $5K early on. I was pleased that the education community had gotten involved and supported me as an educator. Soon, the IEA and IFT, both major teacher unions, made sizeable contributions to People for Eddy. I was informed that these types of union donations were rarely made to a Republican candidate.

Fred led the effort to place signs along well-traveled roadways in all eight counties. In the 109th legislative district, Illinois State Highway 1 was the main thoroughfare north and south, while a variety of east-west county roads needed signage also. When the initial order of a thousand-yard size sign and fifty larger signs were delivered, they filled the entire back room of the campaign office. I never imagined that all of those signs would find a home, but as the inventory dwindled, signs could be spotted all over the 109th.

The signs themselves were bright yellow with big black block lettering. The sign colors were also Jay's idea. Jay knew from experience that when winter set in and during the spring when the mud and grayness set in, these signs would stand out. He was right. I heard about those bright yellow signs everywhere I went, and people wanted them. We had to order at least another thousand yard signs and fifty more large signs to meet demand. The weekend before the Primary, the storage area in the back of the office was nearly empty.

Another thing that was new to me was Lincoln Day Dinners. These gatherings were sponsored by County Central Committees to honor the founder of the Republican Party, Abraham Lincoln. All eight of the counties scheduled these in the spring of 2002 so that the local GOP faithful could meet with elected officials and meet candidates. In the spring of 2002 these dinners provided folks a chance to thank their officials who were retiring or would no longer be representing them. In some cases, the new map had changed the boundaries and due to residency requirements, the official was no longer going to represent that county. More importantly, it provided the Republicans in each county an opportunity to meet the new candidates for office, and in most cases, this was the first time the loyal Republican voters of that county had a chance to meet these new candidates. In turn, it was my chance to meet the voters.

It was very important that I attend all eight of the Lincoln Day Dinners and fortunately, they were all held in the evenings. The first one I attended was in Greenup, Illinois. The Cumberland County Chairman, Jerry Sidwell, called his Lincoln Day Dinner the Annual Meeting of the Eleven-Hundred Club. I never asked why it was called that but this was their version of a Lincoln Day Dinner. The place was packed. The local loyal Republicans wanted to say good-bye and thank you to those individuals they had come to know over the last 10 years as their elected Representatives. Bill Mitchell was their State Rep and Duane Noland their State Senator. They were beloved by the locals and on hand to hear the accolades and good-byes. As expected, in addition to current State Representatives and Senators, current county officeholders were present along with lots of local candidates for county offices like Sherriff or County Clerk. Statehouse candidates for the new 109th were also present. All three candidates for the Illinois House plus State Senate candidate Dale Righter were in attendance as well. The combination of the old and new made for a special evening for any loyal Cumberland County card-carrying member of the GOP.

Each current candidate for office was provided an opportunity to speak. I had written a speech for the occasion. It was my first ever chance to deliver such a dialogue. The speech was full of background information, my stance on issues, my reasons for running and an appeal for their vote. I had written and rewritten portions of the speech multiple times. I had practiced it over and over looking for just the right tenor and tone. The reception was warm and I delivered the message to a crowd that included many supporters. Several had traveled with me from my home county to ensure support. Campaign literature, nail files and refrigerator magnets with my name on them were littered on each table where people sat to hear the speeches and enjoy a catered meal.

My speech lasted about fifteen minutes, and that was after I cut it short. People had to start looking at their watches and squirmed in their seats. There was polite applause when I had finished and I sat down at the head table along with other dignitaries and fellow candidates. Every other candidate apparently knew much more about how to deliver this type of speech than I did. I think they accomplished the same objectives of introduction, the reason for running, stance on issue and appeal for their vote in about 3-5 minutes. The keynote speech that evening was only slightly longer than my missive. I am pretty sure Presidential candidates have been nominated in less time than it took for me to deliver my first-ever campaign speech. My first foray was not good. The next day, State Representative Bill Mitchell called to inform me that my speech was way too long. He reminded me that I was simply a candidate for office, along with others. As he put it, the evening was not meant to be, "The Roger Eddy Show." Thanks Bill, lesson learned.

You can bet at future Lincoln Day gatherings my stump speech was no more than 3-5 minutes long. I adopted a less is more style. I vaguely recall some of the dinners. But in Lawrence County, I met a former State Representative and truly a living legend, Roscoe Cunningham. Mike Neal was the County Chairman but Roscoe was by far the most well-known Republican in the county. In his day, he made eloquent and often blistering speeches on the House floor about how Illinois government was headed in the wrong direction under the Chicago Democrats. He also famously attempted to draw attention to the need for a four-lane highway to connect Lawrence County on the far eastern edge of the State to Interstate 70 in the Center of the State. Although the distance between Lawrence County and Interstate 57 is slightly over 70 miles, never mind that, Roscoe was pictured in the local papers with a wheelbarrow and shovel starting the job himself. It was one of those epic moments in time and is still talked about in Lawrence County.

One of the Lawrence County newspapers was Roscoe's paper. I was called *The Bridgeport Leader.* The paper was a weekly publication read from front to back by folks living in Lawrence County. Roscoe and I had the chance to meet at the Lawrence County Lincoln Day dinner and I immediately become a fan. Of course, he told me that he would not be able to endorse anyone in a contested primary, but I later learned that I was being recommended by Roscoe.

Another memorable dinner took place in Paris, Illinois. Ted Lang, a Veteran, and a deeply patriotic man was the Chairman of the Edgar County Republicans and owned Lang's Service Station. The event in Paris was important, Edgar County, in many ways, was critical to winning the primary.

The VFW in Paris was so crowded with loyal GOP that one could barely walk. The contested House Primary, coupled with some local drama related to the County Sheriff's race made the attendance at this event one of the largest gatherings of the local party faithful ever. One of the Republican Sheriff candidates, Jeff Hodge, was married to a dyed in the wool Democrat named Carolyn Brown Hodge. She would be accompanying her husband to this GOP dinner, and along with interest in other local and state candidates, people wanted to witness Carolyn's presence at this event.

Edgar County was heavily Republican and home to another former GOP legend. Harry Babe Woodyard lived in Chrisman Illinois and was loved and revered in Edgar County. He was a member of the Illinois House from 1979 to 1986 and then served in the Illinois Senate from 1986 to 1997, until his untimely death in January of 1997.

His office had been located along State Highway 1 in his hometown of Chrisman and was in an actual log cabin. After his death, and in his honor, Vermilion County dedicated some acreage near Georgetown as the Harry 'Babe' Woodyard State Park. During the time Babe was in office, Edgar County became a solid Republican County.

As drawn up by Jay Ping and State GOP folks, our strategy for winning the Primary would first of all be to win my home county of Crawford. While it was true that Jim Barnett was also from Crawford County, most people thought I would gain a clear majority in Crawford and Jim could help me there by taking votes that might otherwise go to the person considered to be my main competition, Don Stephen. To offset the perceived likelihood that Stephen would do very well in his home of Clark County, I also needed to win Lawrence County and at least break even with Stephen in Cumberland County. The number of votes in portions of Effingham, Shelby and Wabash counties was smaller compared to the other counties. However, these were highly Republican areas and I would need to win at least one of these and not get clobbered in any of these regions. The key, according to Jay, was to win Edgar

County by a good margin. So, the question became how to gain the edge in Edgar County.

Bob Colvin was an engineer at Francis and Associates in Paris. 'Punk', as he is known, had been born and raised in Paris. He was also one of the key people in a group known as PEDCO- The Paris Economic Development Corporation. This group of local businessmen and officials were responsible for the incredible success Paris was having in regards to attracting business and industry and Bob was one of the folks most responsible for that success. When we began to ask who we needed to talk to in Paris, it was consistent that we needed to meet Bob. There were others to meet, of course, but Bob was the key. So, I called Francis and Associates, asked to talk to Bob and requested a meeting.

I can't remember the exact location of where we met, but I do remember that Bob had done his homework on me. Years earlier, I had interviewed for and been offered the position of Principal at Paris High School. Immediately he inquired of me why I hadn't accepted that offer. Bob bleeds orange and black, the school colors of the Paris Tigers.

I explained to him that at the time, I was Principal at Watseka High School, just south of Kankakee. We had a desire to move back farther south in Illinois and the Paris High School job certainly appealed to us. But after the Paris job was offered, and much discussion with Becca, we decided to stay put for another year. Watseka was a great community and in another year, our oldest and only son would graduate from 8th grade. So instead of accepting the Paris offer, I returned to school to obtain my Superintendent's endorsement. We saw the Paris opportunity as a good one but my ultimate goal was to become a Superintendent. If we had gone to Paris that would have resulted in two major changes, and with our school-age children in mind, we wanted to limit the number of moves. As fate would have it, a year later, I finished my degree and the superintendent position at Hutsonville opened up. Bob understood and accepted the explanation. The rest of the meeting went well and a few days later Bob and I met again along with a few other folks from Paris.

During this second meeting, one of the people I met was Doug Cochran. Doug had been involved in GOP politics for many years and had worked closely with Babe Woodyard during the time Babe represented Edgar County. If Babe was busy in Springfield and unable to attend events, Doug would often appear as his spokesperson. He later became a spokesperson for me as State Representative.

It was during this second meeting that Bob Colvin pledged his full support behind People for Eddy. At the time, I did not fully understand how important this would become to my campaign. As one of my most vocal supporters, Bob and his wife Georgia hosted a meet and greet for me in their home. I didn't realize that so many people could fit into one home! Cars were parked in lines around the neighborhood and into the street. When Bob sent out invitations to meet a candidate, it was important to show up.

Bob and Georgia were among the crowd at the Edgar County Lincoln Day dinner. They wore Roger Eddy buttons and sat at our table. There was no more important support anyone could ask for. His endorsement was pure gold in Edgar County.

The weeks rolled on and the dinners continued, as well as walking of the precincts. I knocked on thousands of doors, shook hands and left everyone I met a walk card which Jay had designed. These two-sided cards contained bio information, stances on key issues and photos of me and my family. Prospective voters also received a fingernail file with my name on it and I told people if they had trouble remembering my name to take the fingernail file into the voting booth with them. I also left two or three small refrigerator magnets at every house. Jay had insisted on these as they were low-cost and people would use them. Many years later, I visited homes of constituents and these magnets were still in place, on their refrigerator, holding up some treasured picture or document.

I visited every newspaper and radio station in the area. There were several weekly newspapers in the region, and all of them ran an introductory story about my candidacy. They would cover many of the local events I attended and would publish information and photos of me, as well as those of my competitors.

An important contact in Clark County became a newspaper editor named Gary Strohm. Gary had also been active in GOP politics and in the past had worked with former Governor Jim Edgar. Gary and I hit it off almost right away. As a newspaper guy, he would remain neutral but he often encouraged me. It was important to me that he thought I might do well in Don Stephen's home of Clark County where Gary's paper, *The Marshall Independent*, thoroughly covered county events.

During the final weeks of the campaign we placed ads in all these weekly papers. We had the money and were not taking any chances. Jay designed the ads and also assisted in the writing of letters to the editor that were sent to local papers by key leaders in each of the circulation coverage areas. Jay also wrote thirty and sixty-second ads that I recorded at local radio stations. The ads were placed and time purchased at several local radio stations including Mt. Carmel, Lawrenceville, Robinson, Marshall and Paris. During the last two weeks, the ads were played 12-15 times per day in each market. Don Stephen also purchased some radio spots. The other candidates could not compete with the resources or match the broadcasting power.

The newspaper ads and radio spots were paid for by another $60K that was raised and added to the early seed money from friends and family plus the larger donations made by the three CRAW-PAC principals. Jack Chamblin, Steve McGahey and Jack Morris were responsible for over half of the funding. The House Republican Organization was a key source of support as well. In the last few weeks, they sent staff to assist locally. By that time, the covert GOP operation had become very obvious. Jay was still in charge of the campaign and I had to make that clear to the folks sent from Springfield. The two mail pieces sent to all likely Republican voters the last two weeks of the campaign were only sent after Jay's approval. I was not interested in any type of negative campaigning and neither was Jay. I trusted him to make sure that the main theme was that I was running *for* State Representative and not running *against* anyone.

My opponents had taken some mild shots at me. Most of the negative comments were aimed at the fact that I was planning to stay on as superintendent. I would be a double-dipper according to comments that were reported back to me as being made by Don Stephen. He claimed that I would be a part-time Representative earning paychecks from two sources and the district deserved better according to him. I call these mild now compared to what was yet to come. As a newcomer, the comments still stung though. My skin did get thicker but I never liked negative campaigning. I especially did not like the fact that nobody was asking if the other candidates were going to quit their chosen professions.

All of the efforts were rewarded on March 19th, 2002. We had a winning hand. At the end of the night, in a three-way Primary, I had received almost 44% of the vote. Don Stephen got 34% and Jim Barnett garnered 22%. There were 7,476 votes cast that night and I received 5,657. It was not a majority of the total votes cast, so it was clear that I would have to capture my opponent's Republican votes to win in the November General Election. It was, however, a solid victory in a Primary that featured two good opponents. Both men called me the night of the victory to concede defeat and wish me well. I also got a call from Leader Daniels and well-wishers from throughout the 109th. Bob Colvin had kept us informed all evening from the Edgar County Courthouse in Paris of my overwhelming win in Edgar County. He was so elated that he drove down to our campaign headquarters that night to help us celebrate. The plan hatched by Jay Ping and the GOP had worked.

The same night I won the Republican Primary in the 109th, a former State Representative and Congressman named Rod Blagojevich won a hotly contested Democratic Statewide Primary for Governor. Blagojevich garnered 36.5% of the vote and narrowly defeated Roland Burris (yes, that Roland Burris). Burris finished with 34.5%. The Blagojevich victory came down to his high level of voter support in downstate counties, plus the majority he won in the metro-east region around St. Louis. Paul Vallas finished third with 29% of the vote. It was notable that both Vallas and Burris were more popular in Cook County than Blagojevich. The flamboyant Blagojevich worked hard in downstate regions and it paid off with the win.

On the GOP side, Attorney General Jim Ryan was victorious, also in a three-way primary. Ryan received around 45% of the vote with Patrick O'Malley and Corrine Wood splitting the remaining vote with 28% and 27% respectively. The stage was set for a November showdown between Ryan and some guy with a hard to pronounce last name…Blagojevich. The Democrats had not elected a Governor in Illinois since Dan Walker in 1973. Many believed that this could be the year since current Republican Governor George Ryan was embroiled in a scandal involving his years as Illinois Secretary of State. The ongoing scandal was believed to be very had for the GOP to overcome.

All that speculation was for another day. It was a good night at the headquarters of People for Eddy on Main Street in Robinson, Illinois across from the courthouse. We had won and it was also was my daughter Brenda's 14th birthday. We had a party and a party!

That night the voters of the Hutsonville School District also overwhelmingly voted in favor of a bond issue that would allow for us to build a new high school in Hutsonville. It was on to the next hurdle. I needed to get some rest; there was school the next day.

Chapter Seven
On a Roll

Winning the Primary was important. As verified by past election results, the 109th district leaned Republican with about 54% of the traditional general election voters as *likely Republican* voters. That did not mean the General election was going to be a piece of cake.

Jim Lane, the lawyer running against me from Robinson had the strong support of the State Democratic Party and House Speaker Michael Madigan, which meant money and resources would be thrown his way. It also meant that, based on reputation and past practices, Michael Madigan and his Chicago-style negative campaign was likely headed our way.

Madigan had been the Speaker of the House in Illinois for all but two years during the previous two decades. He was also the head of the State Democratic Party. Madigan decided who the Democratic candidates would be throughout the State and he was in Jim Lane's corner. Lane also had the support of long time area State Representative Chuck Hartke. Hartke had represented portions of the new 109th District in the past and was well known and well regarded. Everybody liked Chuck and I still do. The CEO of the Illinois Eastern Community College District (IECC), Terry Bruce, was also a supporter of Lane. Bruce had served in the United States Congress and as State Senator as a Democrat and a strong party loyalist.

As Jay Ping pointed out, the democrat winner in the primary for Governor, Rod Blagojevich, performed well downstate and that could mean coattails for downstate democrat hopefuls like Jim Lane. All of these factors meant it was not going to be easy.

An important dynamic regarding the Primary was that while it was exhausting, it provided me a chance to learn how a race is run and gain valuable experience to be used in the General Election. The same could be said for our campaign team. Fred and Kathleen had been tested and passed with flying colors. We had a huge network of volunteers already assembled. I had made countless connections throughout the eight counties that would be incredibly valuable over the next seven and a half months leading up to the November 4th General Election. Jay Ping had also hit his stride. Energized by the solid Primary win, Jay was ready to plot another winning strategy for the General Election. The Primary was at times rough and grueling but ended up being a huge positive for us.

For a short while though, the campaigning could hit pause and we could regroup, bask in some celebratory glory and rest. All of the yard signs needed to be taken down and stored until closer to the fall election. Fred Clatfelter, once again, coordinated that effort. Those signs would be replanted and added to during the fall but for now, everyone took a couple of weeks off from the campaign trail. My Democrat opponent, Jim Lane, did not have a primary opponent.

Late March, April, and May were busy months for a school superintendent. I used the time to complete evaluations, compare actual spending to budget projections and begin plans for the next school year. There are always resignations to deal with and people to recruit and hire for the following school year. In addition to the normal workload, the *Committee of Ten*, looking into the feasibility of combining Palestine and Hutsonville School Districts continued to meet. A final report and recommendation needed to be prepared.

We were all excited about the prospect of a new high school in Hutsonville. The current school was built in 1917 and functioned well for over a hundred years. The heating and cooling systems were antiquated, with necessary major infrastructure upgrades to equip classrooms for emerging technology. The daunting prospect of making the current space the best for our children to provide a high-quality education for the 21st century was at the forefront. Without a new building and major renovations to the entire campus, I was concerned about whether we would be able to provide the quality education that our students needed. The referendum was about more than a new building. In this case, I felt it was about the future including maintaining a school system in our town of Hutsonville.

The huge majority voting in favor of the building bonds on March 19th stoked excitement for the future. As I recall, well over 70% of voters cast votes in favor of increasing their property taxes to make this much-needed investment in the future of children living within the boundaries of the Hutsonville School District. The voters of the school district had spoken and they were willing to pay their part for a new building to adequately house decades of future Tigers. Due to a state capital grant program, the district would be responsible for only 25% of the cost. It was still a lot of money for a district with very little property wealth. This potential cost had been communicated in a series of town meetings before the vote along with the potential benefits of a new school. We were thrilled the voters approved the investment.

The successful referenda provided the Committee of Ten with something more to think about. This Committee was originally formed to study the issue of reorganizing the two districts. The task was to analyze all aspects of how combining the school districts might affect the finances and quality of education of current and future students. Thankfully, Illinois law well spells out the structure and duties of this committee.

The analysis was designed to help determine whether or not the Committee of Ten would recommend placement of a Consolidation Referendum on the November ballot, the same ballot that would include the State Representative contest. The ballot question would ask the residents of the two districts if they wanted to consolidate into one district. This particular committee was made up of ten individuals, five from the Palestine School District, and five from Hutsonville.

The Committee met multiple times during the spring to determine how combining the districts would affect everything from class sizes, bus routes, tax rates and teacher salaries as well as dozens of other details. Not the least these were whether the new East Side County School would be the Tigers or the Pioneers. Or would both current mascots expire and be replaced by maybe a Titan? The fact that Hutsonville was in a position to build a brand new, state-of-the-art high school factored into the discussions of the Committee of Ten.

The March 19th primary election also provided the Palestine Community and School District with a successful referenda vote on whether that district would build a new grade school. The results of the Palestine referendum were positive. Palestine, also eligible for a 75% infusion of state money to fund the project, seemed excited to construct a new education facility and now had the funding source. These pending building projects gave the Committee of Ten lots to ponder when it came to how the proposed new district might house the students.

All of this took time and lots of coordination and effort. I still worked at school every day and continued to attend multiple events all over the region. I was very busy for sure, but nothing like I would be. The school year ended and graduation took place.

After graduation, the school schedule would slow down to a pace that might allow me more time to rev up my campaign work. Days were longer and more daylight allowed me to walk more precincts. The school district switched to our summer schedule hours which meant I could leave most days by 2 PM. I also had some vacation days to use in June prior to July 1st. After July 1st, I would have another full slate of vacation days to use in the late summer and fall leading up to the November election. All of this was taken into consideration as we scheduled events, precinct walking, Committee of Ten meetings and other appearances. The precinct walking was determined to be the most important use of time by the GOP staff and Jay. So, I walked a lot that spring, summer and fall. I followed a plan for this walking worked out by Jay with help from the House Republican Organization (HRO). After I won the Primary Election, I had help from the GOP campaign staff almost the entire time leading up to the fall election.

Another necessary component was to walk in every parade in the 109th District and attend countless other local events. County party chairmen provided us with lists of parades, soup suppers, dinners, chowders and other summertime celebrations scheduled in the area. Some of the events were actually outside of the 109th boundaries but since the events attracted residents of the 109th, I needed to be there. There were over 25 parades scheduled starting in the spring up until the November 4th Election. On many of the dates there were multiple parades. I think the record for one day was four and I was able to make them all based on starting times. Of course, I could not do this without the help of volunteers and supporters who prepared vehicles with my campaign signs and held my spot in line until I arrived. My brother-in-law, John Brooks, was a major parade volunteer. His white pick-up truck was fitted with a two-by-four rack to hold my largest sign. He drove slowly through the streets while I walked behind that truck with dozens of volunteers wearing "People for Eddy" t-shirts. My children were part of the group. In addition to the hundreds of pounds of candy, we handed out a variety of *Eddy Gear*. The most popular summer item was the *Eddy fan*. Again, this hand held fan was Jay's idea. He said that these would be retained by parade-goers and used throughout the warm fall days almost until election-day. I saw the fans at future events all summer and fall.

Looking back, I can say that those were the fun times during the campaign. Often, many of the events became family outings. The chance to get out and meet people and witness the vitality of the wonderful communities in the 109th was a highlight of the campaign.

I met so many fabulous people all over the region. The early summer and throughout June and July, things were quite fun. I ran into my opponent at many of the gatherings and he seemed to be enjoying the experience as well. There was no sign of negativity from either campaign. Perhaps it was wishful thinking that Madigan and his campaign tactics would by-pass this particular election. Unfortunately, that was not the case.

The first hint of negativity came via a mail piece. The hit piece referred to me as, *"Greedy Roger Eddy."* It highlighted the fact that I was planning to continue my work as superintendent and the 109th needed a full-time State Representative. My salary as superintendent was added to the salary of a State Rep and the ad claimed that the combination of both full-time salaries would be my pay. Of course, that was not true. I had already made arrangements with the local school board for reduced pay if I won the election. Later in the campaign, a radio ad was produced and aired with the same theme. Unfortunately, my children heard these ads while they were on the bus on their way to school. Things only got worse.

As the school superintendent of Hutsonville, I also served as a board member of the South-Eastern Special Education Cooperative (SESE). SESE provided special education services to twelve rural school districts in southeastern Illinois. During the year I was running for State Representative, I was also the Chairman of the Board of SESE. The chairman position rotates among each of the 12 school district superintendents and that year happened to be my turn. As Chair, I was responsible for signing lots of legal documents related to the Cooperative. During the previous year there had been some personnel decisions at SESE which caused hard feelings. For example, some individuals were not rehired and I had signed the notices sent to those not rehired. Following these decisions, several administrative employees of the Cooperative came under fire from individuals supportive of those people who had been released. After review of some of the attacks against SESE personnel, the SESE legal counsel felt it was necessary to send letters to those making certain statements and claims about SESE employees. The letter warned the individual that if the personal attacks continued, SESE might be forced to take legal action. As Chairman, and with unanimous support from the Board, I signed the letter and it was sent.

The individual receiving the letter was furious and felt the letter was threatening.

She was also a retired SESE employee. The letter I sent, on behalf of the SESE Board, was later used in campaign material claiming that I had threatened an elderly woman. I was livid at the suggestion that I would ever threaten anyone, let alone someone's grandma. From that moment on, I lost all respect for my opponent. The fact that this was likely the work of the Madigan campaign staff was of no consolation to me. I rightfully blamed Jim Lane for the negative attacks. Either he was directly involved, approved it or had no control over his campaign. All of those possibilities infuriated me.

The GOP's staff from the House Republican Organization (HRO) was eager to fight back. The attack had to be answered and they had uncovered some negative information about Lane. The material they prepared to answer back was very personal. I refused to even think about that type of approach. Then a few days later, the Lane camp claimed to have an endorsement from an important group, an Illinois Right to life Organization. An endorsement letter from that group had been received by People for Eddy. I was confused as to how Lane could make this claim.

I decided that we would fight back with facts, not negativity. Mailers were prepared and radio ads produced revealing the fallacy of Lane's claims regarding SESE and the alleged threats. I was convinced that the voters in the 109th would not approve of Lane's tactics and that the negative approach would backfire.

The HRO staff thought we needed to do more. After a heated debate, HRO staff threatened to use the negative information they had gathered concerning Lane even if I objected. I informed them that if they tried that they would lose me as a candidate. I left the room after telling them that I would rather quit than allow them to go negative. After I had left, one of the staffers said that I was bluffing. Fred Clatfelter was still there in the room. He informed them he had known me for a long time and could guarantee them I was not bluffing. The negative ads were never used. The HRO staff prepared a response based on facts only. Letters to editors were written and sent by supporters all over the 109th, radio ads developed, and mail pieces produced and distributed all highlighting facts and dispelling the accusations. The ultimate payback was when Lane was forced to publically rescind his claim that the Right to Life group had endorsed him.

The strategy worked. After a couple more agonizing weeks, the negative attacks slowed down. I am sure that polling was done that revealed the attacks were not productive. Polls indicated that I continued to indicate I was in the lead. The negative attack, fueled almost entirely with financial resources from Madigan controlled committees and supporters, was meant to diminish the lead but it didn't work. Lane's support actually went down as my poll numbers went up. I was convinced that if we would have gone negative and used the ads first suggested by HRO that my poll numbers would have suffered. The people of the 109th district had soundly rejected these negative campaign tactics that seem to work elsewhere and our strategy of fighting back with the truth prevailed.

The entire episode of this negative campaign was something I have a hard time forgetting to this day. I should let it go but that is hard when people you care about are hurt. I had hoped against that type of campaign and vowed not to lower myself to that level. There was pressure from many to fight fire with fire. I carried a deep grudge against the person that I held ultimately responsible for many years after that. The bitterness has eased but once in a while still comes through. There was never a sincere apology for the lies and slander. In my mind, at the end of the day, the candidate is responsible for the way their campaign is conducted. Campaigns have become increasingly negative since the fall of 2002 when I first ran for office. Innuendo, false claims, downright lies and personal attacks have replaced honest debate over important issues.

There are many other more positive highlights from the general election campaign. One took place when former governor Jim Edgar agreed to keynote a fundraiser for me. The event took place in Casey at a restaurant called Richard's Farm. This converted barn had a banquet room that would hold a couple of hundred guests. I am not sure how close we came to the capacity of the banquet room that night but we could not have fit another person in the room. Fred and Kathleen were responsible for the guest invitation list and preparation, Jay prepared my brief remarks, my brother-in-law John Brooks served as MC, and Jim Edgar delivered an outstanding speech about the importance of public service and citizen legislators.

One of the attendees that night was a State Representative from northern Illinois named Tom Cross who carried a rather sizeable check to support my campaign. The check was from the campaign coffers of Congressman Dennis Hastert. Hastert was Speaker of the United States

House of Representatives. Both Tom and Hastert were from Yorkville, Illinois which is only about 10 miles from where I grew up in Newark, Illinois. It was heartwarming that they would support me due to our ties to Kendall County. They both knew my parents. Little did I know at the time, Tom was planning to run for House Minority Leader after the election in November. He was planting seeds and getting his ducks in a row. At the time, I didn't know much about the politics inside the Republican Caucus of the Illinois House of Representatives.

The Edgar event was covered by all major press outlets in the area. Jim Edgar was a beloved public figure and still carried more weight than anyone who could have supported me. He attended college at Eastern Illinois University in nearby Charleston. Edgar had served as Secretary of State before becoming governor. Most important of all, his integrity was beyond reproach. With allegations of corruption surrounding current Republican Governor George Ryan, and with the history of other governors going to prison in Illinois, Edgar was seen by many as one of the only honest Governors in Illinois in recent memory. His endorsement was more valuable than can be accurately described. This endorsement was highlighted in newspaper and radio ads, many of which we used in the late stages of the campaign. I had other important endorsements by then as well, but the Edgar endorsement was the most crucial. The meeting that the Pair of Jacks had arranged with Edgar resulted in a huge step forward.

(Throughout my campaigns the endorsement of Jim Edgar was always critical- ad produced by People for Eddy)

The resources promised by CRAW-PAC continued through the summer and fall. Jack Chamblin made a personal visit to a prominent individual in Marshall, Illinois named Gerald Forsythe. Forsythe had made a fortune in the electric power generation business. He was originally from Marshall and when he returned to the home farm, he built a large estate and an eighteen-hole golf course he named Canyata.

Chamblin visited Forsythe hoping to get financial support for my campaign. Chamblin left the meeting with a $25K check to People for Eddy. I had never met Forsythe but due to Jack's convincing, he wrote the single biggest check made to the campaign. I later got to know Mr. Forsythe as he continued to support my campaigns and provided great advice during my time in office. He is also a very philanthropic man who has given so much to his hometown and surrounding area. I have a great deal of respect for him and am indebted to him for all the support.

Additional contributions were made by Citizens for Tom Cross as well as another State Representative named Art Tenhouse. He was also planning to run for Minority Leader and against Cross. Leader Daniels and HRO provided tens of thousands of dollars of in-kind support in the way of staff. The Farm Bureau made in-kind radio ad contributions through a political organization known as ACTIVATOR. Plus, I had support from the education community as both teacher unions, The School Board Association, Illinois Association of School Administrators, Illinois Principals Association, and the Illinois Association of School Business Officials supported my effort with important donations.

All total, between July 1st and the end of the year leading up to the General Election, my campaign received over $119K. This, added to the amount raised during the prior six months which included the Primary Election provided me with all the resources I needed. Records show that we spent just under $100K during that period.

The combination of resources, volunteers, a great game plan and, I believe, the decision not to be enticed into a negative campaign, resulted in a resounding win. I garnered 57.4% of the vote and Lane received just 42.6%. It was a landslide victory of almost 15% in a slightly leaning Republican legislative district. Lane called the night of the election to congratulate me but I refused to talk to him. I was still upset that he approved of the negative campaign and held him responsible for this attempt to smear my name. He had upset my children and for no good reason except to run a negative campaign rather than tell people why he should be elected. There was no way I wanted to talk to him on such a joyous occasion. He was not spoiling this night!

There were well over a hundred people at the People for Eddy campaign headquarters that night. The office couldn't hold the crowd and it spilled out into sidewalks adjoining the building. The police came by but simply waived and congratulated me. Bob Colvin made the drive from Paris to join in. Once again, Bob had kept us informed about the vote totals in Edgar County. The figures from Edgar County were incredible. I also won every single county including Crawford, the home county of both myself and Lane. Jay Ping was there along with Fred, Kathleen, Steve McGahey, Bev Turkal, my entire family, as well as and dozens of others who had been so important to the campaign.

I can't recall all of the events of the evening but I do remember dozens of phone calls, including calls from Speaker Dennis Hastert, Leader Lee Daniels, Tom Cross, Art Tenhouse and Jim Edgar. It was truly a night to celebrate.

The same night, voters decided that Hutsonville and Palestine would **not** consolidate. While voters approved of the plan in the Hutsonville District, voters in Palestine rejected it. Illinois law requires that both districts independently approve the merger. The fact that the high school location was planned for Hutsonville was too much to overcome and people feared the loss of the high school would hurt the town of Palestine. Plus, there was a core group of people who were simply against any consolidation. We knew that the high school location would be a tough hurdle.

The result did not disappoint me, although I thought the merger could have potentially provided the students living in the two districts with better opportunities. My main point throughout the effort was that it was time to ask people, after years of discussion, whether or not the proposal should pass. We had our answer. Part of me was relieved. With the general election win and a new school to build, the details and work that it would have taken to combine two school districts would have added to an already full plate.

The same night I won my first election, Rod Blagojevich was elected Governor. He became the first Democratic governor elected in Illinois in almost 30 years. He defeated Republican Jim Ryan soundly by a 52-45 margin. Blago, as he was called, did have coattails downstate, but not in the 109th. The Democrats also captured a majority in the Illinois Senate with a 32-26 margin, with one claiming to be an independent. In the

Illinois House, Madigan increased his majority to 66 seats compared to 52 on the Republican side. The Democrats also prevailed in all but one of the elections for Illinois' Executive Offices. Republican Judy Topinka retained her seat as Treasurer. It was a big night for the Democrats though. They would control the House, Senate and Governor's office. It would be a one-party rule in Springfield with a large freshman class of House Members and I would be among that group, albeit in the minority.

The year 2002 was indeed a memorable one for my family as my campaigns netted primary and general election victories which secured a seat in the Illinois House of Representatives for a Crawford County resident, something that the Jacks always wanted. They were elated and that made me happy.

Of course, lots of other things happened in 2002. The *No Child Left Behind Act* was passed at the Federal Level amid cries for reforms in education. In June, a fourteen-year-old girl named Elizabeth Smart was kidnapped in Salt Lake City, Utah, and was still missing at the end of 2002, ironically the same place where the Winter Olympics had taken place. President Bush also established a new federal agency called The Department of Homeland Security. In October of 2002, former President Jimmy Carter was awarded the Nobel Peace Prize. Popular movies included Spider-Man, My Big Fat Greek Wedding and Star Wars Episode II: Attack of The Mc Clones. Madonna, Pink, Red Hot Chili Peppers, Shania Twain and Celine Dion, among others topped the musical charts. And, I was soon going to take the oath of office as State Representative.

Chapter Eight
A Seat at the Table

On January 8th, 2003 I stood on the floor of the Illinois House of Representatives, along with 117 others duly elected officials and recited this oath of office from Article 8, Section 3 of the Illinois Constitution:

"I do solemnly swear that I will support the Constitution of the United States, and the Constitution of the State of Illinois, and I will faithfully discharge the duties of the office of State Representative to the best of my ability."

As I recited those solemn words for the first time, I can still remember the chills up and down my spine. My wife, Becca, stood by my side, and my mother and father stood behind me on the House floor. I don't think I had ever seen my dad in awe of anything, but he was that day. The meaningful oath I had just recited clearly defined the new role I would have in State government.

The Inauguration Ceremony, while solemn, was also celebratory. It was hugs, flowers and handshakes all around on the House Floor that day. The rest of my family and supporters watched the ceremony from the balcony gallery. Each Representative-elect was provided a limited number of tickets for the gallery but other interested attendees could watch from monitors located in the hallway. I was fortunate to get additional tickets from a few of the veteran House members who, after several terms and inaugurations were not attracting the same first-timers. Jay, Kathleen, Fred, Bev, Steve and the pair of Jacks were all invited to attend and I had enough tickets for everyone, if necessary. Not all of them could make it to the festivities, but there were at least a dozen of my friends and family on hand, including all five of my children. It was a great day and one I will never forget.

At the time, I didn't know how special it was to take the oath in such a historic venue. Due to major renovations to the House Chamber made during the next two years, the Inaugural Ceremony was thereafter held at the auditorium of the University of Illinois' Springfield (UIS) campus. That location proved to be extremely convenient and user friendly to staff and attendees. I still believe that they should move the ceremony back to the Illinois House floor. Having experienced both, I can say without hesitation, there is no comparison. Being sworn into office at a university auditorium compared to the ornate and historical House Floor is like comparing a doll to a real baby.

(A photo of the magnificent chamber of the Illinois House.
Wikipedia, Daniel Schwen-own work)

It was a rather large freshman class due to the new legislative boundaries, which was brought about due to redistricting that takes place every ten years. Along with the twenty-four newly elected members, the 93rd General Assembly included eighty-nine incumbents, one former member (Republican Bob Churchill of Lake Villa), one Senator now elected to the House instead (Democrat Bob Molaro of Chicago), and three returning Reps who had been appointed early to the previous (92nd) House during the time between their election and Inauguration.

I now had a seat at the table. My actual seat on the House floor was the second row from the back next to Representative Dave Winters and Representative Dan Brady. They were both great seatmates.

Winters had a pilot's license and during some slow monotonous times on the floor he entertained me with some hilarious and sometimes dramatic anecdotes from his experiences as a pilot. He quite often warned me about certain legislation and how any single vote could be dangerous politically. Veteran legislators like Winters were more or less assigned to a Member to assist them in identifying potential political landmines. A few times, early on, Winters would look over at me and simply say, "You are a no." Most of the time, I complied as I could also see the danger in the vote and usually opposed the measure anyway. At times though, we had words about it and I voted differently than suggested. I truly *mostly* appreciated his suggestions and I did greatly appreciate Dave's experience and insights.

Dan Brady was a funeral director and previously the Coroner of McClean County before being elected to the Illinois House in 2001. Dan was selected by Leader Cross as a member of his leadership team and sometimes would have to leave the House floor for leadership team meetings while session was going on.

I was supposed to watch his voting switch and vote for him if he were off the floor at a meeting. I found out that this was a common practice and the procedure was that another House Member or even a staff member could vote the switch of a missing lawmaker as long as they were somewhere on the campus grounds of the Statehouse, which included the Stratton building. When Dan was about to leave and turn his switch over to my discretion, I would look ahead at the bills likely to be called for a vote and ask him how to vote on particular bills. He would refer me to the House Daily Calendar that we were provided which contained a symbol with an arrow pointing up for a yes vote, and an arrow pointing down for a no vote. The symbol was next to the bill number on the calendar. Several bills were not accompanied by a symbol. I asked what to do in that case. Brady told me to, "Vote the same way you do." I often teased Brady that he had the best southern Illinois voting record of any central Illinois Representative in the history of the State of Illinois. A couple of times when I debated legislation across the aisle and was opposed to a bill that appeared to not have enough votes to pass, I would tell the bill sponsor that the proposal was, "All but dead," and that they should pull it from the record. My final admonishment was something like, "If you don't believe it is dead, we have a former coroner and current funeral home director on the House floor who can declare it dead." That line was met with roaring laughter the first couple of times I uses it, not so much the tenth time.

Dan became a good friend and that friendship continues to this day. He is currently the Deputy Leader in the House for the GOP. He has a long list of legislative accomplishments and has taken many very tough, but necessary votes as a House Member. I have great respect for him. His wife Teri makes the best chocolate chip cookies ever. I learned during a special session in July a few years later that in addition, Dan is a true Yankee Doodle **DAN**dy as he was born on the fourth of July.

The view from my seat was great, as were my seatmates.

Shortly after the oath and several minutes of celebration, the House Floor was cleared of all visitors and it was time for the newly inaugurated House to get to work. The first order of business was for House Members to elect a Speaker. Michael Madigan, a product of Chicago's 13th Ward, had served as Speaker in the Illinois House for all but two years since 1983. As previously mentioned, Lee Daniels briefly wrestled the title away from Madigan from 1995-97. Madigan's re-election as Speaker for the 93rd House of Representatives was a forgone conclusion. The tradition was that the vote is a unanimous one to demonstrate a spirit of bi-partisanship after a hard-fought general election. On this day, Madigan was indeed voted in as Speaker with a unanimous vote and State Representative Tom Cross was elected as the new Minority Leader by House.

Before this vote, however, both Tom and Art Tenhouse had worked every GOP member hard for their vote to gain the title of Minority Leader. After my election, they had both asked for my support, and since I had nothing against either one, I listened closely to each of them as they explained their plans and intentions. I liked Art a lot, as he was a fellow downstate Member and he had great wisdom and experience. Art was supported to become the new GOP Leader by out-going Leader Daniels. Leader Daniels earlier announced he would not seek to continue as Minority Leader. Daniels had provided critical support to me both in the primary and general elections. Tom Cross also supported me in the general election. This became a tough decision for me.

When I met with Cross, a few things convinced me to support him. First, Tom seemed to have a plan to deal with being in the minority and had done his homework. He knew I would prefer to serve on House Committees that would deal with education and agriculture-related issues. Cross also vowed to do away with a long-standing practice of the House GOP caucus and promised to never require members to vote along what is referred to as a caucus position. In the past, if the Minority Leader directed such a position, all members were required and expected to vote the way the Leader dictated. This provided the Leader with a greater perception of strength when negotiating with other caucus leaders in the House, Senate and with the Governor. The idea was that the Leader would pretty much have a certain number of votes to support him in negotiations and the support of ALL caucus Members if he ever needed to play that card. The other three caucuses still retained the caucus position as part of their procedures. As a new legislator, I liked the idea of being able to vote the way I wanted to so I could better represent my constituents.

Finally, Cross vowed that he would term limit himself as Minority Leader to eight years. A criticism by many was that Leader positions were too powerful both politically and legislatively.

Madigan was the poster child for this theory. Tom's vow to term limit himself made a huge difference to me as well as enough others to secure him the position of Minority Leader.

Both of Leader Cross's promises regarding not taking caucus positions, and term limiting himself as Leader were later broken. Legislation that would have placed limits on liability settlements in medical malpractice cases resulted in Cross announcing a caucus position in favor of liability settlement limits. The caucus meeting before that vote was caustic. While I was in strong support of limits and almost all GOP Caucus Members were also in support of limiting the dollar amount of these judgments, there were a couple of holdouts. Several veteran legislators tried to convince the holdouts to support Cross. They would not change and were roundly criticized.

Cross also went back on his eight-year leader term limit promise, during his seventh year as minority leader. Citing the need to have continuity in that position during an election season prior to the drawing of a new map, Cross announced he would seek to be Minority Leader beyond the term limit promise he had previously made.

I suppose the reasons for Cross going back on his stated promises were the result of other forces evolving during those years. Circumstances change. I certainly do not know all of the pressures he experienced during both situations in which he decided he could not keep the previous promises made. I hold no animus toward him for having changed his position. I am sure it wasn't easy for him. In any event, the promises he made helped him in 2002. Tom Cross was elected the new Minority Leader of the 93rd General Assembly.

With a Speaker and Minority Leader elected, there was still other work to be done on the day of Inauguration. The full House had to vote on the Rules which would govern the body. The Democratic majority authored and proposed the House Rules. Cross, and GOP staff made suggestions for changes in the Rules proposed by the Democrats that were ignored.

The Rules were substantially the same as other previous General Assemblies. These Rules provide for almost absolute power to the majority party, as well as incredible power to one individual, the Speaker.

Under these Rules, the Speaker had the authority to name a majority of members to all committees of the House. He also had the power to replace any Democrat committee member at any time. All legislation that was assigned to any of the committees established by the Speaker must first be introduced through the powerful Rules Committee. The Rules Committee contained a majority of the majority party (Democrats) also appointed by the Speaker. If the Rules Committee voted to hold a proposed piece of legislation, the measure could not move to a substantive committee for a hearing and potentially on to the House Floor for a vote. The Rules Committee had five members, three Democrats named by Speaker Madigan and two Republicans appointed by Minority Leader Cross. Barbara Flynn Currie was appointed as chair of the Rules Committee by Speaker Madigan. Currie was a brilliant woman that I came to respect in later years despite our vast differences in opinion regarding public policy. She could hold her own in any crowd. Currie was tough and seasoned with a great experience. Barbara had served in the House since 1979 and was an integral part of Madigan's leadership team and ruled the committee with an iron fist. Nothing leaked out unless Madigan approved it. Essentially, Madigan controlled all flow of legislation. Even if Currie wanted to support a particular proposal, Madigan could replace her as Chair due to his powers as Speaker contained within the House Rules. The Democrats claimed there was a process available to discharge a bill from Rules Committee contained in the House Rules. And that was technically true. That process to discharge a bill from the Rules Committee required a unanimous vote of the House. Impossible, especially since the Speaker was also a House Member.

I mention this Rule in some detail because it was, to me, the most egregious of the many egregious Rules proposed as part of the House Rules. These Rules, as currently written and practiced, in my opinion, remove a functioning Democracy in favor of the one-person rule. I do not believe the Framers of our Constitution ever envisioned such dictatorial power.

Of course the Rules were adopted along party lines. With advice from Jack Morris, I made it a point to read and become familiar with these rules. The more I read, the more disgusted I became at the blatant lack of transparency the rules required. Under these rules, legislation could come out of nowhere in the form of hundreds of pages of amendments to legislation that had been previously filed without any substantive language. These bills are known as *shell bills.* The amended proposal then moved along in the process without any clue as to what language the end product might contain.

Even the rules requiring bills to be read in separate Chambers (House and Senate), on separate days, meant nothing. When dozens of shell bills are filed by Leaders, the posting requirements could routinely be waived and the legislation could be heard in lightning fashion. No public hearing was required or seldom-used when these amendments are added to these shell bills.

These amended shell bills are often voted on before legislators, or staff, ever have a chance to read the bill. This type of maneuver is also often used with budget proposals. All it takes is a motion by the majority party to waive posting requirements, have the floor amendment introduced and approved by the powerful Rules Committee. The real rule was that there were no rules unless the Speaker wanted something to happen.

The Rules Committee conducted their meetings in the Speaker's conference room behind the House floor in a restricted area. After the secret conclave, the proposed legislation is quickly dispatched to the House Floor for a vote. The entire process taking less than ten minutes sometimes. The same was true in the Senate. The rules adopted by the House might as well have simply said the Speaker can do just about anything he wants. These Rules are a disgusting example of a power grab replacing democracy. Current House Rules can be read in entirety by following this link: http://www.ilga.gov/house/101st_House_Rules.pdf.

After those terrible rules were adopted, the House adjourned for that first day. Members attended luncheons and other celebrations related to Inauguration.

Before the House would reconvene the next day, I had a great afternoon and evening with family, friends and other supporters. There were dozens of inaugural receptions to attend and fellow Representatives to meet. It was a long day and I had learned a lot already.

The next day would be much shorter. The House was called to order January 9th at noon and was adjourned by 3 PM. The House adjourned that afternoon and did not reconvene until January 23rd.

During the interceding two weeks, hundreds of new bills were filed and committee assignments were finalized. As I had hoped for, that first year I was assigned to five personally relevant committees: Agriculture and Conservation, Appropriations-Elementary and Secondary Education, Appropriations-Higher Education, Elementary and Secondary Education, and Computer Technology.

The first bill I filed was back on December 4th, before being sworn in because as a Member-elect, I had that authority. That legislation (HB3) required the certification of stillbirth. This would provide parents legal documentation of fetal death. My wife and I, along with countless others, had experienced this type of event. I felt strongly that there should be some legal record of this human life existing and with the help of GOP staff legal counsel, the legislation was drafted. The bill was referred to the Rules Committee in January and assigned to the Human Services Committee and later re-assigned to the Executive Committee. It was never called for a hearing.

In the next few weeks, thousands of proposals were written and filed.

My first two days were in the books. My family and I returned for the Executive Branch Inauguration ceremony the following Monday, January 13th. It was on this day that day Rod Blagojevich was sworn into office as the 40th Governor of Illinois. I attended that ceremony. At the time he was sworn in as Governor, Illinois faced a $5 Billion Budget shortfall according to Blagojevich. In his inauguration speech, the new governor was inspirational in his words:

"My goal as governor is as simple as it is profound—to create a future as great as our past, a state as grand as our potential and a government as good as our people".

He insisted that despite the staggering debt and corruption that plagued Illinois.

"I did not run for governor to be a caretaker. I did not run to manage a state of decline. I did not run to maintain the status quo. I am not here to serve just a few…"

The speech was widely regarded as well delivered and encouraging at a time when the residents of Illinois were eager to hear about a new chapter and change. He vowed to work on issues that people cared about, among those health care and education. Promising to add new programs, reform education and solve the budget crisis without raising taxes, Blagojevich ended his speech:

"This is my pledge to you. I will tell it to you straight. I will give you my all. I will reach across party lines. I will seek out the best ideas. I will govern as a reformer. It is time for a new beginning. Let that time begin right now."

It all sounded so good, right?

Chapter Nine
A Tough Hand to Play

When I returned for Session on January 23rd, 2003, I was excited about this great opportunity. I was issued an official legislative office in the Stratton Building, complete with my administrative assistant.

Representative, 109th District
ROGER L. EDDY, R - Hutsonville

Springfield: 222-N Stratton Bldg., 62706; (217) 558-1040;
E-mail: reddyunit1@aol.com
District: 108 S. Main St., P.O. Box 125, Hutsonville 62433;
(618) 563-4128; Fax (618) 563-4129
Years served: 2003-present

Legislative assignments: Committees on Agriculture & Conservation; Appropriations-Elementary & Secondary Education; Appropriations-Higher Education; Computer Technology; Elementary & Secondary Education; Committee of the Whole.

Biography: Superintendent of schools; born May 08, 1958, in Ottawa; B.S., education, Northern Illinois University; M.A., Specialist Degree, educational administration, Eastern Illinois University; married (wife, Rebecca), has five children.

(It all became very real when I saw the *2003 Illinois Blue Book* listing)

The Stratton building was located across from the Capitol past an entry road and parking lot. The nondescript, concrete slab building was completed back in 1956, but in many ways seemed older than that. The Stratton was named after Illinois' 32nd Governor, William B. "Billy" Stratton who was first elected governor in 1952. At the time, "Billy the Kid", as he was known, was the youngest governor in America. Stratton was re-elected in 1956. An unsuccessful bid for a third term resulted in a loss to Otto Kerner in 1960. Stratton was charged with tax evasion in 1965. Although acquitted, he continued to attempt to gain a third term and ran once again for governor in 1968, being defeated soundly in the primary. The building now adorned with his name seemed to take on the persona of the defeated soundly version of William Stratton rather than Billy the Kid version.

The structure is home to offices for State Representatives and Senators plus several State Agencies. Over the years many have called for a new building to be constructed. While I was a member of the House, in May of 2004, the House voted 94-18 to close the Stratton Building. At that time, the millions of dollars it would have taken to upgrade the electric, HVAC and other building infrastructure issues convinced most that it would cost less in the long run simply to replace the whole thing with a modern office building. Though, with the State facing a $5 billion deficit that was growing, it was difficult to prioritize new office space for politicians. The fact that the construction of a new office building was not paid for with operating funds but with bonding authority was beside the fact. Politically, it was not the time for it and, although the proposal passed by a good majority in the House, it was never called in the Senate. The Stratton building is still used to this day to house State Representatives.

Like most freshman lawmakers, my office resembled a small storage room. To me, it was much, much more than that. I walked into 222-N of the Stratton January 23rd and was excited to be there. My wife, Becca, had taken some time to decorate it during the few days we spent in Springfield surrounding the Inauguration festivities. There was a desk, a set of *Illinois Revised Statutes*, a laptop computer and a window. No question, there were nicer offices in the Stratton and almost all were more spacious than mine. Some offices had corner windows and much nicer furniture. I found out later that there was a warehouse full of state-owned furnishings that I could peruse to obtain other items. But, it didn't matter. I was happy to be there and ready to get to work. In later terms, I did move to larger offices in the years to come, even one with a corner view. With seniority, the request for specific offices would be granted based on years served. The most senior had office space over at the Capitol. Having an office in the Capitol allowed one to avoid the often bitter cold walk across the parking lot. The saving grace was a tunnel located under the street which served as an escape from the cold and wind of the Illinois prairie.

(Photo of the Stratton Building and Illinois State Capitol.
Wikipedia Strikeforce- own work)

Finding a place to stay during session was also something that had to be tackled. The state allowed a per diem reimbursement for housing and meals. Many hotels in and around Springfield offered legislators something referred to as the *state rate*. That reduced rate took into consideration the amount of the per diem paid to legislators to cover housing. Many people preferred to find something that didn't require checking in and out of a hotel every week. I was fortunate and was able to find a place to rent monthly. The apartment was owned by a doctor in Casey, Illinois (a constituent Bev Turkal knew) who had been on a state medical board for many years. He agreed to rent it to me for the spring. I found another State Rep willing to split the rent with me. Frank Agular, another freshman representative from Cicero, and I were roommates. The apartment was located toward the west side of the city and during the heavy morning traffic was about 15-20 minutes from my office.

My roomie, Frankie, as he preferred to be called, was a treasured anomaly in the GOP ranks. He had been elected as a Hispanic to the Republican caucus. With a growing Hispanic population in Illinois, it was considered important to the party that Frankie had been elected. He was friendly and jovial; it was hard for anyone who met him not to immediately like him. We got along well even though I was from a rural agricultural area and he was a city dweller.

Living with Frankie was great. But, we both wanted to get closer to the Capitol for our second year and we did not renew the lease. During the second year we both did the hotel hop where we moved in and out of temporary rooms and dragged luggage back and forth.

Heavily targeted by Madigan and the Democrats, Frankie faced an uphill battle that he didn't seem to recognize or see coming and he lost his bid for a second term. Madigan knew that any trend resulting in the future election of Hispanics needed to be dealt with, and targeted Frankie with resources and a typical slimy, negative campaign. Since that time, the GOP has not elected another Hispanic to the House. This is a problem for the Republican Party in a state with a growing Hispanic population.

The Illinois GOP has also failed to elect many African Americans. This fact was infamously brought out one day by a Democratic State Rep a few years later. During a heated floor debate she mentioned that the GOP was not representative of the diversity of the population of the State of Illinois. When the GOP's only minority member stood up to be recognized, she referred to him, our House GOP minority Member as, 'a half', in reference to his mixed-race ethnicity. The manner in which she stated this was roundly regarded as inappropriate, at the very least. The fact is that unless the lack of elected minorities in the GOP changes, it will be nearly impossible for the Republicans to regain a majority in either of the two Houses of the General Assembly or win back the Governor's office or other statewide offices.

The early days of any session calendar are short on floor time. Most of the action takes place at the committee level. After all, until various proposals filter through the committee process, not much voting can take place on the house floor.

The entire process all starts with some idea regarding the improvement of public policy being reduced to written form. The ideas come from lots of places. Often, one of the many interest groups representing a wider audience has a legislative agenda that is supported by their membership. Examples include The Illinois Farm Bureau, Labor Union representatives, The State Chamber of Commerce, The Illinois Retail Merchants Association, School Board Association, The Illinois Coal Association, Beer Distributors Association, Illinois Right to Life Groups, Illinois State Rifle Association, etc...., etc....,etc..! There is no shortage of special interest groups represented by hundreds of lobbyists. These groups and the lobbyists that represent them are an important part of the process. They provide valuable insights, research and opinions that should be considered.

Often, constituents from communities back home in the legislative district have ideas for public policy changes they would like to see become law. No matter the origin of the proposal, the process for getting the idea to a committee begins with the Legislative Research Bureau (LRB). The LRB is where the idea or proposal is put into legislative language.

All four caucuses of the General Assembly as well as all Executive Offices and State Agencies have staff members assigned to assist in the development of proposed legislation. Many of these individuals are lawyers. As a legislator, I worked with various GOP staff members on many proposals. These staff members had expertise that would directly align with the subject in the proposal. For education issues, it was likely that the staff members had either a law degree specializing in elementary or secondary education. If the issue was related to agriculture the same was true. The first step was contacting the appropriate staff member. As a new legislator, getting to know these valuable team members was critical. Including GOP staff was a good idea even when contacted by constituents or state agencies to promote a particular change or addition to public policy. Many times, the issue, or a very similar proposal had been brought up in a previous session and there was a history to uncover.

Once a proposal is drafted with the assistance of GOP staff, the draft goes to LRB for the legal teams there to prepare a draft of the idea. Specific language is written which is meant to reflect the intention of the idea. The analysis by LRB includes a study of how the proposal interacts with other laws as well as any Constitutional conflicts. Sometimes, this part of the process reveals flaws with the proposal that must be addressed. In many instances, LRB lawyers make changes to the proposal to address these concerns or sometimes they return the draft for further clarification. I remember instances when the actual language drafted by LRB did not reflect the original intent due to a variety of reasons. Often, changing one word could result in an entirely different suggestion. The final decision regarding language is up to the elected official. Once all of the edits are considered and approved by the bill author, the final language is drafted by LRB and returned to the member. Then the proposal is signed by the member and filed with the Clerk of the House. Bills can also be filed by staff after receiving authority from the appropriate member. Upon filing with the Clerk, the proposal is finally assigned a bill number.

After the proposal is filed and assigned a number, it is read for the *first time*. The first reading of a bill often takes place during a session called a *perfunctory session*. Members of the House are not present during these sessions. The House Clerk, or Assistant Clerk, stands on the House

Floor and after calling the Perfunctory session to order, the Clerk reads into the record the bill number and a brief review of what the bill is intended to accomplish. It is then assigned to the all-powerful Rules Committee for further discussion and hopefully positive action. Any changes, referred to as an *amendment,* must also pass through this same Rules Committee.

Committee and Floor Amendments are the most common way to change the language content of the original bill during the process. Amendments heard in Committee provide for the most transparency and public input. That is why, toward the end of Session, or as deadlines approach, Floor Amendments are often used to avoid full transparency. This is especially true regarding perhaps the most controversial, yet most critical decisions. As mentioned, the hundreds of pages of both the State Budget and Budget Implementation Bills (BIMP) are good examples of how this Amendment process is abused with Floor Amendments.

Unfortunately, the same can be said about lots of other substantive legislation. This lack of transparency was made famous at the federal level when Nancy Pelosi years later uttered the famous words, "We need to pass it so we can see what's in it." The same thing happens in Illinois.

If the bill makes it out of the Rules Committee, it is assigned to one of the *substantive committees.* Sometimes these committees are referred to as *standing committees.* Earlier I mentioned five of these committees that I was assigned to my first two years. Committee hearings are advertised and assigned legislation which is supposed to be posted publically 24 hours before any hearing on the final version of the proposal. HB3, the Vital Records- Stillbirth proposal I mentioned was first read January 8th, 2003 during a Perfunctory Session, and referred to Rules Committee that same day and then assigned to a substantive committee called Human Services. The Human Services Committee was chaired by William Delgado. I asked the Chairman about having the bill called for a hearing. He was friendly and informed me that this particular proposal was not a priority among the dozens of bills assigned to his committee and that it would not likely be called for a hearing. He was kind during his explanation. Willie, as he was known, was a nice man and we later worked together on several education issues across the aisle.

The stillbirth proposal was soon thereafter reassigned to Executive Committee then back to the Rules Committee where it languished until the two years marking the period of the 93rd G.A. ended. In other words, the legislation was never called for a hearing and died when the session ended. The timeline for any bill filed during a legislative session is two years and until the General Assembly officially adjourns *Sine Die*. For the 93rd General Assembly, the first day was Inauguration Day, January 8th, 2003 and the Session ended officially January 11th, 2005.

Many of the 37 Bills I had drafted and introduced during my first session died without even a hearing. I was not alone in that club. Thousands of bills were introduced by House Members and only a fraction were called for hearings and only a few hundred were eventually passed by the required House majority of 60 votes, the Rule of Sixty, was an important lesson learned in my first two years. Remember, the GOP had only 51 votes. We had no real power to force any committee hearing for our proposals, let alone move bills out of committee without Democrat votes. The majority party could, and did, move proposals without any support from any GOP House Members. As they say, elections have consequences.

I learned a lesson of the Rule of 60 in my first spring session. Five of the proposals that I nursed from the idea stage, through drafting at LRB, the Committee process and a vote of at least sixty on the House floor became law, or Public Acts (PA). What also bears mentioning is that after the proposals pass in the House, the entire process starts again in the Senate by finding a willing Senate Sponsor. For me, fortunately, my corresponding Senator Dale Righter often sponsored my successful House proposals.

The five successes, after securing Governor Blagojevich's signature were: P.A. 93-0239, P.A. 93-0110, P.A. 93-0166, P.A. 93-0691, and P.A. 93-0682. The number 93 stands for the 93rd General Assembly. The second number in the sequence refers to the order in which it was signed among all of the Public Acts enacted during that General Assembly.

Some of these successful measures were simple and made no earth-shattering changes to public policy. One of the proposals dealt with how driver education claims could be submitted to the State Board of Education. Another made a slight change to existing law regarding falsification of academic degrees, and another a definitional change as to how speech pathologists could be employed by special education coops.

Two of the new public policies were a bit more important in my view. One of them enhanced the penalty for reckless driving in Illinois and included a provision where intentional ramping of a vehicle over an embankment if death occurred, could result in enhanced charges. This idea came from a tragedy in Mt. Carmel, Illinois where a teenager was killed when the driver accelerated purposely to cause the car to become airborne. This dangerous practice of ramping carried more serious consequences and enhanced penalties after this law was passed.

I worked closely with the parents of the young man that was killed. His parents were invited to the Governor's mansion and stood beside me during the ceremony while Governor Blagojevich signed the bill. Their devotion to making something positive come from their heartbreak still moves me.

Another piece of legislation I considered important that was signed by Governor Blagojevich during my first two years dealing with the growing issues related to a serious drug problem we were experiencing in rural Illinois. Meth was becoming a common drug of choice in our rural regions because it was inexpensive to purchase and relatively easy to make. The main ingredients for meth were available over the counter at local convenience and drug stores.

The meth scourge prompted the formation of various community groups to fight the growing epidemic. One of the most well-organized and passionate groups was from Paris, Illinois. It was led by a lady named Kristen Chittick. She was not only committed to fighting this scourge but was also highly determined. The name of the group was *Citizens Against Methamphetamine Abuse* (CAMA). During the time I was in office, I worked with Kristen and CAMA countless times to address issues related to meth and other drugs.

The first successful effort came when the group made me aware of products being sold which could intentionally mask efforts to determine drug use. A number of these products were advertised and sold in Illinois. The purpose of these products was to assist people who wanted to pass a drug test while using drugs by masking or fraudulently affecting the results of the test. Keep in mind that school bus drivers are among those subject to random drug testing, as are most individuals on probation for drug-related offenses.

When the legislation to end the sale of such products was introduced, it immediately drew opposition. I was shocked that any group could oppose the removal of these types of products. I was, of course, naïve and just learning the way things work. It seemed that retail merchants had a problem with the removal of these items from their inventory. They were especially upset that any inventory currently existing would not have the chance to be sold. The business owner would incur losses if the once legal product were suddenly illegal to sell. After some negative press, they agreed to remove opposition if I delayed the effective date of the legislation. It seemed to me that they wanted to sell off inventory before the proposal became law.

I refused to delay the effective date, they eventually backed down, and after some additional negative press, and the proposal became law. Later, when I worked on additional restrictions related to meth manufacturing, like limiting the use of precursors, I ran into more opposition from retailers and others. These were important lessons because no matter how reasonable something appears to be, some groups will likely be opposed.

About halfway through the legislative session calendar, important deadlines occur. There are deadlines to get Bills out of Committees. During those times, committees meet long hours and often twice a day to handle the increased workload due to the deadline. A *third reading* deadline also must be monitored. This is the deadline for House Bills to have been heard on the floor at least three times before a final vote. Remember, the first reading is when the bill is read into the record during the perfunctory session. The second reading allows for other House Members to ask questions about the legislation and propose any changes to the measure before it is moved to third reading. If amendments are added, the bill goes back to the committee for approval and then is moved to the house floor to be called again on second before moving to third reading. Sometimes bills are moved back and forth from second to third more than once to make necessary changes. After being amended after a return to the committee for approval, the proposal comes back to the house floor, gets read again a second time on second reading with the amended language and then finally gets moved to third reading. All of these motions have accompanying rules and deadlines. I studied the rules very closely during my first term.

Interestingly, all of these rules and deadlines can be waived by a majority vote of the House Members. That also provides the majority party with another advantage. They can simply not agree to waive deadlines, posting requirements or other rules for minority legislation while assuring their members of receiving favorable consideration. Did that happen? Yes, often.

I must also admit that sometimes the same consideration to waive deadlines was provided to Members of the minority party, though not nearly as often. Once again, elections have consequences.

As the third reading deadline approaches in the House it is understood that unless the bill is acted upon favorably on third reading, it is likely dead for the session. Leading up to that deadline, it is hectic. Often, the early weeks of the session are slow and it seems like a lot of time is wasted during committees and on the house floor. The opposite is true when the deadlines approach; the entire climate of the General Assembly changes. There is also a tendency for House Members to watch Senate action on legislation just as Senate members watch for House Bills. As I mentioned, it is often the case that the Senator associated with the House Member sponsors the legislation passed by that House Member in the originating Chamber, and vice-versa. I contacted Senator Righter anytime I was ready to pass legislation on third reading so he could file to sponsor the legislation. There is also a process that allows for pre-filing for legislation. Plus, anyone can file to sponsor a particular bill, party affiliation does not matter.

Sometimes, someone will file to sponsor a proposal to slow it down or even stop it in the other Chamber. It does not happen often. There are rules about that as well.

During my first two years, I was learning a lot and did not sponsor many Senate Bills that came over to the House. I only picked up two successful Senate Bills. One was sponsored by Senator Mattie Hunter, a Democrat. It dealt again with some minor changes to laws regarding Speech-Language Pathologist Assistants. This proposal passed the House with a unanimous vote and became P.A. 93-1060.

The second proposal I picked up was one passed unanimously in the Senate by Senator Righter. The measure was assigned to Rules Committee and despite my efforts to move it in the House Chamber, it died when the 93rd General Assembly ended Sine Die. The proposal would have simply allowed for the use of the higher of two grant indexes in cases where consolidation was to take place between school districts. There was grant money available to build schools and there was also a desire to encourage schools to consolidate. Senator Righter and I thought this idea would remove any opposition to consolidation in instances when the grant index differential inhibited the possibility of consolidation. To me this was common sense if folks were interested in removing obstacles for reducing the number of school districts in the state. What I did not count on was the fact that there was considerable and deep competition for available School Construction grant money. There was not an appetite among Democrat House Leaders (Madigan and others) to see any change in how these funds might be distributed. I was extremely frustrated by this and even filed a motion to discharge the bill from the all-powerful Rules Committee. I figured that there should at least be a vote on the matter. After all, it passed the Senate with a unanimous vote. Of course, the motion to discharge failed because it took unanimous consent to discharge a Bill from that committee according to the Rules of the House at that time. Ugh! I would not give up on this idea though and in a future session, years later, I successfully passed a version of this original legislation.

I also sponsored several House Resolutions during the 93rd General Assembly. Most of these were congratulatory. For example, the Oblong High School Math Team finished second in the State, the Martinsville Lady Bluestreaks won the IESA State Championship, and a young man named Robert Quick, from Robinson was named by the Illinois VFW as Eagle Scout of The Year. Some of the Resolutions honored the contributions of various individuals to the community. Tony Cork, a veteran Track and Field Coach from Robinson was inducted into the Illinois Coaches Hall of Fame. Long-time Coach and Principal of Palestine Grade School, Jerome Jochim, passed away and subsequently the gymnasium in Palestine was named after him. As State Representative, I was able to sponsor resolutions congratulating and honoring a number of people and events.

Unfortunately, the war in the Middle East resulted in numerous House Resolutions memorializing young men and women who had given the ultimate sacrifice. Charles Lamb, of Casey and Shawna Morrison of Paris, both members of the 1544th National Guard Unit located in Paris, Illinois were both killed during a mortar attack on September 5, 2004 in the outskirts of Baghdad. Shawna was twenty-six and Charles was only twenty-three years old. All too often these types of Death Resolutions were necessary. Often, members of the family were on hand while their loved one was honored. I will never forget seeing these incredible families as they withstood the grief that accompanied the loss of their son, daughter, brother, sister, husband, mother, father or wife.

In March of 2003, only a couple of months after Inauguration, the United States invaded Iraq. The date was March 19th, 2003. I will never forget that day. I had just gotten off the phone after wishing my daughter Brenda a Happy 15th birthday. It was a Wednesday and the House was in session late that day as we faced one of the deadline weeks. Word quickly spread through the chamber that the United States was beginning an invasion of Iraq. It was then, that Jim Sacia, another freshman State Representative, stood and asked for a, "Moment of personal privilege."

In an emotional speech, Jim asked for prayers for his son who was an Apache Helicopter pilot involved in the invasion. You could have heard a pin drop in what was normally a very noisy Chamber. The entire rest of that evening bore an eerie silence as we watched and waited.

The 93rd General Assembly, over the two years, resulted in 1,102 new Public Acts. Some of these originated in the Senate and some in the House. They all traveled the same constitutional pathway to success.

The devil, however, is truly in the details. Many of the most critical and controversial proposals did not follow the transparent path I felt was in the best interest of the citizens. I often made that statement on the House floor during discussion and debate. I was often, as many of my colleagues, frustrated and angry that the obvious intent of Rules and the Constitution were ignored in favor of political power.

Early in my first term, I expressed my frustrations to Jack Morris regarding what I considered to be outrageous rules. He reminded me that this was the reason it was so important for me to learn the House Rules thoroughly. There were also so many unwritten rules. So, I committed myself to learn more about the procedures both written, as well as learning and applying unwritten rules, to get important proposals through the House, the Senate and to the Governor's desk.

Often, when Jack made important points, he did so with a steeple-fingered gesture. His second point, and one that I never forgot, was that I was responsible to my constituents first and foremost. He admonished me that I should never vote for, or propose anything that would harm the people I represented.

Part of the effort to provide constituents the type of service they deserved, was to ensure that my office properly responded to needs that arose with constituents regarding state agencies. Kathleen Rankin was doing a good job on that front. After the campaign, she became my legislative office assistant and quickly learned the system, and more importantly, who in the various agencies she could count on to solve problems. Fred Clatfelter also assisted with constituent services. He established traveling office hours in the remote areas of the 109th. Fred would set up times for constituents to be heard by securing space in public courthouses.

I reminded Jack of these efforts. While he agreed these were important, he also urged me to take on a challenge he felt was equally important. Jack thought I needed to make sure citizens knew what was going on in Springfield. He thought I should write a regular correspondence which outlined what was happening at the Capitol. Together, an idea was hatched. I would write a weekly newspaper column and offer it to the many newspapers in the 109th district. The column was intended to be an update about what was going on in Springfield. I asked citizens to stay in touch and let me know what they were thinking about key issues we would be voting on. That way, citizens would know what was going on and could provide me with input. I started writing a weekly column early in the spring of 2003 and wrote hundreds of these columns during the time I was a State Representative. To my surprise, almost all of the daily papers and virtually every one of the smaller weekly papers printed the columns. Most often the columns were printed verbatim, but a few times the obvious partisan language was edited. At one time, around twenty publications carried these articles. People in the 109th loved the columns. Jack was often on target with his suggestions, and this was a grand slam. Of course, the other important by-product was constant name recognition between election cycles. Jack was aware of that advantage as well. Every week, I would send the information to the papers and overnight the folks of the 109th districts had the latest news from Springfield. There was never a lack of material to relay.

Perhaps the most important thing that I learned during those first two years of my first term was that if I was going to be successful, *I could not allow perfect to become the automatic enemy of good.* Things were often not likely to go as I wanted them. To start with, I was in the minority and had no seniority. Although, as a school superintendent, I was used to making decisions and giving direction, I needed to understand that to get anything accomplished in the future, I would have to work with the other side of the aisle and within the rules, no matter how terrible the rules were. There were many people at the table and my hand was weak comparatively. There was a way to make the most of it and I was committed to doing just that.

Of course, this rule had a major caveat. Some issues and policies would never be open for compromise which would gain my support or vote. Some things were either politically or philosophically so poisonous that I could never support the legislation, even if it was 99.999 % good. If the legislation expanded abortion or provided for public funding of abortion, I would never support such an effort. I also would never support policies regarding civil unions or same-sex marriage. I held no personal animosity toward those seeking such legalization. I just felt that the government should not become involved in this issue. The civil and legal rights of all people should be respected and protected. I would also never support any attempt to diminish Second Amendment rights. I have high regard for the U.S. and Illinois Constitution and the 2nd Amendment to the U.S. Constitution is very clear on this issue. These, among other proposals were poison pills in my eyes and I would never support legislation that contained language that in any way was oppositional to my beliefs. Yes indeed, don't let perfect become the enemy of good **while never compromising certain basic principles.**

As mentioned, I also learned early on, from GOP Representative Bill Black that there was something he called, "The Rule of Sixty". Simply put, it means that nothing gets out of the House of Representatives and on to the Senate without 60 votes. During the five terms I served, the GOP was never in the majority, so this rule was critical.

Over in the Executive branch, the new Governor had hit the ground running in his first year. To show the public that he was going to cut government spending to provide money for education and health care, he froze the salary of Judges with an *Executive Order*. This order was later found to be unconstitutional. Nobody was surprised by the fact that a panel of judges would find freezing their salaries unconstitutional. Blagojevich though had made his point; he was going to fight government spending so he could instead provide more funding for programs for the people.

The freshman governor also made what he and supporters called a bold move to demonstrate his commitment to lowering the cost of health care for Illinois citizens.

In a letter to the head of the federal department of Human Services, Tommy Thompson, he asked for permission for Illinois to import drugs from Canada. Thompson denied the request but that did not stop Blagojevich from attempting to purchase drugs from Canada. After several court battles and appeals, the practice was finally found to be illegal in 2006. Once again, Blagojevich was fighting for the people and the drug company lobbyists had thwarted his efforts by influential contributions to Congress.

There were also early signs that Blagojevich was going to push all of the rules regarding campaign fundraising. On October 29th of his first year, he flew to New York for a fundraiser accompanied by Joseph Cari and Stuart Levine. Make a mental note of these names as they will come up later in this book. Levine had been named to the Teachers Retirement

System (TRS) Board by Blagojevich early on in his first term and Levine provided the airplane. A month later, during the Veto Session of the General Assembly, Blagojevich flew to other fundraising events out of state. On certain trips, he used a state-owned plane and traveled at taxpayer expense to these campaign events. After public criticism, he later reimbursed the state for this expense. These were early signs that Blagojevich did not draw a hard line between fundraising and his public service. Most people chalked it up to simple innocent errors made by a first-term governor. Any loud criticism was dismissed as partisan political banter.

The year 2003 was an exciting year. It was also the year Arnold Schwarzenegger was elected Governor of California. Lance Armstrong won his fifth Tour de France, and the Space Shuttle Columbia burned up upon re-entry which brought about a two year suspension for the NASA space program. Saddam Hussein was captured in Tikrit by the U.S. 4th Infantry and President George W. Bush announced on May 1st the end to all major combat in Iraq.

Hurricane Isabel hit the United States killing 40 people; Michael Jackson was arrested and booked on suspicion of child molestation and the last old-style Volkswagen Beatle rolled off the assembly line, Bruce Almighty and Finding Nemo were popular movies and folks were listening to P. Diddy, Nelly, Clay Aiken, Kelly Clarkson, and Hillary Duff. Gas was $1.83 a gallon.

Chapter Ten
Reading People's Faces

While I was busy learning the Rules, I was also learning to balance my work back home as superintendent with my duties in the General Assembly. The Board of Education at Hutsonville hired an interim, Jim Koss, to be present on days that I was in Springfield. Jim was a highly respected, recently retired superintendent from nearby Casey and the arrangement worked very well. I worked many weekends to catch up and Jim left copious notes regarding the events of the week including his thoughts about various items. If necessary, we spoke by phone during the week, and overall, things were working out the way we had envisioned.

In addition to what was going on at school and in the General Assembly, the new governor was establishing his style, as well as his aggressive populist agenda. Since I knew that I was going to have to work with the Executive branch and the governor, I tried to find out more about him. What I learned was interesting. After enrolling at and then spending two years at the University of Tampa, Blagojevich transferred to Northwestern University on the north side of Chicago. In 1979, he graduated from Northwestern with a B.A. in History and then went on to Pepperdine Law School from which he graduated in 1983. The History degree gave us something in common, but that was where the similarity ended. I used my degree to teach History and coach. He entered law school. He once famously quipped that he attended the law school in Malibu, California to surf, spent little time at the law library and even made fun of the low grades he received. Most people would agree this fact was evident throughout his time in public office. Another unique part of his growing up was his foray into boxing. While attending Foreman High School in Chicago, his Golden Gloves record was 6 wins with 1 career-ending loss to a guy named Patrick Porter.

After obtaining his law degree he left sunny California and the beach to return to Chicago, where Blagojevich worked as an Assistant State's Attorney in Cook County. At the time, the State's Attorney was Richard M. Daley. Perhaps the most important break for Blagojevich politically came in 1980 when he married Patricia (Patti), Mell. Patti Mell was the daughter of influential Chicago Alderman Richard (Dick) Mell. Dick Mell was Alderman of the 33rd ward for 38 years and during that time built his political clout into something of a legend. In 1982, Dick Mell proposed a handgun ban ordinance that required the registration of certain handguns. Mell owned a collection of guns and was later found to have violated his ordinance. No, problem. Mell, along with Mayor Daley, proposed an amnesty period during which Mell quickly registered the guns. In July of 2013, when Mell finally left the Chicago City Council, his daughter Deb was named as his replacement, as proposed by then-Mayor, Rahm Emmanuel. Deb also served in the Illinois House of Representatives during the time I spent in the General Assembly.

It was with that type of clout and political backing that Blagojevich ventured into politics. In 1992, he ran for and won State Representative in the 33rd House District which is located in Chicago along the North Shore. During his two terms in the Illinois House, Blagojevich was not particularly productive. He used his experience in the Cook County State's Attorney office to work on drafting and filing several judicial reform and crime bills, but his efforts did not result in anything substantial being passed into law. He was, by all accounts, a back-bencher. As governor, Blagojevich later called out members of the General Assembly not willing to back his proposals by calling them, "wallflowers", when it was he that resembled one during his time in the House.

After his second term as State Representative, Blagojevich seemed bored with his situation. Another opportunity arose and he decided, once again with the strong support of Dick Mell, to run for U.S. Congress in Illinois' 5th Congressional District. This District had been represented for many years by Dan Rostenkowski. Rostenkowski had served in the United States Congress since 1959 until his departure in 1995. Dan himself was the son of a Chicago Alderman, and his participation in the famous Congressional Post Office Scandal led to his downfall. The conspiracy involved laundering Post Office money using stamps and postal vouchers. Not deterred by an investigation, Rostenkowski ran for re-election but was defeated in 1994. The scandal was so bad that a Republican, named Michael Patrick Flanagan, defeated him in a largely Democratic Congressional District. That would change when Dick Mell and the Chicago Democrats decided it was time for Mell's son-in-law, Rod Blagojevich to run for Congress.

In the very next election after Rostenkowski's loss, Blagojevich was elected to Congress in the 5th Congressional District in 1996 and was elected two more times. During his time in Congress, Blagojevich was most famously known for his 2002 by a vote in favor of the invasion of Iraq. During his time in Congress, he kept a close eye on what was happening politically in Illinois and an obvious opportunity was presenting itself as the scandal involving the Republican Governor, George Ryan, continued to heat up. Once again, with the support of Dick Mell, Blagojevich entered the Democratic Primary where he defeated the two other Cook County contenders.

(Blagojevich takes the oath of office as Illinois Governor for the first time- Roger Eddy personal photo)

As a first-term Governor, Blagojevich began to push an agenda centered on education, health care and ethics reform. After the widely heralded scandal involving George Ryan, ethics reform was fertile ground. He was a brash, young good looking governor in a large Midwestern State which had produced several Presidents in past years. Many thought that Blagojevich ultimately wanted to ride a wave of progressive reforms into a national spotlight and later run for higher office, even the presidency. It is interesting to note that when Blagojevich returned to Illinois as Governor, another reform-minded Democrat by the name of Barack Obama was a member of the Illinois Senate.

Obama had joined the Illinois Senate in 1997, just as Blagojevich was leaving the General Assembly to serve in Congress. Of course, Obama's star rose quickly as everyone knows and in 2005, Obama was successful in his run for U.S. Senator from Illinois.

While a member of the U.S. Senate, Obama and I made joint appearances in my legislative district to discuss agriculture and education issues. I joined him and we toured a new ethanol plant in Palestine, Illinois followed by a discussion of state and federal agriculture issues. After that morning session we traveled to Paris, Illinois and held a forum regarding education issues. As a downstate Republican State Representative, I took some negative criticism from a few local and state GOP members for appearing with Obama. I never regretted the day. Both venues were packed and attendees had a chance to hear from their elected officials regarding issues that were important to them.

(Representative Eddy, Legislative Aide Kathleen Rankin and then U.S. Senator Obama in Palestine, IL- Roger Eddy personal staff photo)

Obama was a U.S. Senator for only a couple of years and then rode a rocket sled into the White House as the 44th President of the United States. The fact that Obama was elected President during the middle of his term as U.S. Senator provided Blagojevich the opportunity to name his replacement. From 2003, when Blagojevich was inaugurated until 2005 when Obama left for the U.S. Senate, the two shared mutual policy interests and were often on the same page pushing the same progressive agendas, especially having to do with health care expansion. They both wanted to be President of the United States.

(Blagojevich and Illinois Senate President Emil Jones from his days in the Illinois Senate, together they pushed for universal health care in Illinois. *Wikipedia* photo by John Mintier)

The real problem for Blagojevich was that Illinois revenue was down and health care costs for the poor were rising much faster than the state could already pay. The idea of expanding the State of Illinois healthcare coverage seemed unlikely. How could revenue be found to provide additional funding for healthcare and education? He desperately wanted to expand funding for early childhood education. Yet, Blagojevich was against any type of income tax increase and refused to raise taxes, "On the backs of the hard-working people of Illinois."

In his own words, he wanted to, "Shake things up."

Along with Blagojevich, a staff of other cocky and creative individuals joined him in the governor's office. A guy named Bradley Tusk became Chief of Staff and another guy named John Filan became budget director. Blagojevich, always talking in superlatives, called the Illinois fiscal situation, "The worst budget crisis the state has ever known." At that time, the deficit was estimated to be around $5 Billion. John Filan, according to Blagojevich, was just the person to solve the problem. In his first budget, Filan intended to balance the State Budget with a combination of downsizing, operational cuts, fund sweeps, and other borrowing schemes. The number of state agencies was reduced from 66 to 46 in the first two years.

Illinois had 649 *Dedicated Funds* which were intended to support specific expenses and these funds had been created through legislative action. The funds held various amounts of money accrued over the years from legislative proposals intended to fund various specific pet projects. The fact that funds had to be protected like this says a lot about how legislators, over the years, trusted the spending in the State Budget to go for its intended purpose. Filan proposed unprecedented power to transfer and borrow from these dedicated funds to fund State spending and help balance the budget. This power later led to several lawsuits claiming that some of these funds were protected. The centerpiece of the plan was to issue $10 Billion in Pension Obligation Bonds. As part of that scheme, the scheduled payment of over $2 Billion in the first year of Blagojevich's term was paid for with the borrowed money. The idea of arbitrage for some of the pension debt was a notion many financial experts thought to be a good plan for the pension funds. However, using the money to pay current debt, while certainly creative, was a one-time infusion of money and not any type of solution to the fiscal issues facing Illinois.

Of course, to Blagojevich, the Democratic majority, and even some Republicans who supported the bond scheme, this smoke and mirrors approach was acceptable.

Kick the can down the road regarding real sustainable revenue while expanding spending (especially on health care) seemed to be the strategy and remained the practice for the next several years until the crisis became so bad that fellow Democrats could no longer support the creative strategies. The expansion of a health insurance program for poor kids, started under the Jim Edgar Administration, was expanded to what was called the *All Kids* program and later expanded health coverage to family members of poor children. The types of health care issues and costs were also expanded in his plans.

As mentioned, a major influencer in the early days of the Blagojevich administration was a brash, young, bright and enthusiastic young man named Bradley Tusk. Tusk was a native of New York, having grown up in Brooklyn and Long Island. He earned his undergraduate degree from the University of Pennsylvania and then a JD from the University of Chicago Law School in 1999. His first real experience in politics came as an undergrad in the administration of Ed Rendell when Rendell was the Mayor of Philadelphia. After graduating from the University of Chicago, Tusk worked as the Commutations Director for New York Senator Chuck Schumer. He gained a solid reputation handling communications for Schumer after the September 11th attack on New York's World Trade Centers. Tusk then became a special advisor to New York City Mayor Michael Bloomberg before being named Deputy Governor by

Blagojevich. He shared the desire, along with other Blagojevich allies, of bringing universal health care and *Preschool for All* to children in Illinois.

There was no question that Tusk was front and center in the new administration. In a book he authored in 2018 entitled, *The Fixer: My Adventures Saving Start Ups from Death by Politics,* Tusk included one very telling story about his experiences with Blagojevich. He recounts that in 2003, the first year of his first term, Blagojevich was scheduled to be on a telephone call with the head of Homeland Security, Secretary Tom Ridge. The call was important. Governors from around the country would be on the call to consider various scenarios that might result in a declaration of a State or National Emergency. Keep in mind this was an important call because of tensions across the U.S. regarding terrorist activities. According to Tusk, in a story retold in his book, Blagojevich was not all that interested in being on the call and instructed Tusk to sit in on the call for him. As various scenarios were described by Homeland Security Secretary Ridge, governors from around the country chimed in to respond. The question became what would each of them do if the described scenario took place. When Illinois was called upon to respond, Tusk would respond. He wasn't sure if anyone would notice it was not Blagojevich's voice but in what might be described as a muffled and quick reply, he remembers saying something like, "I'd declare a state of emergency", in response to one of the scenarios.

In the same book, he describes how he would even be left in charge of signing or vetoing certain pieces of legislation. Not yet 30 years of age, this was the strong influence of Bradley Tusk on the early administration of Rod Blagojevich. Tusk would leave the Blagojevich administration at the end of 2006 before serious legal issues popped up and political walls began to close in on Blagojevich. Undoubtedly, Tusk must have had concerns by then about what was going on in the Blagojevich political operation. He was later called to testify against Blagojevich in a criminal trial regarding an instance when Blagojevich asked him to hold up a government grant until after a fund-raiser was held. To his credit, Tusk, at that time, put an end to the plans of holding up the grant, did not comply with Blagojevich's wishes and reported the incident to the Chief Ethics Officer.

It is also interesting, and worth noting that after serving as Illinois Deputy Governor, Tusk went to Lehman Brothers where he served as Senior Vice-President and created a lottery monetization group and was in charge of efforts to set up a system whereby states could monetize their lottery systems. Whether this came from Tusk's creative mind or not, the theory of monetization or privatization of the state lottery to raise money to pay for state expenses became a focus of future revenue proposals by Blagojevich.

Whatever the future of Bradley Tusk, the populist agenda formulated by Tusk and Blagojevich was robust and became the cornerstone of the Blagojevich policy foundation and legislative agenda. Beyond the expansion of health care, this agenda included support for previous executive action of former Republican Governor George Ryan's suspension the death penalty in Illinois, the importation of less expensive prescription drugs from Canada, the conversion of the Illinois Tollway system to the nation's first Open Road Tolling system, and, ironically enough, **ethics reform**.

(Former Illinois Governor, George Ryan attended Blagojevich's first Inauguration. Ryan would soon be in prison on corruption charges. Blagojevich extended Ryan's initial ban on the death penalty in Illinois. Wikipedia Flickr user spsarge)

Looking back now, it may have been the height of hypocrisy that Blagojevich was sounding the trumpet on ethics. In his first year, the Governor signed into law the State Officials and Employees Ethics Act. Calling the package, "The toughest, most comprehensive ethics reform package is the state's history," Blagojevich claimed to be cleaning up state government. An earlier version of ethics reform passed by the General Assembly had been vetoed and in an Amendatory veto he inserted what he described as tougher language. Included in his version were enhanced enforcement measures, additional violations and punishment related to the existing Gift Ban Act, rules regarding the appropriate use of public service announcements, required ethics training for officeholders and state employees and even an ethics hotline.

The General Assembly did not act on the Governor's veto. Instead, the original legislation simply was not addressed after the veto. During the fall, the General Assembly and along with the Governor's staff, re-wrote the proposal as part of two separate bills, one was SB702 and the other HB3412 and later, after signed by Blagojevich, became P.A. 93-0615. It was signed into law on December 9th, 2003. Six years later, on December 8th, 2009, Rod Blagojevich was in handcuffs and leaving his home to be charged with various crimes related to public corruption.

However, in the late fall-early winter of 2003, Blagojevich was playing the part of the reformer quite well. The ethics reform legislation he signed contained many lauded components including a ban on taxpayer-funded public service announcements, newspaper or magazine ads, bumper stickers, billboards, buttons, magnets and stickers that feature the image, voice or name of constitutional officers or members of the General Assembly. The measure prohibited state workers from leaving government employment and immediately accepting jobs with companies they regulated or licensed or were involved in the awarding of state contracts over $25K. This ban lasted one year but had a waiver clause. It is important to note that this was not an actual revolving door ban and did not include lawmakers. Numerous exemptions that had been a part of the State Gift Ban Act were removed, which meant that a lobbyist could no longer gift a round of golf or tennis, and lobbyist spending on any state employee or official would now be limited to $75 per day. An existing limitation on the use of state employees for political work was strengthened and the new law banned making political contributions while on state property. Documentation of State employee's work hours was also implemented, and each of the constitutional officers was required to appoint an executive inspector general to review complaints of corruption or wrongdoing.

New and tougher penalties were also established in the law. Those in violation could be charged with a Class A misdemeanor plus fines and potential dismissal. Of course, members of the General Assembly could still not be removed unless convicted of a felony. Retaliation against State employees reporting misbehavior was also part of the legislation. Each caucus leader named two members to a new Legislative Ethics Commission which would review allegations. And, there was much more. The entirety of the legislation can be read online at the Illinois General Assembly website- www.ilga.gov. The language of the law is contained in P.A. 93-0615 and can be found by clicking on the link entitled, *Previous General Assemblies,* and following prompts from there.

All the while this public display of reform was taking front and center, Blagojevich was working on his campaign fund to ensure he would be very well-funded for his next campaign, whatever that would be. He worked with two men by the names of Stuart Levine and Antonin (Tony) Rezko. These men also worked to raise money for Barack Obama. Rezko was an engineer, real estate developer and contributor to Blagojevich's first campaign for governor. He opened the first Subway sandwich shop in Chicago and also opened chains of Panda Express and Papa John's Pizza restaurants in the city. Patti Blagojevich was a business partner of Rezko's and received real estate commissions for work with his firms.

Stuart Levine was a long-time political insider who had been previously associated with Republicans and switched sides when Blagojevich was elected. He was also an admitted drug user and later he was sentenced to prison for various crimes. Levine also later testified against Blagojevich and numerous others in exchange for a more lenient sentence.

Another individual heavily involved in raising money for Blagojevich was Chris Kelly. Kelly used a brash, tough-guy style to raise millions of dollars for Blagojevich. He and Blagojevich became what Blagojevich described as best friends. Years later, after being indicted on charges related to extortion and bribery, Kelly committed suicide just before reporting to prison to serve a long sentence.

These were the people in the inner-circle. These were the folks setting up the campaign enterprise of Rod Blagojevich during the early days of his time as governor. They started working on raising money quickly and the results were impressive, if not all-together above board. As early as 2003, the *Friends of Blagojevich* campaign account received large campaign contributions that seemed to be connected to either appointments to government agencies or some type of preferential treatment.

For example, in July of 2003 a $10K donation came from the Elevator Constructors Local 2 PAC. That same month, three associated union Officers were named to state positions and this was just the beginning. For the next few years, Blagojevich continued to receive large contributions from individuals and entities that would then benefit from being appointed to boards or commissions, be awarded state contracts, awards and/or grants from state agencies.

In February and March of 2004, Joseph Cari and Stuart Levine were involved in a huge pay to play scheme. A Virginia based company wanted to obtain an $85 million contract doing investment business with TRS. This company was subsequently asked to pay a phony consulting company $850,000, to help raise campaign money for, "A high ranking public official." In May of 2004, Cari delivered this request to the Virginia based company.

The toughest ethics reforms in history were being implemented while the governor and those surrounding him were busy setting up perhaps the biggest extortion, bribery ring and pay to play operation in the history of Illinois.

Amid all of this, Speaker Madigan was surely watching and aware of the enterprise that was being established. He watched a young governor play the system while attempting to convince the Illinois public he had some type of golden touch and could provide all kinds of public programs without raising taxes. Madigan was a supportive partner early on as budgets passed that were not close to being balanced, and some identify him as an accomplice since he seemed reluctant to intervene and often received campaign contributions from the same benefactors. I doubt that was entirely the case. Madigan long ago perfected the art of campaign contributions while adhering to the law. After all, most of the current campaign finance laws in Illinois were written and passed while Madigan as Speaker. Likely during those first two years, some of the craziest requests from the governor and his budget guru, John Filan, were rejected by the Speaker and Members of the General Assembly were really not made aware of some of the proposals.

(Long-time Illinois House Speaker Michael Madigan.
Wikipedia- illinoislawmakers)

After wrestling with Republican governors for many years, Madigan could see the political and policy advantages to having a Democratic governor. It was also a chance to promote party platform principles such as movement toward universal healthcare, preschool education funding and support of labor union issues. It was also a chance to consolidate even more power which would result in more support and increased fundraising for his campaign accounts and other members of his caucus. It was a chance to build on his majority and guarantee party dominance into the future. With a democratic majority in the House and Senate, along with a democrat governor, there were a lot of possibilities. Madigan could put up with the antics of Blagojevich at least for a while. The positives outweighed the negatives.

During this time, most rank and file lawmakers really were not that knowledgeable about these schemes. The first public indications that feds were watching the Blagojevich campaign became known much later. What everyone did know was that by the end of the second year of his first term that Blagojevich had chosen a path that would find him constantly talking negatively about members of the General Assembly whenever anyone dares challenge him. The General Assembly was the problem, according to Blagojevich, when his policy proposals failed. After all, he had inherited such a bad situation created by these inept, corrupt lawmakers. He was the guy to clean this all up and usher in a new era of Illinois government centered on serving the people of the state. All of this negative bluster took place while smiling and greeting lawmakers with a handshake as if he was their friend.

In January of 2004, as part of his budget address, Blagojevich suggested that the State Board of Education (ISBE) should be, "taken over," by the Governor's office. As always, his plan to make this major change started with an attack on the agency. After calling the State Board of Education a "Soviet-style bureaucracy," he then worked with Senate Democrats to introduce legislation to allow for the Governor to completely control the State Board of Education and make all of the board appointments. Later on, this tactic became a clear indication of his desire to control these appointments to exchange state board appointments for campaign support. In any event, the larger scheme of the complete takeover of ISBE was not acceptable to lawmakers. However, a restructure of how and when a Governor could appoint members to the State Board of Education did pass. The new law would allow the office of the Governor upon election, a majority of appointments to the Board while maintaining some independence of the Board from the Governor's office.

It was not the complete takeover that Blagojevich wanted. However, it did provide him the opportunity to appoint new members more quickly and gain a majority of the Board by appointments he would make. Many people thought that this was a positive change in public policy that would make the Governor of the State more accountable for the education of children. Often, the Governor is held accountable for the performance of students on things such as testing when, in fact, the Governor had no real control over the Agency which was responsible for the education program. I voted in favor of the plan. I thoroughly regret that vote as do many others. The agency lost some of the independence to advocate for the best interest of students at times and has become increasingly political.

After the FY04 Budget was passed in the spring of 2003, which included a $10 Billion Pension bond sale scheme, it also included fund raids and dozens of new fees. Blagojevich was against raising taxes but did not feel the same way about fees. The FY05 Budget constructed in the 2004 spring session was even more difficult to assemble and clearly out of balance using any reasonable accounting application. A large part of the problem was the desire to build in permanent spending for health care expansion and education funding increases while using one-time revenues such as bond proceeds, shorting the State's share of the pension payment, and sweeping funds from accounts which were supposed to be dedicated to paying other expenses. These were all one-time revenues. What would happen when it was time to repay and replenish these various dedicated funds? The simple fact is that a dollar can only be spent

88

once and many of the dollars used to get by in FY04 were simply not available and counted on the erroneous theory that somehow money dedicated for other purposes could be counted as revenue.

It was clear that if the increases in spending in the FY04 State Budget were to be maintained in FY05, plus any expansion of health care or additional money for things like Early Childhood and K-12 education was to take place, additional **real revenue** was needed. And, it was not just a small amount of revenue that was necessary to balance the state budget. Several billion dollars would have to be added to support the proposals made by the Governor. His budget address and public comments supported all of the spending without any plan to pay for it. According to him, finding the revenue was the responsibility was that of the General Assembly.

There are few sources of sustainable and reliable revenue for any State. The obvious ones are income and sales tax. In Illinois, gaming revenue is also a source of funding state operations along with lots of fees. However, it was obvious the kind of spending that Blagojevich wanted would require much more than dedicated fund sweeps, some new fees or expanded gaming. It was eventually going to take a sustainable and reliable source of revenue to support this kind of spending. When some Democrats floated the idea of an increase to the 3% flat income tax rate in Illinois, Blagojevich lashed out at the General Assembly and promised that he would veto any effort to raise taxes on the hard-working people of Illinois. He also warned that a sales tax increase would result in a veto. In the media and on the stump, he did a great job of making the General Assembly the enemy because they would not find ways to support his great ideas while completely demonizing any of the sources where the type of revenue needed could be generated.

The spring session of the Illinois General Assembly typically wraps up by May 31st. The session dates in May are considered as days to complete the budget. The Illinois Constitution requires a balanced budget, and if the budget (supposedly balanced) is not passed and signed into law by May 31st, a super-majority of votes (2/3) is then necessary for a budget to pass after that. While the Democrats had a majority in the House, they did not have the super-majority of votes necessary to pass a budget on their own. It was clear by mid-May of 2004 that there was likely not going to be a budget passed by May 31st.

The Democrats, led by Madigan, simply were not going to use the clear majority they had to pass such a rotten budget without requiring some Republicans to join them. The strategy of going into overtime was clear. To pass a budget after May 31st, some GOP House Members would be forced to eventually vote yes.

So, in June, dates were added to the spring calendar to facilitate the passage of a budget. A group of GOP Representatives would meet with the Democrat majority behind closed doors in an attempt to come to some type of agreement. These were normally more experienced legislators who were well versed in revenue and spending. The designated appropriations committee chairs were included in these discussions. The goal was to come to an agreement and call the entire House membership back to vote on the agreement. The stalemate would drag on when it became very clear that Republicans were not interested in voting for any new taxes. The month of June passed and the end of the fiscal year, June 30th, 2004, came and went without a new budget to start FY05 on July 1st.

The State could continue to operate for a while into a new fiscal year, even without a budget. But, that could not happen for very long. Appropriations for FY05 were not available for agencies until approval of a new spending plan was signed into law. Pressure built further when State employee pay was threatened. Pressure was added by calling lawmakers into special session. Blagojevich called for most of the special session days, publically calling on rank and file members of the General Assembly to get involved and be the ones to force an agreement. Finally, in mid-July, the then record-setting special sessions came to an end when a budget was passed. The proposal did not solve the real problem. Pension payments were once again put off (shorted), unrealistic income projections were made and the continuation of fund raids was part of the plan. More smoke and mirrors amid a dog and pony show.

While this had been a record-breaking length for a session (at that time), it was nothing compared to what was coming. As mentioned previously, the budget problem for Illinois was not solved. The fact that revenue did not even come close to matching expenses meant providers were not going to get paid promptly and schools were not going to receive critical state aid, special education and transportation funding. These delays forced borrowing by providers, especially health care providers. When the State did make payments, interest was also paid for the late payment. In many cases, the interest rate paid by the state was more than the rate providers were charged by financial institutions to provide cash to operate. Short term, providers could even come out ahead.

As the State's fiscal crisis droned on, financial institutions became worried that the state would never provide the money it owed. School districts that did not have enough property wealth to support educational operations also were forced to borrow. Working Cash Bonds became a very popular form of borrowing for school districts to pay operational costs. State aid payments were not only months late, but there were also concerns that maybe the full amount would never come. Fears and rumors of discounted state aid payments that were already late, or possibly even skipping a couple of payments were widespread. Schools were forced to lay off staff and while record education funding was being touted, education was suffering negative consequences due to larger class sizes and smaller operating budgets. Plus, all of this borrowing would have to be paid back, with interest. The long-term effect of all of this was not fully realized in the summer of 2004. After breathing a sigh of relief that catastrophe had been averted with a budget deal in late July, the General Assembly adjourned. However, it would soon become evident even to the most optimistic, that the crisis was just beginning. The worst was yet to come in terms of fiscal issues and overtime sessions.

It was also in 2004, after that much-heralded Ethics Bill had outlawed the use of public funds to promote officeholders, that Blagojevich spent $480K of state money to have signs erected on tollway entries proclaiming *Open Tolling* in Illinois, along with his name in big bold letters. Later, this practice was declared illegal and the signs were changed, removing his name.

In 2004, Blagojevich tried something else that was considered quite controversial.

Illinois, like many other States, was experiencing a shortage of flu vaccine. Blagojevich ordered the Department of Health in Illinois to purchase $2.6 million in flu vaccine from overseas. The vaccine was coming from a country that had not gained the necessary federal approval to allow for the importation. The Food and Drug Administration had blocked the vaccine from entering the United States. The payment had been made through and there would not be a refund. Eventually, the vaccine was donated to support earthquake victims in Pakistan. Sadly enough, the vaccine expiration date passed before the vaccine was used by anyone. The $2.6 million spent by Blagojevich's administration was a total waste.

In another effort to provide drugs to Illinois residents, Blagojevich attempted to allow drugs manufactured in Canada to be used in Illinois without FDA approval. Some of the drugs were also in short supply in Illinois, but some were not. They all were less expensive. He contended that the drugs were safe and less expensive. He was, in his mind, fighting for the hard-working people of Illinois and attempting to deliver health care reforms. Many Democrats were supporting the effort. However, before the drug purchases could be made, the FDA once again shut down the plan.

He also attempted to require pharmacies to dispense a drug known as, "The morning-after pill." This drug would terminate a fetus in a suspected pregnancy. Many pharmacists would not fill prescriptions for this very controversial pill. However, in 2004 Blagojevich issued an Executive Order requiring pharmacies to dispense the pill to anyone requesting it. Many Pharmacists still refused and went to court to block the order and won.

Some of those who supported Blagojevich's efforts to reform healthcare in Illinois were also clearly upset that he was using powers he did not have to implement these reforms. In the case of the morning-after pill he gained enemies he would never win back. This was not only a healthcare issue, it was an issue related to the termination of a life. Many downstate Democrats who are typically pro-life were outraged by the action of their governor. He was intentionally using the power he did not have to circumvent the law and push a liberal agenda regarding the termination of a pregnancy.

Blagojevich was especially close with one downstate State Representative named Jay Hoffman. Hoffman was a bright, likable and friendly down-Stater from the metro-east area of St. Louis. Hoffman served with Blagojevich during the time Blagojevich was a State Rep in the early 1990s. He provided a lot of assistance to Blagojevich in the downstate rural areas where Blagojevich had performed so well in his initial campaign for governor. Hoffman became a close ally of Blagojevich and often carried legislation that was crafted by the administration. There was no question that Representative Hoffman was the top legislative ally of the governor. He presented the Governor's argument on the House floor during the budget stalemate, even though privately, Jay had a hard time defending some of the Governor's tactics.

Hoffman still serves in the House of Representatives and is a well-respected lawmaker. His deep loyalty to Blagojevich eventually cost

Hoffman dearly as he fell out of favor with Speaker Madigan when the feud between Blagojevich and Madigan reached its' pique. The powerful House Transportation Committee which Hoffman chaired did not have legislation that would have typically been assigned to it assigned for a long time. Some thought Madigan might remove Hoffman as Chair. However, it was far more embarrassing to simply allow Hoffman to be Chairman of a Committee without a purpose. That was vintage Madigan.

I often wondered if Hoffman knew everything that was going on behind the scenes.

I doubt it, especially those early years. Any criticism of Blagojevich was identified as partisan whining or undue attacks by lawmakers against the guy coming in on the white horse to clean things up. And likely, some of the criticism was partisan politics.

Behind the policy curtain, much more was happening related to Friends of Rod Blagojevich and his political and fundraising operation. The early pattern of large contributions by donors who ended up with state contracts and/or board appointments continued. Back in September of 2002, a law firm by the name of Myron M. Cherry and Associates made a $25K donation to the Blagojevich fund. Another $25K donation was made on June 18, 2004. The Illinois Department of Financial and Professional Regulation hired this firm for legal services and the firm was paid over $900K for these services, according to a story in the Chicago Tribune. Perhaps not illegal, but it sure looked bad. Another group, ACS State and Local Solutions started contributing to the Blagojevich campaign fund on July 23, 2003. The first $25K donation was followed by additional amounts totaling $25K. ACS State and Local Solutions was paid around $17 million in state-contracted work in the next six consecutive fiscal years. Again, not illegal but the connection between the contributions and the contract awards is noteworthy. A company called Environmental Design International made two $25 K, one on July 25, 2003 and one on June 21, 2004. In FY 2004, Environmental Design International gained State contracts worth $560K. These were but a few of the large contributions made to the Blagojevich campaign fund with had some direct correlation to an award of State contracts or the appointment of individuals to boards or commissions. Seemed, I guess, at the time, business as usual in Illinois.

As I finished my first term, I was certainly not completely aware of the extent of the Blagojevich campaign activities. There were by this time a few newspaper stories and some whispers about how much money

Blagojevich was raising. Records were being set. To put this all in some perspective, comparisons are helpful and hindsight makes things a bit more clear. During his last six years a Governor of Illinois, Jim Edgar raised around $11.8 million. Only eight of the individual contributions to Edgar's campaign were $25K or more, and those eight contributions totaled around $422K. In a similar six-year period, Governor George Ryan, who preceded Blagojevich, raised around $20 million. Ryan's campaign received 35 individual contributions of $25K or more totaling around $1.6 million.

When Congressman Rod Blagojevich decided to run for Illinois' Governor and a Political Action Committee (PAC) was formed called the Prairie State Committee which was meant to support his effort, the PAC was very successful in fundraising efforts. In August of 2001, when the Prairie State Committee changed their name to Blagojevich for Governor, it had around $2.2 million in collected donations. From the time of the creation of the original Blagojevich for Governor fundraising committee which used the $2.2 million as seed money, through the next eight years, Blagojevich raised $58.3 million, including 435 contributions of $25K or more. These 435 contributions totaled $20.6 million or over 35% of the total funds accumulated. This was certainly enough to hold off any challengers.

However, the extent of this pay-to-play was not widely known in 2003 and 2004.

After all, it was the first two years of the governor's first term and he had done a great job of convincing the public that he was sent to Springfield to fix the mess and straighten things out. Sure, his methods were controversial, different from the way things had been done.

But, that was the reason he was sent there. He was going to clean things up. He had overseen the passage of epic ethics reform and even vetoed a weak ethics bill, demanding more. The fact that he forced lawmakers to make tough choices and pass what he termed as a balanced budget using his creative budget techniques should, according to him, be lauded. Any attempts to point out flaws, including the collection of a record amount of campaign funds linked to donors benefitting in some way, were merely political attacks by those jealous of his success.

As mentioned, I was among those not really aware of the corruption right in front of us all.

The construction of the new high school in Hustonville was well underway by the time my first term was completed. On evenings, weekends, and even holidays, I would pour over bid documents, change orders and the state Capitol Development grant paperwork. The construction work was in addition to the regular workload in a small rural school district for a superintendent. The assistance of interim Jim Koss was essential as was the hard work of my Principals and Secretary Lori Crumrin. The Board of Education was also very supportive and understanding. Things were working as planned. I wanted to continue to perform both jobs and it certainly seemed that things were going so well that a second term should be sought. Of course, I kept accurate records of the days I worked and the days I was in session. That came in handy as the local county Democrat Party leaders attempted to cause problems in my first couple of years. In a meeting requested by a couple of these individuals, I remember Board President Tina Callaway presenting these individuals with records which indicated that I had not violated any laws and the Board was very satisfied with the arrangement and the job I had done. When they began to question the wisdom of the Board, Tina reminded them politely that they were not residents of the Hutsonville School District and wondered what difference it made to them as long as the Hutsonville Board was satisfied. They left and never returned with any complaints.

After making sure everyone was still on board, especially at home, I announced my campaign to run for a second term during the first few months of 2004. The Board was satisfied, we would soon find out if the *people* were satisfied.

When I was not at school, in session or at one of the ballgames my kids were playing in, I was busy attending parades and trying to raise money for People for Eddy. It was important to make sure that there were funds available for the next election. The pace was hectic for sure. The fact that the budget stalemate required additional days in Springfield during the summer of 2004 for special sessions added to the already busy schedule.

Some days I would drive the two and a half hours to Springfield early in the morning, attend the Special Session which would begin around 10 AM. On most days, the session ended after only a few minutes since there was nothing to vote on. Once in a while, some minor Bill, long since presumed dead due to the original session ending date, was brought back to life with a series of House Rules being waived. Often the measure was not controversial and passed with the super-majority needed after May 31st. It at least appeared that something was being done, however inane.

The working group is known as 'The Budgeteers' had not agreed on anything. They were supposed to come to some agreement and then the full House would be called in to vote.

The special sessions were called by the Speaker or the Governor to exert pressure to agree. The public had to know that the budget was a priority and lawmakers would have their feet held to the fire. But in reality, as mentioned, most of the time, we took roll call around 10 or 11 AM, and then would adjourn very soon thereafter. I remember times we were in special session for 10 minutes or less.

I would then drive the 140 miles back to Hutsonville, often arriving in the early afternoon to continue my day at school. There were days that I was asked to stay for budget meetings related to the K-12 Education Budget. I was not the GOP Minority Spokesperson for the House Education Appropriations Committee at that time, but I did know the issue very well.

The fact that I was asked to stay, at first, did not sit well with the more senior member assigned as the Minority Spokesperson at the time. Seniority was king.

My work at school would often last into the early evening to stay caught up with the workload of building a new school, in addition to the normal requirements of the job. In the summer, we did not have an interim, that was for session only and nobody could have predicted the special session days that were added. At the time, everyone figured this overtime and these special sessions were something unique. Likely, in the future, summers would be clear of all of these extra trips to Springfield. Of course, time would prove that notion wrong.

Despite all of the additional days and long hours, things were going well. Most of that was due to the hard work of others, especially my wife. She took everything in stride and often kept me from becoming negative. My family was very understanding. They continued to support my efforts by walking in parades and attending my events.

My fundraising base had widened and two successful golf outings brought in tens of thousands of dollars. My fund-raising consisted mostly of small donations. Many of those who donated had an interest in education, agricultural and economic development. There was never a thought that any donation I received was tied to any particular vote I would make. Folks knew where I stood on the issues and by the end of my first term, I had a voting record. If people liked the policy issues I supported then they might donate to help me with my campaign. Plus, as an incumbent who had been elected by a wide margin in the first election, interest groups and many individuals were pleased to send support for reelection. Of course, the efforts were still being strongly supported by CRAW-PAC and the Jacks.

I did not have a Primary opponent this time but despite a 15 point win in my first general election, I did have an opponent in the 2004 general election. The Democrats slated a guy named Terry Edwards to run against me. The campaign was much more low-key. Edwards did not raise any real money and there was no negative campaigning. Even though my opponent did not spend money, we did spend some. It was still important to further establish my name and make sure that newspapers and radio stations I had established positive relationships with made some money.

This time, I won by a 67-33 margin. After getting an orientation to the life of a Representative, learning some of the rules, both written and unwritten, and starting to learn how to read people's faces, I was going back for another hand to be dealt with.

In 2004, the Boston Red Sox won the World Series for the first time since 1918 and ended the curse of the Bambino, Hurricane Charley hit Florida killing 12, Condoleezza Rice was named U.S. Secretary of State, and a CIA investigation revealed that before the invasion of Iraq in 2003, there was no evidence of weapons of mass destruction. Despite the report, George W. Bush was re-elected President defeating John Kerry. The Mars Spirit Rover landed on Mars in 2004, the first same-sex marriage took place in the U.S (in Massachusetts), Martha Stewart went to jail for insider trading, Ken Jennings won $2.5 million on Jeopardy, and Janet Jackson suffered a wardrobe malfunction at the hands of Justin Timberlake during halftime of the Super Bowl. Along with some college roommates, a guy named Mark Zuckerberg launched Facebook and the 60th anniversary of D-Day was remembered. At the box office, Oceans 12, *The Passion of Christ, Meet the Fockers* and another *Harry Potter* movie, along with *Spiderman II* was popular. Green Day, Usher, R.E.M., Britney Spears and Scissor Sisters were hot on the music charts.

And, gas had risen to $2.10 a gallon.

Chapter Eleven
If You're Gonna Play the Game...

On January 12th, 2005, Members of the House of Representatives of the 94th General Assembly were sworn into office. By this time I had a much better idea of what was going on.

Things were more familiar including the fact that Madigan was about to be reelected Speaker of the House. This time his majority was 65-53. Even though the Democrats had lost two seats in the House, they still held a healthy majority and the *Rule of 60* still meant that any legislation from the GOP side of the aisle must have Democrat votes to pass out of the House to the Senate.

It also meant that the Democrats still controlled all committees. My seating assignment on the floor of the House was virtually the same, near the back of the Chamber.

Of course, when the House Rules were proposed to govern the House, we once again strongly objected. The House Rules, with very few changes, passed once again along partisan lines.

Jack Morris urged me to study the rules and make sure that I was well versed in the application of those procedures. I did recommit myself to that task. I also made it a point to employ the unwritten rules I had already learned. These unwritten rules were just as, if not more, critical to the success of a Member of the minority party.

There was a slight change in my committee assignments. I was on the same education committees as the first term but this time was appointed to the Labor Committee. I had requested that committee assignment since labor issues often crossed paths with education. The Labor Committee appointment was highly sought after by caucus members and thanks to Leader Cross, I was fortunate to get that particular requested assignment.

I was also named to a special sub-committee related to education. That sub-committee was supposed to filter the many bills filed dealing with school code waiver requests. There was a process in place whereby K-12 school districts in Illinois could request a waiver of state laws on a case by case basis. Sometimes, schools would request a waiver from a designated school holiday for students to attend on that day. Often schools would request a waiver of the $50 fee limit for driver's education.

There were dozens of other popular waivers that were almost always routinely approved. I had trouble finding an instance certain waivers were *ever* denied. My thought was that these waivers took time and resources from local school district personnel and amounted to nothing more than red tape since the waivers were granted in an almost automatic fashion.

I filed legislation that would have allowed schools to waive these types of laws locally. I was interested in less red tape. For example, the State Board of Education always recommended the approval of waivers of the law governing the fee charged by local school districts that restricted the fee to $50 as long as the requested increase was not above $250. It made sense to me to file legislation that raised the limit from $50 to $250 or even allows locals to determine the fee. The legislation I filed to increase the limit to $250 was never successful because politically it was a problem for anyone to vote for a bill as it would be characterized as a fee increase in the next election. Many times I was told by my colleagues that the legislation made perfect sense... but they could never vote for it. A voting record is heavily scrutinized and votes are the perfect fuel for negative, attack style campaign ads.

There were many other possible instances where school code waivers could easily be applied. The sub-committee met and approved several bills to be recommended to the Elementary and Secondary Education Committee. Some made it to the House floor but most died due to the lack of willingness to vote on controversial issues. One idea that came out of these meetings was the waiver of residency required for students of parents-guardians that worked in one district while their children attended school in another district. That waiver is popular to this day. If a teacher works in one school district but resides within another district's boundaries, the student can attend the school where the teacher works, as long as the school district has requested and been approved for that waiver. Several years later, there was finally succeeded in reducing the red tape involved with some waivers. There is still much more that can be done in this area.

I was assigned a similar office in the same wing of the Stratton for my second term.

My seniority had not increased much. I think it gained me maybe 40 additional square feet in office space. My parking space was the same. I was never really concerned about those types of things. At least my new office had a window. Some Reps spent days looking around at offices and planning for the day they could move to a particular spot. As soon as someone announced retirement or was defeated in an election, the office buzzards started to circle. My Illinois House license plate number went from 104 to 90. I had moved up 14 spots in seniority in one election cycle.

I was happy to be back but disappointed that my roommate and friend Frankie Agular had been defeated. I had to look for a new place to live and stayed in hotels for the most part. I remember that the state rate allowed General Assembly Members to get a flat discounted rate at most Springfield area hotels. I quickly learned that hotel life was the housing choice of many. I had the standard complimentary hotel fare breakfast at several of the hotels in and around Springfield in my search for the most comfortable place. Pastries, coffee, at times eggs (often boiled) plus some bad bacon.

I vividly remember one of the places I stayed quite often early on in the hotel hopping was a hotel on the south side of Springfield; I am not going to mention it by name. That hotel was one that had exterior entry doors facing the parking lot from both floors.

I was staying in a room on the second floor one night and about 2 AM I awoke to the sound of someone turning the doorknob. That was followed by tapping on the door and another more forceful attempt to open the door. In an instant I shouted something like, "Frankie, get the gun, someone is trying to break in!" As soon as those words left my mouth, I heard the sound of someone running down the outside aisle way and a flight of stairs. I did not have a weapon and Frankie was not around. The person attempting to open the door did not know those facts. After calling the police, I did not sleep for the remainder of the night and I never could bring myself to stay at that location again. Never again did I stay at a hotel with exterior entries facing parking lots. To this day, I avoid those types of places at all costs.

A few new GOP members joined us. David Reis had been someone that CRAW-PAC and I had supported during his election to unseat a Democrat in a district just on my western border. He defeated an appointed Rep who had replaced long-time Representative Chuck Hartke after Hartke had been appointed as Director of Agriculture by

Blagojevich. He was one of several downstate members of the General Assembly rewarded for their support of Blagojevich with a nice agency appointment. Hartke, who had a solid background in Agriculture, was named Illinois Secretary of Agriculture. He was replaced in the General Assembly by Bill Grunloh. Bill was very likable and easy to work with. His expertise was in the construction industry.

Reis' background was as a pork producer so he had strong support from the agriculture community. David worked extremely hard to win and his opponent, Bill Grunloh, had been stuck in special sessions during the summer leading up to the general election which hurt Bill's ability to get out and campaign. Campaigning is not easy and requires a candidate to knock on doors, meet people and stay committed to a door to door program for months. Some candidates either are timid, lazy or otherwise unwilling to engage enthusiastically in this type of political work.

They call these activities *retail politics* and it pays off. David knocked on more doors and worked as hard as I have seen anyone work to win a campaign. While Grunloh was in Springfield, David was knocking on thousands of doors. I do believe David would have won this election anyway, but the fact that Grunloh was tied up helped David.

Another new Member was former McHenry County Board Chairman, Mike Tryon. Mike and I became close friends almost right away. He stopped by to say hello early on and told me that he was born in Terre Haute, Indiana. Terre Haute was the largest city in the Wabash Valley near where I lived in Hutsonville. He graduated from North Vigo High School in Terre Haute. After high school, Mike attended Indiana State University, also in Terre Haute, earning a degree in Environmental Science. After graduation, he moved to McHenry County to accept a job with the county health department. Later Mike started a successful water treatment testing company.

After once working for the county health department, he went on to be a county board member and then chairman of the county board. Best of all, he knew lots about my home area. In fact, during our first visit, we had great fun discussing a very popular local restaurant in West Union, near my home called Earl's Supper Club. Earl's is known far and wide for the best deep-fried catfish filets anywhere. Anyone who knew about Earl's was a friend of mine.

Mike also knew more about tax levies than the average member of the General Assembly.

As county board chair, he understood the process and filed legislation that would improve the levy process for all governmental units, including school districts. On a couple of occasions, his proposals drew objections from GOP leadership. Despite that fact, Mike worked hard to gain support and several key improvements became law. Mike once traveled to a little town called Neoga, Illinois to speak at a crowded town meeting to clear up issues related to an erroneous levy filed by local officials. Neoga was in my legislative district, and since I was unable to attend the town meeting due to a conflict, Mike drove five hours to substitute for me. No doubt he did a much better job explaining tax levies than I would have. He was that outside expert who is often listened to closely. Often, close to home one is not much of an expert but a couple of hundred miles away from home, a genius.

During his time in the General Assembly, Mike and a couple of other members of the General Assembly formed a band called *The Boat Drink Caucus*. Mike played guitar and the band performed in various venues throughout Springfield. From The Globe Bar located at the Abraham Lincoln Hotel to The Butternut Hut, they provided entertainment to fellow General Assembly Members, lobbyists and others. This group had quite a following. Fellow Rep Chad Hays (more on him later) also played guitar and was a lead singer while Senator Don Harmon played bass guitar. Harmon is now Illinois Senate President. Mike retired in 2017 and we remain great friends to this day.

In many ways, Springfield was becoming more and more comfortable and familiar.

In addition to many colleagues in the General Assembly who became friends, I also met dozens of staff members and lobbyists I counted on. What happens over a period of time is that one develops sort of a second or surrogate family of people that you get to know and rely on. That was certainly true for me. When you spend three to four days and nights a week away from home, you begin to cultivate routines regarding people you hang around with and places you go. The days are very busy with committee work, office hours and action on the House Floor. At the end of the day, life goes on and a life-style begins to take hold.

For me, the fact that a sort of second life evolves resulted in a friendship that I will never forget. A lobbyist named Dean Sweitzer was extremely kind to me and a great friendship developed quickly. He never described himself as a lobbyist, he preferred the term hobbyist. Hobbyist probably isn't even a word. Dean made up lots of new words. He was a veteran of over 25 years in Springfield as a lobbyist or hobbyist, whatever he preferred to be called. His specialty was nursing home and health care of the elderly. He was passionate about those issues and nobody knew more than Dean about that industry. Nobody cared more about the treatment of the elderly. He endeared himself to countless legislators over the years. His giant personality with the booming voice hollering "YO!" as you walked into his 'office' at the Globe Tavern in Springfield were trademarks. Yes indeed, he had an actual assigned chair and phone designated for his use at the bar. I cannot count the number of nights that Dean, myself and usually three or four other legislators had dinner together. As Mike Tryon often very accurately stated, "Dean could work an appetizer menu like Michelangelo painted the Sistine Chapel."

There are tough days at the Capitol and campaigning is sometimes brutal and Dean was always there to lend an ear or give you just the lecture you needed. He held court every night at the Globe and worked well with the well-known bartender named Kathleen, whom Dean referred to as *Evil*. Kathleen is a very special lady as well. She was named bartender of the year so many times in the Capitolfax blog annual poll that the award was named after her. She is the best, there is no question. They were best of friends; Dean had some sort of name for everyone. I was simply 'Sir' to him. After I retired from the General Assembly, we remained very close friends. Sadly, Dean was diagnosed with cancer at age 60 and passed away far too young.

I still miss him this very moment. I am sure everyone has had friends like that.

I continued to work on education, agriculture, and economic development-related issues during these two years. Some of the highlights for me were passage of P.A. 94-203 which established The Eastern Illinois Economic Development Authority, P.A. 0082 extended State Employee health insurance to hospitals with under 100 beds, and P.A. 94-0129 allowed retired teachers to return to teach in designated shortage areas. Similarly, P.A. 94-0914 allowed for retiring teachers to return to any teaching assignment (shortage area or not) to teach or substitute teach for up to 120 days. This growing teacher shortage in Illinois only worsened in the future and additional leniency was eventually passed into law to staff classrooms, especially in rural areas of the State.

Of course, I also introduced many bills that were not successful. Of course, they were very good bills, they just didn't have enough support.

103

That is always going to happen. At times, it was very frustrating to see what I considered to be a completely common-sense change to Illinois laws soundly rejected by my peers. Illinois is such a diverse State and it often difficult for rural, urban and suburban lawmakers to have the same priorities or see things the same way.

One of the bills I introduced is a good example of the problem. As already mentioned, I introduced a measure in 2005 to allow school districts to raise the amount charged as a fee to charge for Driver's Education students from a $50 cap to $250. This one deserves a little more explanation and highlights some of the frustration felt by lawmakers.

A waiver process which school districts could use to waive the $50 fee limit existed in Illinois. This waiver was applied for often and it was considered common practice for this waiver request to be permitted as long as the request for the fee increase was $250 or below. Again, this request was routinely approved hundreds and hundreds of times. My common-sense approach was to simply pass a law that was consistent with the current practice, thereby eliminating red tape paperwork for school districts and the State Board of Education.

The measure came out of the committee process to the House floor with what appeared to be some minor opposition. The fact that such a common-sense change was opposed at all sort of surprised me. Once it hit the House Floor it was tagged by legislative staff as a 'fee increase bill.' That type of designation, I found out later, is difficult to overcome.

I even argued with our own GOP staff that the legislation did not increase a fee. This proposal simply allowed for the local school district, through a locally elected board of education, to establish an increase in the fee which was being summarily allowed anyway. Despite my best efforts to convince me, colleagues, that the measure was a reinforcement of current practice without the unnecessary paperwork, the measure failed. It wasn't even close as it went down with a mere 44 yes votes and 64 no votes.

Early in the voting, the tally was much closer and yes votes hovered around the magic 60 number. When the vote total fell slightly below 60 and members saw that the 60 was not likely, the Speaker recited the warning that the vote would soon be officially recorded. The House Rules state that the person in the Speaker's Chair must announce three times that the official vote is being recorded. "Have all voted who wish? Have all voted who wish? Have all voted who wish." During the time the roll call is being announced three times, often Members watched the board and might change their vote depending on how the vote is going. In this case Members started jumping off the bill when it appeared that the bill was not going to get 60 yes votes. The eventual result was 44 yes votes. In their mind, there was no sense in voting yes and being accused of supporting a fee increase if the bill wasn't even going to pass. Some people who had originally stated they would support the bill ended up voting no. I learned a valuable lesson that day about a *hard roll call* as opposed to a *soft roll call.*

Once in a while, as a bill begins to slide backward from anywhere near 60 votes, so many Members start to vote no that a bill becomes in danger of getting 100 no votes.

If that happens, the Representative is awarded a traveling trophy and enshrined into the *Century Club.* The designation of being a Century Club Member comes with a special hat and lots of playful cheering. A Rep named Ken Dunkin was awarded this dubious distinction several times and there were rumors that the award might be named after Ken. Ken always handled this honor well. Thankfully, I was never enshrined.

The fact that the driver's education fee waiver bill did not pass was disappointing.

However, I learned another valuable lesson about fee bills and how difficult these were to pass. Common sense, not being all that common, it was necessary to get a hard roll call for my legislation and not assume support.

Another disappointment came after I introduced HB2734. I intended to save school districts money on a practice that was required but seemed outdated. At the time, the law required school districts, along with other public bodies, to publish certain items and information in a local newspaper. The original idea was that certain business performed by elected bodies should be shared as reasonably as possible with taxpayers and the public. Many of the notices required by law had to do with taxation, budgeting, bids, meeting notification and the like.

In my mind, the problem schools and other public bodies faced was twofold. First, the newspaper as a method for ensuring that information would be distributed in the best possible manner was questionable for many reasons. Some people didn't subscribe to the paper advertising the information required to be advertised. I felt there might be more effective ways for the information to be transmitted that would increase transparency. The second issue was that there was no limit as to what

105

newspapers could charge to perform this requirement. The way the law defined which paper had to be used for the required legal advertisement pretty much guaranteed the business to a certain newspaper without a limitation on the charges. My proposal could have allowed taxing bodies to save money, while remaining transparency.

I planned to make some common-sense changes to an antiquated law that I felt could be improved. Doesn't saving money while increasing transparency make sense? The current law provided an unfair balance between the newspapers being able to charge whatever it wanted and school districts having no other options but to pay the fee. This is the very definition of a monopoly.

The Illinois Press Association, along with their vast media membership, did not appreciate either the suggestion that some papers were out of line with the charges nor the notion that there might be better alternatives. The opposition they mounted was fierce and formidable. Within days I was being charged with attempting to allow public bodies to hide critical information from the public and taxpayers. Of course, the legislation still **required** that the information be disseminated, just by different means. In fact, in some areas of the state, posting the information on a website or including it in a newsletter that went directly to the constituency, or even mailing a notice to every citizen was a much more effective and cost-efficient way to ensure that people were informed. That charge made by the newspaper, about attempting to hide information, was ridiculous. I was, however, dealing with those that created the news and their version was hard to fight. This was *fake news* before fake news was a thing. The old saying that it is not smart to fight with people who buy ink by the barrel applies to this situation. I was vilified in papers all across the State for this proposal.

Despite all of the opposition to my original Bill, I was able to pass something that improved the situation. After I gathered information revealing that some newspapers in the state were charging thousands of dollars for such ads, the Press Association was willing to make some type of change to the current law. They claimed that they had no idea that this type of gouging was occurring. Once I developed the list showing the wide variance in the amount charged for a pubic body to fulfill this civic responsibility, it became obvious, even to the Press Association, that something had to change.

An amended version of the measure eventually became P.A. 94-0874 and the Press Association did not oppose it. The only thing we were able to accomplish was to set a maximum rate for these required ads. It was an improvement but in my mind more could have been accomplished to provide this information to taxpayers than the current mandate. The mantra that I had adopted, "Don't Let Perfect Become Enemy of Good," definitely applied to this situation. It was better for public bodies, but far from perfect.

Another highlight occurred during my second term in the fall of 2006. While the Illinois House Chamber underwent a renovation, the Fall Veto Session needed to be held elsewhere. We were all thrilled to hear that the historic Old State Capitol in Springfield would be our home for the 2006 Fall Veto Session. The historic building was fitted with proper technology to allow the business to take place and we used the famous site to consider potential overrides to legislation that the governor vetoed. The space was cramped but nobody complained. It was surreal to sit in that Chamber. The desks and chairs that we used were original to the time when the Illinois General Assembly met there. The historic Chamber was fitted with electronic boards to display the vote, a new sound system with microphones at each desk, laptops, and Wi-Fi. I wondered what the Representatives and Senators who used the Chamber in the 1800s would have thought!

Abraham Lincoln had served in that very Chamber and occupied one of the seats.

On one of the final days, we were in the Old State Capitol; the very chair that Lincoln occupied was identified. It just so happened that I was seated in that exact chair. Chills ran up and down my spine, I felt so honored and I will never forget that day. It was one of the most memorable days of the nearly ten years I served in the House. It was not in the front row as I recall, maybe the third row right of the aisle. But, that day, it was the **best seat in the House.**

While I was working on my legislative agenda, Governor Blagojevich was midterm of his first four-year term. After establishing an adversarial relationship during his first two years as Governor and attempting to portray the General Assembly as evil, everyone wondered what type of session we were in store for. By this time, in the early months of 2005, the State was already behind in payments to health care and other providers. School state aid payments were delayed and the State's economic picture continued to be bleak and getting worse.

But, based on the 2005 State of the State Address, delivered by Blagojevich in late February, nobody would suspect anything was wrong.

Unlike his first two State of the State Addresses or Budget Addresses, Blagojevich seemed to take a toned-down approach while praising his first two years' accomplishments. He acknowledged challenges ahead but there was no boogie man identified.

Much of this Budget Address contained policy suggestions that Republican lawmakers could support. Blagojevich spoke of the need for rooting out corruption in worker's compensation as well as medical malpractice reform. He mentioned the need to lower health insurance costs for employers, especially for small businesses. The speech was heavy on promoting job growth. He would support the construction of a third airport in the southland of Chicago. An airport site in Peotone, Illinois had been proposed many years earlier. He proposed spending over $5 billion on transforming the tollway system in the suburban region of Chicago. For Southern Illinois, a $1.7 billion clean-coal power plant was proposed. After once proposing to do away with a State Council supporting the development of the Wine Industry, he now declared that Illinois should establish September as Illinois Wine Month. Perhaps some of the Illinois Members of the General Assembly had invited Blagojevich to sample the various award-winning wines produced in Illinois? The Illinois wine industry, especially in southern Illinois, has developed into a very lucrative and popular market.

There was little mention of how all of these publically funded projects would be paid for. It all sounded good. He once again echoed strong support for more money for K-12 Education efforts and healthcare expansion. On cue, Blagojevich once again stated that he would not support any attempt to raise income or sales taxes.

Both the State of the State Address and the Budget Address seemed like an attempt to tone down the rhetoric and work with the General Assembly on a rather aggressive agenda which Blagojevich insisted centered on job creation. There were hints of support, although also skepticism, from business groups and Republican leaders.

He held back on most of the typical harsh rhetoric he was known for during the first two Budget and State of the State Addresses. His need to battle something took control though and Blagojevich attempted to make headlines by vilifying something new. In 2005 his crusade was against the violent video gaming industry. His disgust was centered on a video game called *JFK Reloaded*. A bill was introduced that was drafted by LRB for the Governor's office to ban the sale of certain video games deemed to be excessively violent.

Although many legislators were concerned that the law could very well be unconstitutional, the legislation passed and was signed into law by Blagojevich. He had done such a good job of using the bully pulpit of the governor's office to reveal the violent nature of many video games that even those lawmakers who knew it was likely a law that could never be enforced voted for it. Once it became law, Blagojevich banned the sale of *JFK Reloaded*. The video gaming industry filed a lawsuit claiming that the ban was a violation of freedom of speech and the court agreed. Not satisfied, the Governor's office appealed that decision to higher courts, only to be defeated. In the end, the Governor's crusade against the video industry cost Illinois about $510,000 in legal fees. To him, it was money well spent. His public persona rose and this time he didn't even have to pick a fight with the General Assembly to look like a hero and it appeared as if Blagojevich enjoyed taking on the Court System.

It became the hallmark of the Blagojevich operating strategy- always fight with someone, or somebody, or something. This time, in his mind, he had identified multiple villains: the judicial process, those demons that protected the violent video gaming industry and the violent video gaming industry. Violent video games were damaging our children then and still are today. It was a convincing argument; as I too hate those games and wish they were not available to our children.

Overall, it seemed like a different Rod Blagojevich in 2005. He seemed less interested in confrontation. He even served as the Federal Liaison to the Democratic Governors Association from 2005-2006 and was the chairman of the Midwestern Governor's Association in 2005. Maybe it was the fact that he was no longer fooling the public as much as he had in the past. During his first two years he was popular and his confrontational attitude toward the Springfield establishment was equally popular. Three years in, public polling numbers showed that people were growing tired of his populist act, starting to understand the budget crisis Illinois faced and were beginning to pay more attention to the campaign pay-to-play activities he was involved in.

A combination of factors brought his approval rating down and, more importantly, revealed a steady increase in his disapproval numbers. These disappointing numbers did not look good for a mid-term governor intent on being re-elected to another term. He also had his eyes on running for higher office. Many thought he had his sights on the Presidency. Could that be the reason for the change in attitude?

The new, more pleasant tone and demeanor must have at least meant something to some Democrats. Early in 2005, then Illinois State Senator Barack Obama, endorsed Blagojevich for re-election to a second term as Illinois Governor. Obama was not alone as many prominent Democrats from throughout the State endorsed Blagojevich's re-election. Even after the loss of millions of scarce and valuable state dollars related to the flawed purchase of a foreign vaccine, the attempt to allow Canadian drugs into Illinois contrary to federal law, some questionable fundraising and very questionable board appointments and state hiring practices, Speaker Madigan agreed to serve as his re-election campaign chair. This surprised some people. The feud between Madigan and Blagojevich was evident by this time and very real. One could even call them political enemies. Why then the support?

I could never figure out why Blagojevich had established such a negative relationship and on-going feud with Speaker Madigan. Perhaps it was because Madigan was the Speaker of the Illinois House of Representatives and Blagojevich had worked hard to make the House his sworn enemy as he fought for the people. No matter the reasoning, it was just plain stupid. Madigan had more political experience than anyone, worked harder, knew the rules better, and was much more intelligent than Blagojevich. Plus, Madigan was famous for his patience. Madigan had an excellent staff and, while Blagojevich did have some bright people on his staff, most of the Department Chiefs, Board appointees and other staff were political appointees and not the best choice for the job.

If these positives traits mentioned about Madigan seem to infer that he was doing a good job using his skills for the betterment of Illinois as the leader of the Illinois House; that could not be further from the truth. His arrogance, stubbornness, desire to punish others, brandishing his power, make deals and otherwise ignore the fact that Illinois was headed into a deep fiscal crisis, was inexcusable. The single most constant factor from the time Illinois was in decent shape fiscally until the State sank into the worst fiscal condition in history is that Michael Madigan was the Speaker and ran the Illinois House with absolute control.

The point is that Madigan was not going to be bullied by Blagojevich. Madigan is himself the ultimate bully and he surrounded himself with people that were bright, extremely hard-working and deeply loyal to him. Rod Blagojevich was no match. Those familiar with future Illinois governor's feuds with Madigan would attest to the fact that Blagojevich's replacement, Pat Quinn, was equally ineffective when crossing swords with Madigan. Quinn, in my opinion, often simply capitulated.

There is also the highly publicized attempt by GOP Governor Bruce Rauner to wrestle power away from Madigan. Once again, despite coming into office with a boastful arrogance about how he had, in his own words, "never failed at anything," Madigan reduced Rauner to a one-term, almost totally ineffective governor. In the eyes of many, including **in the Republican Party,** Rauner is thought viewed by many as perhaps **one of** the worst governors in the history of Illinois.

Rauner had money and after using over a hundred million dollars to become governor, he attempted to use campaign contributions, coupled with threats toward legislators, to control GOP Members of the General Assembly. He also tried to take on Madigan by attempting to influence House Democrats with threats of overpowering them with money to defeat them in the next election. It was such a bad plan and a pathetic example of a public service. Rauner was also going to, "Shake up Springfield." Once again, just like with Blagojevich, Madigan's combination of patience, with no concern about the welfare of the people of the State, coupled with Rauner's inability or unwillingness to take good advice from people much more experienced and brighter than he was, defeated Rauner. Madigan emerged from the four-year scuffle with Rauner stronger than ever. Worse yet, the State GOP was left in shambles by Rauner's four years of tyrannical reign. It will take a long time to recover.

I was truly surprised that despite the deep and bitter feud that was forming between Blagojevich and Madigan, Madigan had agreed to support Blagojevich in his bid for a second term. Maybe Mike enjoyed the fight just as much as Blagojevich seemed to.

There was a notable exception to the parade of Democrats endorsing Blagojevich.

Illinois Attorney General, and daughter of Speaker Madigan, Lisa Madigan declined to endorse his re-election bid. There was a good reason not to. As she stated that it, "Would be a conflict of interest for her to endorse him while her office was part of investigating serious corruption charges against him."

Another Democrat, Senator James Meeks, appeared to be a threat to Blagojevich politically. Meeks was chirping about a third party run in 2006. The Reverend Senator James Meeks was elected as an Independent to the Illinois Senate. However, Meeks attended Democrat Senate caucus meetings and was for all practical purposes a Democrat. Meeks ran for State Senate because he was very concerned about education funding inequity in Illinois and truly wanted to make changes to ensure a more equitable funding system for Illinois schools. He was the pastor of a very large church congregation in Chicago. I worked with Senator Meeks on several education issues in the General Assembly.

To eliminate the possibility of Meeks running as a third-party candidate, Blagojevich made a deal with Meeks. Blagojevich promised Meeks that he would support leasing the Illinois Lottery system and dedicating the lease proceeds to education funding equity. Meeks agreed and did not run as an Independent. The removal of Meeks's threat as a third party candidate was important to Blagojevich. Meeks was popular enough to attract enough Democrat votes to possibly hurt Blagojevich in what could be a close General election in November.

Of course, the Lottery was never leased but Blagojevich made good on his promise and later proposed the sale. Meeks, by the way, did not stop his advocacy for a more equitable funding system and a few years later he even endorsed Republican, Bruce Rauner for governor.

After Rauner was elected, Meeks was rewarded by being named Chairman of the Illinois State Board of Education.

The FY06 Illinois Budget passed without a great deal of controversy in May of 2005 as scheduled. This time, there would not be an overtime session. Perhaps the Governor's change in tone, or the fact everyone was looking forward to a summer without interruption by special sessions, resulted in an agreement. Expansion of state-supported health care even took place as part of the agreement. Never mind the fact that there was no money to pay for the expansion. A program called All-Kids was signed into law in October. It would take funding in future budgets to make the plan a reality, but this was a victory for Blagojevich as he announced his re-election.

The FY06 Budget was not even close to being balanced. The structural deficit in the budget remained and the payment cycle for providers and schools was simply being extended. The State's calculated share of the pension payment was once again not made in full.

In later years, although workers and employers made pension payments on time and in full, politicians would blame the workers for the poor financial conditions of the system. School employees and state workers are not responsible for the pension debt. Every law governing the structure and all benefits related to the five State Retirement systems

112

were passed by the General Assembly and signed by a governor. Teachers and state workers have always paid their designated share into the systems as well. The State has not made the required payment and the systems have accrued a large debt because of that fact. In FY06, this practice of underpayment continued.

Madigan's march toward the financial crisis continued. It was evident to all that even tougher choices were ahead. Despite that, nobody was interested in fighting in the summer of 2005 and a deal was struck which included Republicans votes. Another bad budget!

As the summer of 2005 wore on, more stories began to emerge about the campaign questionable fundraising tactics of the Blagojevich insiders. Newspapers across the state started to report more and more about the numerous investigations by Federal and State law enforcement agencies. Someone labeled, "Public Official A", was mentioned in several documents filed in Federal Court. Not many people were paying attention yet, but some people were. By the end of 2005 Blagojevich had only a 36% approval rating and a 56% disapproval rating. Even with the more conciliatory tone, Blagojevich saw his poll numbers drop to new lows. Blagojevich, of course, was later identified as 'Public Official A'.

It might have been that Blagojevich was trying a different approach in 2005. However, it was obvious by the spring of 2006; this much more mellow version of Blagojevich did not result in any change in public perception. Blagojevich must have decided that with only a weak Primary opponent by the name of Edward Eisendrath. It was time to go on the attack again and stir up some controversy. He no longer needed to be civil toward his campaign co-chair, Speaker Madigan. And, James Meeks had been dispensed of as a third party candidate with the promise of supporting the leasing the Illinois Lottery.

It was clear that Blagojevich was going to be the Democrat nominee for governor in November. Blagojevich defeated Eisendrath in a landslide in the 2006 Democratic Primary, receiving 72% of the vote.

As a result of this newfound confidence, the Blagojevich agenda for 2006 was both aggressive and controversial. In early January, during his State of The State Address, he called for a $3 Billion Capital Bill to fund various infrastructure projects. There was widespread agreement that Illinois needed a large dollar capital program to repair roads and bridges, build and renovate schools and expand crowded suburban tollways. The problem was always finding a way to pay for the program. This time, Blagojevich suggested an expansion of gambling, specifically making a game called Keno legal in Illinois. This was a lottery-like gambling game and the proposal allowed for a vast expansion of where the game could be played, including bars. This particular version of gaming was seen as one of the most addictive and dangerous forms of gambling. It was often referred to as the crack cocaine of gaming.

In addition to the concerns regarding how the capital program was going to be funded, there was growing unease that the $3 Billion in projects would be fertile ground for Blagojevich's fundraisers to extract more money for his re-election campaign from potential contractors competing for the money. By this time, the news media was reporting numerous instances of questionable grant awards as well as odd appointments to state boards and commissions. Any attempt to pass such a large spending program is always difficult because paying for the program requires tough votes to produce the revenue necessary to make bond payments. In the political climate that was so poisonous at the time, it was going to be almost impossible to pass a capital bill. These facts did not faze nor detour Blagojevich. As always, when lawmakers hesitated to support his proposals, he went on the attack.

Blagojevich was also a master of playing to his base and portraying himself as the ultimate populist. Nationally, the Democratic Party platform was heavy on expanding public health care, climate control and gun control. To help secure his base, Blagojevich proposed various concepts related to all of these. In February of 2006, he called for a ban on semi-automatic weapons and throughout the spring, he floated various ideas as to how state-sponsored healthcare should be expanded. In October, he issued an Executive Order creating the Illinois Climate Change Advisory Group to study greenhouse emissions and made recommendations to the General Assembly to protect the environment. I think he would have loved the political possibilities of the Green New Deal.

The 2006 (FY07) Budget proposed by Blagojevich was roundly criticized as out of balance the very day he delivered his address to the General Assembly. As expected, spending increases included more money for education, expansion of Pre-K education programs and an enormous expansion of State-sponsored health care.

Just a year earlier, Blagojevich, sounded like a strong supporter of small business.

In 2006, that rhetoric was replaced by proposals to place massive taxes on businesses in Illinois to fund health care expansion. He also, as promised, proposed the sale or lease of the Illinois Lottery system, following through on an agreement he made the previous year to eliminate James Meeks as an opponent in the Democratic Primary.

Simply put, the FY07 Budget proposal outlined by Blagojevich was dead on arrival in the House. While he still had a strong ally in State Senate President Emil Jones, Madigan was having none of the shenanigans. Of course, Madigan had already agreed to co-chair the Blagojevich re-election committee and Blagojevich was the Democratic candidate for governor. It appeared that Blagojevich figured at some point Madigan would have to compromise and provide support to Blagojevich's budget scheme once again. He was dead wrong.

Madigan was not about to be forced into a corner by Rod Blagojevich. Even though the Democrats had a clear advantage in the House and could have passed any budget measure with their 60 plus majority, Madigan also knew that putting votes on these types of new business taxes that would be necessary to pay for the proposed program expansions in the budget would be politically risky. Madigan was not about to expose his House majority to the reckless budget proposals of Rod Blagojevich. In the fall of 2006, in addition to the election of a Governor, all 118 Members of the House were up for re-election. Above all, Madigan was not going to take any risk with his majority.

Remember, having the majority of votes for the party was the source of all power in the Illinois House of Representatives. The House Rules completely favored the majority and allowed for an all-powerful control of legislative proposals which also meant control of fund-raising and that fueled the continuation of majority control. That meant all-powerful control for Madigan himself. This is the vicious, ugly political reality that continues to this day.

When the 2006 regular session of the Illinois legislature once again failed to pass a budget in time to avoid an overtime session, it was not a surprise. The fiscal condition of Illinois was so terrible after three years of irresponsible budgets which were structurally way out of balance, nobody wanted to be responsible for supporting either the deep cuts necessary to balance the budget or supporting the revenue increases (taxes and fees) necessary to support all of the additional spending the Democrats had piled on during the previous two years. The smoke and mirror machine had malfunctioned and there was no appetite for the charade to continue. Above all, this was an election year.

Madigan knew that after the deadline passed, at some point, the House Republicans would be forced to provide votes to help pass a budget. House GOP Leader Tom Cross knew it too. In an election year, the blame game would intensify and the fact that Democrats had a majority would be, at some point, forgotten.

Without a budget, as the spring became summer and June turned into July, the State would once again face the prospect of not being able to pay providers of healthcare and education. At some point, state workers could not be paid without budget appropriations and authorization. The Illinois government would be forced to shut down. If that occurred, how would it eventually affect voters and who would they blame? The unvarnished truth is that both sides were, at some point, going to get the blame. The fact that Democrats could have passed a budget alone would be replaced by the reality that it would now take a bi-partisan agreement to enact a budget. The issue would become the inability of the General Assembly to pass a budget, and that meant the entire General Assembly. The truth was that after the deadline passed, the GOP was in the hot seat along with the Democrat majority.

Just like two years earlier, in another election year, the Illinois General Assembly steamed into an overtime session. Madigan dug in and waited for a budget agreement that would include the governor, and the House Republicans joining House Democrats in the vote to pass a spending bill. Madigan figured that this budget was so bad that everyone had to share in the pain of passage. Without additional revenue or deep cuts, or some combination of the two, a budget could not be passed.

Blagojevich publicly continued to support the expansion of healthcare and education spending and also wanted a capital program. While Madigan, as head of the State Democratic Party, supported the Democrat platform ideals of expanded healthcare and increased funding for public schools, he also insisted that the budget must at least appear to be balanced. He called for the governor to declare what he supported as far as revenue to get a deal passed. The governor stuck to his very shaky yet unpopular revenue ideas. He repeated that he would not support any increase in the state income or sales tax. One time revenue from a lottery sale or lease combined with potential revenue from the expansion of gaming is not sustainable and reliable revenue sources in the mind of Madigan and many others.

Once again, a hallmark of extended overtime sessions are meetings of working groups held to work out possible solutions. So, in June of 2006, budget experts and appropriation committee chairs met almost daily to work on some sort of solution. Because the vote to achieve a super-majority had to include House Republicans, meetings included members of House Appropriations Committees. I was a member of the Elementary and Secondary Education Appropriations Committee. Although I was not the GOP minority spokesperson, my knowledge of the K-12 education budget coupled with the fact that I was a downstate House Member resulted in my being asked to work on the budget solution. This process included multiple meetings held at the Governor's Mansion.

This time the House GOP Minority K-12 Education Committee Appropriation spokesperson was a lady named Suzanne Bassi. Suzzi was a likable, very dedicated education advocate who often railed against unfunded mandates in speeches on the House Floor. She would get out a list of unfunded mandates passed into law and begin to recite the list every time another mandate was being voted on. This was a list I loved to hear Suzzi recite.

Also in that working group for education was a fellow school administrator named Jerry Mitchell. Jerry was a great mentor and friend during the time I was in the General Assembly. He had been a school superintendent for many years, then retired and ran for State Representative and served multiple terms. Because I was a school superintendent and still on the job,

Jerry and I often discussed education legislation pending in the House Elementary Education Committee. He was never threatened by my presence and welcomed input. Our education budget team was pretty strong as we worked to find some common ground solutions with Democrats.

The K-12 Education portion of the budget is just one part of a larger puzzle. As we met, it became clear that many of the issues we faced in attempting to make suggestions regarding a solution were similar to the problems faced by other working groups who were meeting to hammer out details related to Higher Education, Public Safety, General Services, and Human Services. The diversity and diverse needs of various regions of the State were exposed during these meetings.

Our orders were to look for ways to reduce spending. In K-12 Education, for any serious cuts to be made, general state aid (GSA) or mandated categorical spending would have to be cut. GSA supported, on a per-pupil basis, basic essential support for educational operations including classroom and administrative costs. Mandated categorical spending supported reimbursement to school districts for mandated costs such as transportation and special education.

GSA is vital to school districts in which property values were low and local tax levies could not support a decent minimum funding level of spending per pupil. The minimum level of spending was referred to as the *foundation level*. The suggested foundation level was calculated by a group called the Educational Funding Advisory Board, or EFAB for short. EFAB members took into account the types of operations and support necessary to provide a child with a minimum quality education. Once that minimum was established, an effort was normally made to increase state aid toward that foundation level number. The EFAB recommended funding level was never met during the time it was in use as a measure. This negatively affected school districts in regions of the State with very little property value.

Many schools in Illinois operated at a per-pupil spending level far below the amount suggested by EFAB. If the minimal level was calculated at $6,500, often the actual funding level based on the appropriation for this line item in the budget was much lower. Money was paid to school districts in the form of state aid payments on a schedule throughout the fiscal year. In school districts that lacked property tax wealth, and therefore local revenue created by tax levies applied to this property wealth, state aid was critical.

Because of all of these factors, in Illinois, due to the heavy reliance on property taxes to fund education, there is a wide range in spending per-pupil. In 2006, there were districts in Illinois that spent as little as $6K per pupil and, in property wealthy districts, located mainly in the suburban collar counties of Chicago, where per-student spending surpassed $25K.

Mandated categorical spending supported mandated costs such as transportation and special education. Formulas were established for these cost reimbursements. All school districts received these funds on a per-pupil basis applied to a particular formula depending on the number of students receiving the service. The only exception was Chicago. In 1995, as part of a school reform package, Chicago received a flat 20% of the amount appropriated for these services. In 2006, the 20% allocated to Chicago represented an amount larger than the amount Chicago should have received based on the actual calculation. The student population in Chicago had decreased since 1995 proportionately to other parts of the State. However, Chicago continued to receive 20%. In addition, property wealthy school districts, mostly in suburban areas, also received mandated categorical funding despite the fact the districts met or exceeded the per-pupil foundation level established by EFAB.

As a member of the working group, I suggested that since there was not ample revenue to support an increase in the foundation level, the mandated categorical spending that was going to wealthy districts and the amount Chicago was receiving which was above their actual calculated total be appropriated to increase State Aid for poorer districts. Of course, the suburban members of the working group and those representing Chicago rejected this idea. Education was one of the most important issues facing Illinois and they would not support any cuts to their piece of this pie.

I suspected the other working groups were having the same issue. Illinois, as mentioned is very diverse. Funding for public services reflects that diversity. To maintain funding in one area, it often affected funding in another region of the state. Making any reduction in spending, especially in an election year, is difficult. It was made more difficult because the governor publically called for increases in education spending. He claimed the increases were necessary to support the education of our children and continued to call for expansion of healthcare as well. He blamed the General Assembly for not being able to come up with a budget that would support what he called common sense spending proposals. Once again, the Governor called the General Assembly into Special Sessions to show himself as the hero who was pushing Members of the General Assembly to get their job done.

Just like in previous years, June rolled into July without a budget and tensions continued to rise. Blagojevich called lawmakers back to Springfield over and over again. During his time in office, he called 36 special sessions, by far a record for any governor. This figure likely surpassed the total of all other special session days combined by all other governors. One lawmaker, fellow Democrat Representative Joe Lyons, insinuated that Blagojevich was insane and called the governor a, "mad-man." But, the most renowned name-calling took place at the Governor's mansion one day when Blagojevich accused Madigan of, "acting like a Republican. Madigan's angry reply was for Blagojevich to, "Knock it off." It was a memorable standoff.

Tensions were indeed very high. Meetings at the Governor's mansion resulted in shouting matches between lawmakers and the governor. Foul language, threats and childish behavior replaced governing.

In early July, as tension grew and Blagojevich called the General Assembly into yet another day of the special session, a report surfaced that the governor was jogging near the Capitol in Washington Park. The pettiness between the Governor and Speaker reached a new low on July 7, 2006 when Blagojevich even attempted to control the **exact time** that the House was to convene by inserting a specific time for the House to meet in his Executive Order calling for the special session. Madigan ignored the time Blagojevich inserted into his Special Session order. It was extremely tense on the floor of the Illinois House when news that the Governor was seen jogging in Springfield's Washington Park made it to the Chamber floor. Several House Members stood once again requesting to comment with what is referred to as a 'point of personal privilege.' House Democrat floor leader Lou Lang delivered a fiery speech calling for the governor to get serious and stop the nonsense. Others vented their frustrations as well.

It was then, in early July of 2006, for the **first time publically,** the idea of impeaching Blagojevich was uttered. State Representative, Mike Bost, a fellow downstate Member from Murphysboro, had enough. Mike, a former firefighter who also ran his family's trucking business, had a plain-spoken manner and got right to the point. He asked for the House members to be quieted and then stated that the House should consider starting impeachment proceeding against Blagojevich. He finished stating, "I don't say it lightly. I'm not joking."

I had requested the opportunity to speak and I was called upon to speak next. Not knowing what Representative Bost was going to say, earlier that day I had thought about what behavior would the governor need to demonstrate for the House to consider impeachment. I looked up the issue of impeachment in the Illinois Constitution that I kept on my desk. I found what I was looking for in Article IV, Section 14. I remember reading these words, "**The House of Representatives has the sole power to conduct legislative investigations to determine the existence of cause for impeachment and, by a majority of the members elected, to impeach Executive and Judicial officers.**" I read the passage over a couple of times and decided I wanted to make a statement right then on the House floor. According to the Illinois Constitution, Members of the House had the duty to determine the existence of cause for impeachment.

I was standing at my desk with a copy of the Illinois Constitution opened to the passage regarding Impeachment. As I stood and spoke, I held up the Illinois Constitution and echoed Representative Bost's comment stating, "This is not said lightly," I paused and continued. **"We're talking about the potential of using these sessions to remove the executive officer of the State of Illinois for malfeasance in office. At some point, we have a responsibility to consider that."**

The seal had been broken regarding the matter of impeachment in a very public way, on the floor of the House and the media took notice. I was surprised when immediately, GOP Leader Tom Cross attempted to tone things down saying that it was not time to go down that road. Cross said that disagreement on the budget was not a basis for throwing someone out of office.

Of course, I was not suggesting that Blagojevich be thrown out of the office for budget disagreements. By this time, everyone knew about the $25K contributions for appointments and State contracts, and the highly questionable fund-raising that had taken place. Many of the Executive Orders Blagojevich had delivered were also questionable constitutionally, at best. Cross had completely missed the point. If the General Assembly was going to be called into meaningless special sessions, we might as well use the time and taxpayer money well and begin to investigate the behavior of Blagojevich to determine if he was fit for office. I was puzzled by the fact that Cross would come to the quick defense of Blagojevich. To me, this was a great opportunity to separate the House Republicans from the entire Democratic Party and do it in a very public way.

When Bill Black, legendary House Republican Floor Leader from Danville rose to speak on the issue after our comments, I listened carefully. Black helped deliver Cross's message when he said, "I don't think we should go down that road, *at this time*." I have the highest regarding and respect for Bill Black. Although, I still believe to this day that an investigation was warranted at that time and we should have used upcoming special sessions to begin an investigation. There was already plenty of *cause* for an investigation in my opinion. Unfortunately, the matter of impeachment was not pursued for quite some time.

The FY07 Budget was eventually passed in late July of 2006, just before a complete government shut down. A carefully developed and structured roll call to approve the budget and accompanying implementation bill took into consideration any vulnerable candidates on either side of the aisle because of the upcoming fall election. I was asked to vote yes by Leader Cross and I did. My House seat was considered safe and the madness had to end. Without an agreement, payments to health care providers and schools would not be made. Some schools, faced with borrowing limitations, might not even be able to open. My vote was yes to help avoid a catastrophe.

Keep in mind there were very clear signs in 2005 and 2006 that Blagojevich was engaged in unethical behavior. Back in 2005, two of his closest advisors and operatives, Stu Levine and Joseph Cari had been indicted on various federal charges related to accepting kickbacks.

While not directly connected to Blagojevich at the time, both men took plea agreements in exchange for cooperation with federal agents in a wider corruption probe. As early as June of 2005, U.S. Attorney Patrick Fitzgerald publically stated that he had, "Witnesses to very serious allegations of endemic hiring fraud in the Blagojevich administration." In October of 2006, Blagojevich fundraiser, Tony Rezko, was indicted on federal charges of taking kickbacks for arranging state contracts and Stuart Levine pleaded guilty to mail fraud and accepted a reduced sentence agreeing to cooperate with federal authorities in the investigation of Rod Blagojevich's fundraising operation. Multiple news outlets were reporting numerous allegations of potential wrongdoing by Blagojevich. People in leadership, as well as others had to know what was going on!

"And in the naked light I saw, ten thousand people, maybe more. People talking without speaking, people hearing without listening; People writing songs that voices never share, and no one dared, disturb the sounds of silence... "
Simon and Garfunkel- *The Sounds of Silence*

Blagojevich chalked up all of the media reports and noise to politics as he denied any wrongdoing. He used the millions of dollars donated to his campaign fund, much of it in chunks of $25K from those receiving board appointments or public contracts to defeat Judy Baar Topinka on November 3rd of 2006. Ironically, using the millions and millions of dollars in campaign contributions, Blagojevich attempted to tie Topinka to convicted former GOP Governor, George Ryan. Ryan was sitting in a federal jail in Terre Haute, Indiana by that fall and Blagojevich did a pretty good job of associating Topinka with Ryan using lots of his ill-gotten gains.

Topinka was extremely well-liked and had found consistent success running for office. She served in the Illinois House and Senate before winning three consecutive terms as State Treasurer in 1994, 1998 and 2002. Even after losing as the GOP candidate for Governor in 2006, Topinka was elected twice more to statewide office in 2010 and 2014 as State Comptroller. She was a formidable foe who was simply outspent by a wide margin. In my opinion, Judy was one of the finest and most dedicated public officials I ever worked with. In the summer of 2006 Jerry Mitchell and I assisted her staff in developing her education agenda. I also often traveled with her to campaign events throughout the state. In my eyes, nobody was a better public servant than Judy. The attacks against her infuriated me. Sadly, Judy passed away far too early in 2014 while serving as State Comptroller. Blagojevich outspent Topinka $37 million to $6 million in the 2006 General Election. Much of the money spent by the Blagojevich campaign was on vicious attack ads.

(Former State Treasurer and Comptroller Judy Topinka.
Wikipedia open source official State photo from State of Illinois Comptroller's office.)

Another factor hindering Topinka was a third-party candidate named Rich Whitney who did not help her chances. As you recall, Blagojevich had talked James Meeks out of running with the promise of leasing the Illinois lottery system to infuse money into education. Any chance of the third party run by Meeks harming Blagojevich had been eliminated. Blagojevich defeated Topinka by 11%, a large margin under the circumstances, and was re-elected to his second term.

Another two years had ticked by and the 94th General Assembly, spanning the years 2005-06, was coming to an end.

What had those years been like in America while Illinois slipped deeper and deeper into a fiscal crisis?

In 2005 the average cost of a gallon of gas rose to $3.18 a gallon. A few industrious employees at a company called PayPal started You-tube. It was the year Disneyland celebrated their 50th Anniversary, Lance Armstrong became the seven-time champion of the Tour de France, and George W. Bush was re-elected to his second term as President of the United States. One of the deadliest hurricanes in history hit the United States when Katrina formed in late August in the Gulf of Mexico and made landfall in Florida on August 25th killing fourteen. Katrina wasn't finished though, after returning to the Gulf and being refueled by the warm gulf waters, it grew to a category five monster and after diminishing to a category three hurricane, it hit New Orleans with devastating force killing 1,577 in Louisiana and 238 more in Mississippi. That same year, an F-5 tornado hit Evansville, Indiana and killed 25 people. Another Star Wars Movie made the box office scene along with *Hitch*, and a very controversial movie called *Brokeback Mountain*. Michael Jackson was found not guilty of those previous charges of child molestation. The music industry featured Cold Play, Kenny Chesney, Toby Keith, Foo Fighters, Rascal Flatts, 50 Cent and Weezer.

In 2006, Google purchased You-tube and Nintendo released the Wii gaming system to the U.S. market. NASA launched a new spacecraft, New Horizons, intending to reach Jupiter in 2007 and Pluto by 2015. Although now vilified as a cheater using steroids, Barry Bonds surpassed Babe Ruth's home run record on May 28th when he hit number 715. On the television, a show called *The Bachelor* was popular along with *CSI Miami, The Apprentice, Boston Legal, Family Guy, The Office* and another show called *Survivor*.

Bands like Nine Inch Nails and performers like Bon Jovi and Mariah Carey sang while the world went by and Illinois rambled down a path toward fiscal crisis while re-electing perhaps the most corrupt Governor in history.

Chapter Twelve
You Better Learn to Play it Right

On January 10th, 2007, House Clerk Mahoney began the Inaugural Ceremony to swear in 117 of the 118 Members of the 95th General Assembly of the State of Illinois. A recent vacancy between the election in November and the Inauguration date had left one seat vacant at the time of the ceremony.

He began, "All assembled...all assembled in the auditorium, give attention. All assembled in this auditorium, please give attention."

Due to remodeling at the State Capitol a few years previous, the event was now being held at the auditorium of the University of Illinois at Springfield and it simply lacked the majesty of the House Chamber. Although more people could be accommodated as guests, parking was more plentiful, and the facility allowed for easier travel access than the downtown Springfield avenues with the confusing array of one-way streets, it was rumored that the staff responsible for the event liked this venue more based on how much less work this site entailed for them. Whatever the reasoning behind the decision to continue meeting at the Springfield U of I campus for Inauguration, I do know, it was not nearly as memorable as being sworn in on the House floor.

With the auditorium-style seating, Clerk Mahoney was having trouble getting everyone's attention. Doorkeeper Lee Crawford attempted to assist. Crawford announced that all Representative-elect should assemble on the auditorium stage. Getting the Representatives settled would assist in Mahoney's plea to begin the proceedings.

Mahoney, like a sixth-grade class substitute teacher attempting to gain control continued, "May I have your attention, please. May I have your attention, please?" Then, finally, after some decrease in the noise level he continued, "The Secretary of State, the Honorable Jesse White sends greetings and proclaims that this day, the second Wednesday of January 2007 is the day fixed for the convening of the House of Representatives of the 95th General Assembly of the State of Illinois under Article IV, Section 5 of the Constitution."

As Jesse White stood at the speaker's rostrum, I thought about this extremely popular public Illinois figure. A former paratrooper in the United States Army's 101st Airborne Division and founder of the Jesse White Tumblers, White was 72 years old in 2007 when he presided over the oath of office administered to the 95th General Assembly. He was first elected as Secretary of State in 1998. In the year 2020, as I write this, White continues as Secretary of State, now age 86. White understood the duties of the office of those he was about to swear in as Members. He served in the General Assembly from 1974 until 1990. I had met White numerous times before this day. While I was Principal at Watseka High School, the Jesse White Tumblers annually performed in front of our students.

White stepped to the microphone and began, "Thank you very much. The House of Representatives of the 95th General Assembly in and for the great State of Illinois will come to order." Finally…silence.

After Reverend George J. Lucas led the gathering in prayer, White called on Speaker Madigan who then led the group in the Pledge of Allegiance. Then, upon instructing all to be seated, White introduced officeholders present for the ceremony. Among those in attendance: Lieutenant Governor Pat Quinn; Attorney General Lisa Madigan and Comptroller Dan Hynes. A roll call was taken of the 117 individuals about to be sworn in. After roll call, White announced that "117 Representative-elect having answered to the roll and are being in attendance, a quorum is present and the House of Representatives of the 95th General Assembly is officially convened."

Secretary of State White introduced The Honorable Alan J. Grieman, Justice of the Illinois Appellate Court to administer the Constitutional Oath of Office. Grieman began, "If each of you would now stand and raise your right hand and repeat after me. I, state your name…" I stood, and after raising my right hand as instructed, began a most historic oath:

"I Roger Eddy do solemnly swear that I will support the Constitution of the United States and the Constitution of the State of Illinois and I will faithfully discharge the duties of Representative of the General Assembly according to the best of my ability."

This was the third time I had taken this solemn oath and, as each time before, I felt a deep sense of duty and commitment to the task. Little did I, or anyone else at the time, fully understand the historic importance of the words we had spoken. Member of the Illinois House would be the individuals called upon to undertake the most difficult of Constitutional duties. It would be this group who would study evidence and decide, for the first time in Illinois long history, the ***impeachment of a governor.***

As had become routine, two names were nominated for Speaker of the House. Tom Cross was nominated by longtime colleague and friend Brent Hassert plus several others including a very young State Representative from Peoria named Aaron Shock. At age 19, Shock was elected to the Peoria School Board as a write-in candidate becoming the youngest School Board Member in Illinois. At age 23 he was elected as a State representative and at age 28, in 2009, Shock was elected to the U.S. Congress. His political career ended amidst allegations of misusing campaign funds a few years later.

Michael Madigan was also nominated for Speaker by Representative Barbara Currie and four others. The nomination speeches were flattering to both Cross and Madigan with excellent depictions as to why each should be elected Speaker.

Of course it would not have made any difference who nominated Cross or Madigan.

The vote was predetermined. The time taken to dwell on the qualifications and leadership skills was a long-held tradition and not at all critical to the outcome of the election of Speaker. What mattered was that there were 66 Democrats and 51 Republicans voting.

Nobody understood this better than Tom Cross. So, in a traditional display of bi-partisan cooperation, Cross was recognized by Secretary of State White for a motion. Cross made a motion to elect Michael Madigan by acclamation to once again become Speaker of the House. As per tradition, Cross asked for one person to withhold their vote so he would also once again be elected Minority Leader. Madigan obliged and then voted for Cross as Minority Leader. The official vote was 116-1 and Madigan was again elected Speaker of the House.

After Speaker Madigan was sworn in as Speaker by Grieman and White ceremoniously escorted from the rostrum, Madigan addressed the crowd and the Members of the House. When he had finished acknowledging about two dozen dignitaries, Madigan finally admitted that Illinois was facing some very difficult fiscal problems. Referring to the fact, "That tough votes might be necessary," he hinted that revenue increases were likely necessary as part of the solution. Almost everyone knew that another budget without additional revenue would mean catastrophe for healthcare providers and many schools. By this time, payment cycles were as much as six months or more behind.

Another, more memorable portion of his remarks that day had to do with moving the date for the Illinois Presidential Primary. By this time, it was widely known that Illinois Senator Barack Obama was seriously considering and likely going to announce his candidacy for President of the United States. In 2007, Madigan used this Inaugural event to announce that he intended to introduce legislation that would change the date of the Illinois Primary from March 18, 2008, to February 5th, 2008. Madigan reasoned that with the Illinois Primary being so much later than other states, the disadvantage could hurt Obama's run for president.

True to this announcement, Madigan indeed introduced a Bill that was passed and signed into law that changed the Illinois Primary from March to early February in 2008. This momentum proved crucial to Obama's early success and helped him eventually defeat Hillary Clinton to become the Democratic nominee for President in 2008. The vacancy Obama left in the Illinois Senate when he was elected President becomes an important part of this story.

Tom Cross also made some remarks that day. He pledged to work together with the Democrats to solve the fiscal problems facing the state while also mentioning that there very well could be differences in philosophies as to how those fiscal problems should be solved.

He welcomed five new GOP members: Sandy Cole, Dennis Reboletti, Jil Tracy, Michael Fortner and Franco Coladipietro. These five were now part of the group that would also face these fiscal problems. They ran for office knowing about the fiscal challenges and like everyone else on that stage, they knew about the rumors surrounding Blagojevich and his associates regarding fundraising tied to appointments and contract awards. Many had used these well-known accusations in their campaigns, as there were stories about the ongoing federal investigations in the media almost daily. Little did they know they would be part of removing a governor from office and making history in Illinois.

For my part, I ran opposed in 2006 and received 30,067 votes. I was starting my third term and was much more comfortable with the House Rules and the process. I had also moved up in seniority. Members of the House are provided the opportunity to purchase license plates bearing the House of Representatives designation and also prominently displaying a number. The less seniority one has, the higher the number. My first set of license plates were numbered 109. New members were always the highest numbers and ranked by the last name. At least having an "E" as the first letter in my last name kept me from being number 118. By the time I was sworn into this third term, my plate number was 80. My seniority increase was tied to the fact that several Reps had retired or had lost their elections.

My committee assignments for this term were still heavily associated with education issues, and I was also reappointed to the House Labor Committee. I was named minority spokesperson for the Ethanol Production Oversight Committee. Normally after three terms a Representative was eligible for a spokesperson position. In most instances, due to my expertise and knowledge of education issues, I would have been named as a minority spokesperson on one of the education committees. However, seniority still was the determining factor and Jerry Mitchell and Suzzi Bassi were still around and continued in those spokesperson roles. I had no problem with that and enjoyed working with both of them. Plus, I had worked with local agriculture leaders on many bills related to Ethanol Production. The assignment as Spokesperson for Ethanol Oversight was a good match. At that time numerous new Ethanol Plants were springing up in Illinois.

Things at school were busy but going still going very well. The school construction program and the aftermath which had taken so much time were complete and students were into their second year in the new building. We no longer needed to employ an interim because one of our administrators, Julie Kraemer, an assistant principal, had returned to school and earned a specialist degree and became qualified as a superintendent. She had earlier been promoted to the role of high school principal when the current principal, Monte Newlin, was named Regional Superintendent of Schools.

Since Julie was now qualified as a superintendent, the School Board designated her as acting superintendent on days that I was in Springfield. Her decision to return to school and earn a specialist degree came at just the right time. The interim superintendent that had been employed decided after a few years he wanted to have more free time and freedom in retirement than the interim arrangement provided him.

In many ways, the new arrangement was better. Jim Koss had performed well as the interim but a retired superintendent at some point really would like to fully retire. Julie was eager to begin her career in administration. As an alumnus of the Hutsonville School system, she was especially dedicated to doing a great job. It was easier to meet with her on days I was in the district since she was there every day as HS Principal. This arrangement also provided Julie an opportunity to prepare to become superintendent upon my eventual retirement. That is exactly how things worked out a few years later.

When I retired from the superintendent's position at Hutsonville in 2012, Julie was named superintendent and still serves in that capacity. Looking back, it was truly incredible that things fell into place so well for me to be able to be a superintendent and a State Representative for almost ten years. Without the contributions of countless staff members, the continued support of the school board, good planning and a little luck, there was no way I could have done both jobs.

The new arrangement turned out to be good fortune as well because as a fourth term State Representative, my responsibilities and workload in the General Assembly also increased. I was, by then, although not by title as the Minority Spokesperson on any of the Education Committees, the go-to person regarding education issues. I had a reputation as someone who would work across the aisle and help anyone with legislation that would support improvement in education policies in Illinois. I became co-sponsor of numerous proposals that even originated on the Democrat side of the aisle.

If I opposed a particular piece of legislation as written, I would still work with the lawmaker to improve the bill, if possible, to achieve the goal they were seeking. Most of the time, it was a matter of removing a mandate from the proposal and allowing the school districts to make the decision. Many of the proposals were good ideas for their area or some school districts in their region. But, as pointed out many times previously, Illinois is diverse and the best approach is to allow school districts to determine what is best for the students in their local school district. After all, voters elect people from their towns, cities and villages to a local school board that is responsible for making decisions regarding the education programs and success of students. These elected officials also make determinations, with administrative input and expertise, about how to best use available financial resources to deliver the best education possible.

Unfunded or underfunded mandates regarding curriculum, administration, programs and operations remove these critical decisions from local control. The proposal made by a State Representative might be well-intended and even a great policy proposal that should be shared.

I emphasized to my colleagues that the idea can be proposed in such a manner that the idea is supported but not necessarily mandated.

I know that some can point to problems with a small number of elected school board members, and even school boards. Many point to poor test scores and schools in financial difficulty and seem to be run poorly. Often, schools in financial straits are in that shape due to inadequate or delinquent state funding or having to comply with unfunded mandates.

I also understand there are times that some basic oversight is necessary. However, my strong belief is this - locally elected school board members care more about the children in their communities than State Reps, Senators and bureaucrats at the state or federal level. For the most part, unless there must be intervention, schools should be left alone to govern themselves.

I am sometimes irritated but mostly amused when those who have never taught a class or ran a school think they know the best solutions for education. I was always pushing back against those individuals and organizations attempts to force their beliefs upon local schools.

Many others feel that they have the answer to poor test scores in reading or math. Most of the time, the issue of poor performance is coupled with poverty or other identifiable demographic issues. Wealthy, well-funded school districts with low levels of poverty perform better on standardized assessments for a reason.

I was always willing to talk about education issues and policies with my colleagues despite our differences in opinions or differences in demographics. Because of this, my plate was full in my fourth term with multiple education-related bills.

The Regional Superintendent's Association requested that I carry legislation outlining new policies for deactivation of school districts. I was the chief sponsor of legislation for the Teacher's Retirement System (TRS) which required notification by a local State's Attorney to TRS of the conviction of a job-related felony. Several State Senators requested that I sponsor successful Senate Bills. PA 95-0496 and PA 95-0793 were bills that provided various repeals, and cleanups of the school code and both sponsors were Senate Democrats. I was also asked to be the House sponsor of a measure that provided for changes related to bond issues to allow for the conversion and formation of a school district in southern Illinois. The Senate sponsor of that measure was also a Democrat. I can't even recall the number of House Bills regarding education for which I was a co-sponsor. I was busy but I liked the role.

Besides education issues, I also passed other bills that were important to my local constituents during that term.

One of the bills dealt with a local problem faced by the City of Paris that went back almost 8 years. A local state prison work camp, The Ed Jenison Work Camp, opened in 1993. It had been shut down in 2002 due to budgetary issues. The work camp was located on the north end of Paris and had been shuttered for a few years when we tried to take some action to use the relatively new facility.

Our first attempt was to attempt to get funding in the state budget back in 2003 and 2004 to reopen the camp and bring the prison guard jobs back to the community. With the state budget mess, the attempt to reinstate the funding for the work camp failed. The longer the facility was closed, the less chance that it would ever reopen. The camp was still maintained by the State though and that still cost money.

Once local leaders came to a point in 2007 they were convinced that it would likely not reopen as a work camp, they became concerned as to what the state might use the facility for. There were even rumors that it might be reopened as an early release facility for sex-offenders. Although relatively new, the building was deteriorating as any empty building would. If something didn't happen soon, it would become an eyesore- or worse.

Bob Colvin, the guy who had been a supporter since back in my first election, and several other Paris civic leaders came to me with an idea that the City of Paris should own the work camp and take over the responsibility for the facility. By this time, city leaders, along with local school officials were also talking about the possibility of building a new high school in Paris.

One of the preferred sites for the new high school was near the site of the existing work camp. Thought was that the building could be incorporated into the education campus for perhaps vocational education purposes. There were other ideas, but the desire for the City of Paris to somehow obtain the work campsite was clear. So, I went to work on legislation to make it happen early in 2007.

During the time my office investigated the possibility of the camp becoming the property of the city, we discovered that a process existed which required state property to be the subject of open bidding. Getting the property listed for bid was the first step, and after working with various state agencies, that was accomplished. Since there was no real hope that it would reopen as a work camp, it was simply costing the state too much money to maintain. But, getting it listed as surplus saleable property took some time.

Once the property was for sale, there were other rules regarding the bidding. At the first auction of the property, Colvin traveled to Chicago where the surplus property sale was to take place. When the work camp property came up for bid, Colvin discovered the minimum opening bid was $250K and the state would not accept less than $1.38 million during the initial bid process. The city was perhaps willing to come up with $25-50K, but $250K was ridiculous, even as an opening bid. He called me that day very frustrated about the price being so high and said that the process was so complicated. I won't use the exact language he used to express his frustration, but fortunately, there were no other bidders for the property.

As the process moved along and certain time requirements were met for the property price to be lowered, Bob and I stayed in touch. I was concerned that the land conveyance may never take place. Then, an opportunity came along.

By the spring of 2008, Rod Blagojevich was failing in his second term as governor.

He had few friends and some crazy ideas. There was even a very public attempt and a lot of support for a recall provision to be passed by the General Assembly. Short of Impeachment, which Madigan was not interested in pursuing, recall seemed like a good plan to many people. In any event, Blagojevich needed support for any plan, however suspect, to increase state revenue.

I don't even recall the dumb idea that he was attempting to get passed but I do recall the conversation I had with someone from the Governor's staff about the need for support for the dumb idea. I initially told the staff member that the idea was not something I could support but as he walked away, I thought about the work camp in Paris and how important it was to get support from the state Department of Corrections, under the Governor's control, to pass any legislation to transfer ownership.

Maybe, I could look at the governor's proposal if he would look at the Paris Work Camp legislation that I was proposing to have the camp transferred to the ownership of the City of Paris?

I called the governor's staff member back and indicated that maybe I needed to take a closer look at the governor's proposal. After all, the state was in dire financial condition and any idea should be considered and not dismissed without more thought. We made an appointment during which I half-listened to the governor's idea for adding revenue. We discussed the problems facing the state and I brought up the fact that the state was still spending money to support a facility in my legislative district that had been closed for many years. I mentioned that the property would likely never be used again, had gone through the required bid process without any successful bids and was a money pit for the state.

Maybe we could work together to find ways to improve the State's dire financial situation. I could possibly support the governor's idea but I would appreciate it if the governor looked at my legislation as another creative way to save the state money. I emphasized that we should be working together on the fiscal problems we faced.

I had previously filed legislation in February of 2007 (HB5768) which would have conveyed the work camp to the City of Paris for one dollar. Of course, at the time, nobody thought that the transfer would take place for a single dollar bill. The number was a place-holder until negotiations would take place once the state determined they were willing to sell the camp. The city was still hoping to somehow get the land for less than $50K. I was able to get the legislation out of the House and over to the Senate prior to the deadline to move bills to the Senate with the understanding that the price for the land listed in the bill would likely change.

The bill was assigned to the Senate Rules Committee on April 2nd and sponsored by my associated Senator, Dale Righter. The legislation sat idle until April 29th. I had kept Senator Righter informed about the discussions I was having with the Governor's office regarding the cost of the camp and that conveying it would save the state money at a time when every dollar counted. When I told Righter about the meeting I had regarding the bill the governor wanted support for, he laughed at the governor's idea that I was considering supporting.

He did understand what was going on though, and what I was attempting to accomplish.

On April 29th I called Senator Righter to inform him that an amendment was being drafted to HB5768 and it was going to be delivered to his office to file.

The Department of Corrections (DOC) had found some technical drafting error and the amendment corrected the problem and also removed the opposition of the DOC. The legislation was far from becoming law but the bill had new life.

On May 8th, the bill, as amended, was passed by the Senate Executive Committee and sent to the Senate Floor. It sat there as budget negotiations went on behind the scenes.

As mentioned, the governor was desperate for support for any of his ideas to increase revenue to get a budget deal done. One afternoon in mid-May, I received a call from the governor's office with a request that I come to his office for a meeting. These types of meetings were regularly occurring with the governor's staff. His staff was attempting to meet with groups of lawmakers directly and by-pass House and Senate leaders to get support for his budget plan. I walked down to the Governor's second-floor office from the third floor of the capitol where the House of Representatives was in session. When I entered the reception area and gave them my name, I was told to go into the office, the Governor was expecting me. Instead of meeting with the staff, my meeting was with Blagojevich.

For a few minutes he railed about Madigan, the fact that he was not able to get support for any of his proposals related to the budget and bemoaned his predicament. He explained a piece of legislation that he thought would help with revenue without raising taxes. To this day, I don't recall the specifics of the proposed legislation. I do recall that there seemed to be little support for the proposal and it had something to do with gaming. I explained that I would take a look at it and keep an open mind. He then thanked me for my idea to convey the idle state work camp and save money. It was something he was looking at and might be able to support.

A day later, I received a call from his staff and agreed to vote for the governor's proposal. Then on May 29th, just two days before the May 31st budget deadline, HB5768, the legislation that conveyed the work camp to the City of Paris, passed the Senate unanimously and went to the House Rules Committee.

As budget talks heated up May 30th, the Rules Committee sent the Paris Work Camp bill directly to the House floor where it passed 115-0 on May 31st just hours before the scheduled end of the session. Soon, the Governor's bill was introduced and voted on. Keeping my agreement, I was one of the yes votes. The bill the governor wanted support on failed with less than 50 yes votes.

The work camp conveyance measure had passed both the Senate and the House and just needed the governor's signature. Since his bill failed, even though I kept my promise to support it, would the governor still sign my bill? I was concerned but still cautiously optimistic.

I called Colvin to give him the news. We had not spoken about the details of the final version of the bill although we had discussed the highest amount that the city would pay to make the conveyance happen. When I told him that the final amount was **one dollar**, he couldn't believe it. He was ecstatic. I then informed him that we still needed the governor to sign it into law and there was never really a guarantee with Blagojevich that he would follow through. But, on July 9th, 2008 he did sign the legislation and PA 95-0730 officially transferred the property to the city of Paris…..for $1.

Another similar opportunity arose during this session of the General Assembly to assist with a problem developing in my home county of Crawford. Robinson, the county seat, was home to a small airport in the rural part of the county. The airport was important in supporting our local industry. Marathon Petroleum Company has a large refinery in Robinson that provides over 700 great paying jobs to folks in the area. Hershey Candy Company has a huge production facility in Robinson, and a new Ethanol Plant had recently been constructed in Crawford County. The airport was used by many of these businesses for executive travel in and out of the area. The airport was also used by others for recreational flying purposes.

The airport had severe financial problems. Those financial issues dated back to when the airport authority was formed. The original boundaries of the Robinson Airport Authority included only the original city limits of Robinson. The tax base from which the funding to support the airport was derived was limited to the area within the original authority. Although the entire county used and benefitted from the airport, a very small geographical tax base supported the operation. The revenue produced through levies applied to the small tax base needed to maintain and operate the airport dwindled to a point that it was becoming almost impossible to keep the runways and other parts of the airport, safe, well maintained and intact. The local airport board struggled with the issue for years. They were at a critical point and faced the possibility of the airport not being certified. Other attempts to increase the tax base were futile.

Several members of the airport authority and the Robinson Chamber of Commerce knew the seriousness of the problem and had informed me about how important the airport was to the entire county. So, when a Senate Bill came over to the House that was entitled, *Airport Authority-Peoria*, I immediately got in touch with the House Sponsor, Representative Aaron Shock. That was the easy part; he sat directly behind me on the House floor.

In the Senate, the Bill was introduced by Senator David Koehler, who represented the Peoria territory involved. It turns out that an airport authority in Peoria was experiencing much the same problem as the one I represented in Crawford County. When I explained the situation in Crawford County to Representative Shock, he contacted the Senate sponsor to see if he would agree to allow an amendment to the measure to include the tax base territory expansion needed in Robinson in his bill. Koehler, after discussing the issue with Senator Righter, agreed to have the bill amended to include the Robinson airport tax base expanded.

I filed House Amendment 1 to Koehler's Senate bill after discussions with officials from Robinson. They agreed to travel to Springfield to testify before the Local Government Committee to support the proposal. Steve McGahey, Bob Berty (Director of Crawford County Economic Development) and a couple of other business and airport authority board members traveled to Springfield and testified. They did a great job of explaining the fairness of expanding the airport authority tax base and the critical need for additional funds that would be created by the expansion. These local representatives specifically identified several important projects with projected costs that were needed for the airport to continue safe operations and support jobs in the county.

On May 10, 2007, the amendment was added. The bill went back to the House floor for final House Action. Since it had been amended, it had to also return to the Senate for favorable consideration to be sent to the governor and signed into law. Both Schock and I were Republican State Representatives, clearly in the minority, and getting the bill back to the Senate would be a challenge. This bill was seen as a tax increase bill since the tax base was being expanded. It is never easy to get this type of legislation passed. Often, both GOP and Democrat Leaders do not want to expose their membership to a vote to increase taxes or the tax base.

For almost two weeks, Shock and I worked a roll call to see if we had enough votes to get the measure back to the Senate. This time, I made sure we had a *hard roll call.* Fortunately, we were able to garner 73 yes votes and the legislation went back to the Senate for final action on May 22nd with a 73-42 favorable vote. On May 29th the bill was passed in the

Senate by a 48-9 margin and the Governor signed it into law on August 23rd. The effective date of the new law was January 1, 2008. PA 95-0365 created both the *Greater Metropolitan Airport Authority* serving the Peoria area and the, which serves Robinson as well as the entirety of Crawford County to this day.

In my third term, a better understanding of the Rules, applying the principles I had learned, working across the political aisle, working with local officials from both Paris and Robinson, legislation was passed that helps these communities to this day.

The Paris work campsite eventually supported educational efforts in Paris and the new Crawford County Airport Authority now had the tax base to maintain and expand the airport. The airport remains a critical part of current and future economic development in Crawford County. Just the other day, a large plane flew over while I was working in my yard and was set to land at the airport. That would not have been possible without this legislation. I just looked up and grinned. These legislative successes to support local causes made me feel like I was truly making a difference in my role as State Representative.

Another legislative success that session was even more difficult and very controversial.

During each of my elections, a common theme I heard from constituents was that property taxes were too high. Reducing expenses is one way to lower property taxes. But when local governing bodies, like school districts propose cost reductions, there is normally an outcry from the same folks that wanted property tax relief. They are also against the cost reductions being proposed. After the actual cost reductions are proposed, the opposite usually happened and local voters, by local referenda, vote to increase their property taxes to maintain the educational or extra-curricular programs threatened by cuts funded. The same is true for police, fire and ambulance services. Everyone wants great schools, law enforcement, well-maintained roads, sidewalks, and other public services, but the problem is, all of that must be paid for. I have heard it put this way, "Everyone wants to go to heaven but nobody wants to die."

None the less, there is widespread public support that local costs related to education and other public services and infrastructure costs are too reliant on property taxes. One way to reduce this burden on local property taxes, besides cutting expenses, is to shift the funding burden to other revenue sources.

State Senator Harry Babe Woodyard, mentioned earlier in this book, made several proposals in the 1990s that would have allowed a shift away from dependence on property taxes by allowing voters in a certain taxing area to vote to increase their income taxes to pay for school-related costs in exchange for property tax reduction. The notion was fairly simple; let the locals decide if they would rather pay the expenses with income tax or property tax revenue. The idea drew some support but lots of criticism because people were concerned about whether or not the increased revenue would be used to offset expenses. The proposals just did not catch any momentum in the General Assembly at that time.

In neighboring Iowa, legislation had passed which would provide local voters a similar option to reduce property taxes. In Iowa, local residents, by referenda could vote to impose a retail sales tax that was to be used for school facility expenses that would, in turn, take the pressure off of property taxes. Two legislators from the northeast area of Illinois took notice. Senator Mike Jacobs and State Representative Pat Verschoore decided to make a similar proposal as an option for local voters in Illinois. Verschoore asked me about the idea early on and asked if I would take a look at the proposal.

The original proposal was contained in HB410. The proposal would allow local voters, by **front door referendum**, to impose up to a 2 cent sale tax on retail sales. Everything that was currently included in the municipal and county sales tax code was included with some exceptions. The measure exempted car, truck, ATV, boat, Mobile Homes and RV sales along with unprepared food, drugs (including over the counter and vitamins), farm equipment and parts and farm inputs. Just like with the already existing retail sales tax, services were also not subject to the tax.

The use of these new sales tax revenues was also limited. Schools could only use the revenue for new facilities, additions and renovations, security and safety, technology infrastructure, architectural planning, durable equipment (non-movable), land acquisition, energy efficiency, parking lots, demolition, roof repairs, and other capital projects.

The money could not be used for any direct instructional costs, textbooks, buses, any detached furniture or equipment, computers, any movable equipment, teacher or administrative salaries or other operating costs. The purpose was clear; the revenue could only be used for capital costs.

I looked over the proposal and really liked the idea. I especially liked the idea that this was a **local option.** It gave local voters an option to reduce local property taxes by establishing a sustainable revenue source by shifting to local sales tax as an option. Most importantly to me, it required a local referendum to be passed. This measure **did not raise taxes**, it simply allowed for discussion, debate and control.

I spoke with my colleague Jerry Mitchell about the bill and decided that this idea at least deserved discussion and debate. I informed Vershoore of my support of his proposal for local taxpayers and signed on as a co-sponsor to HB410. Three other House GOP members also signed on: my good friend Mike Tryon, Rep Ron Wait and my mentor Jerry Mitchell. All thought the idea merited discussion.

It was a struggle to get HB410 through the House but together, in a bipartisan fashion, we managed. It took two amendments, but we got the bill out of the House on May 18th, 2007, with a 65-45 vote. A *hard roll call* was once again necessary, but people stuck with us. With such a thin margin, House floor debate on third reading revealed some additional concerns about the legislation. After the legislation passed the House, Pat Verschoore and I both had concerns that it might not pass in the Senate due to remaining concerns expressed in the House during floor debate. Senator Jacobs, with input from Verschoore related to the concerns that arose in the House, crafted an amendment to the measure and attached it to a Senate Bill that could be used as a vehicle (shell bill) to get the now amended proposal out of the Senate and back to the House in time to be acted on before the end of May.

It was important to get the bill passed in both the Senate and House before the end of May for two reasons. First, budgeteers were still working on the FY08 Budget and, while there seemed to be growing concern that an agreement would be made by May 31st, it was possible May 31st could be the deadline. The calendar still showed the adjournment date for the spring as May 31st. What we didn't know then was that the impending budget battle to take place in the late spring and summer of 2007 would be the worst yet. But more importantly, after May 31st, any legislation had to pass with a super-majority and we had a very thin margin.

It was critical to get the bill passed by May 31st.

As a member of the majority party, Senator Mike Jacobs had no trouble finding a Senate Bill to use as a vehicle to attach the amendment to. SB835, originally a measure intended to make a minor change to a section of law concerning the Municipal Code, was resurrected. The original contents of SB835 were completely removed by what is known as a 'gut and replace' Amendment and Senate Amendment 1 to SB835 became the *Local Retail Tax Option, Bill.* Due to his majority party status, Jacobs was able to get the bill through the Senate quickly and on May 24th SB835 passed by a vote of 31-24. My Senator, Dale Righter, voted against the bill in the Senate. In a phone call to me, he warned that there would be some strong opposition and likely a political price to pay for supporting this measure.

He was always much better at sniffing out the political side than I was.

When it reached the House, Vershoore was also in a position to get the bill a hearing in Rules Committee, and quickly assigned to Revenue Committee for a hearing.

After a successful vote in the Revenue Committee, SB825 was placed on the House Calendar on May 29th, just two days short of scheduled adjournment. While it still looked like the General Assembly might be in Session in June due to another budget stalemate, it was still imperative that the bill gets out of the House and on to the governor before May 31st at midnight. On May 30th, the legislation was put on third reading and ready for a vote.

I was pleased to see that a couple of additional House Republicans signed on as co-sponsors during the debate. Both Sandra Pihos and freshman Rep Mike Fortner became sponsors. Fortner was a fellow educator and college professor; he was a rocket scientist. Several times on the house floor during the contentious debate, I would insert Mike's name into the debate reminding everyone that it shouldn't take a rocket scientist to figure this out, but we had one handy if needed. Pihos was a former school board member and understood the need for local a local property tax relief option.

The amendments made to HB410 before the final language was inserted in SB835 addressed some concerns of House Members and, in the end, added a few votes. On May 30th, with a full day to spare, SB835 passed by a vote of 74-41, an additional 9 votes from the 65 votes on the original version of the proposal (HB410). While, at the time, we had no reason to believe this proposal would be vetoed, it was nice to know that the bill had a veto-proof, supermajority of votes. As it turned out, we would need that cushion.

Our bill was to become part of a larger and very nasty political skirmish unrelated to the actual merits of our legislation.

During the late spring of 2007, as legislators considered and debated various proposals made by Blagojevich related to health care expansion and revenue increases, tensions rose to a fever pitch. Blagojevich began to threaten members of the General Assembly who were questioning the policies he proposed. One of the more tense exchanges came when he attempted to get the support of Senator Jacobs to vote for universal health care coverage in Illinois. The plan, called *Illinois Covered*, was very costly and lawmakers on both sides of the aisle were cautious about supporting additional costs for health care when the state was several billion dollars behind in paying health care providers.

While he was a member of the Illinois Senate, Barack Obama was among the original chief architects and co-sponsors of universal health care expansion in Illinois. Obama, though, was not around in the Illinois Senate during this attempt to expand health care coverage in Illinois.

By the spring of 2007, Obama had moved on to the United States Senate after defeating Dan Hynes in the Democratic Senatorial Primary back in the spring of 2006. Republicans had nominated Jack Ryan in the GOP Senatorial Primary in 2006. However, after it was discovered that there were controversial photos of Ryan and his wife, he dropped out of the race. Ryan's wife, Jeri (Zimmermann) Ryan was an actress. She played the Borg drone named Seven of Nine, in *Star Trek; Voyager.* She also appeared on a TV show called Boston Public. Her celebrity status fueled the fire and Ryan eventually was forced to drop out of the race. This was even before Twitter.

After Ryan dropped out, eventually, in a very controversial move, the Illinois State GOP replaced Ryan with a candidate from Maryland named Allen Keyes. Keyes unsuccessfully ran for President of the United States in 1996 and 2000. Before that, Keyes was the Republican nominee for U.S. Senate in Maryland twice. He lost both of those Senate races by large margins. In the 1988 Maryland Senate race, he only received around 38% of the vote. In the 1992 unsuccessful Senate race, he attracted considerable negative press by paying himself over eight thousand dollars a month from his campaign fund. Why he was chosen as the Republican replacement for Ryan puzzled many and enraged others.

Many people thought former Chicago Bears Head Coach Mike Ditka would have been a better candidate. After former Illinois Governor Jim Edgar pulled his name from consideration though, the GOP decision-makers, at the State Party level, chose Keyes. The rest is, as they say, history. Obama thrashed Keyes by a margin of 70-27% to become U.S.

Senator Barack Obama. Many believe that Jim Edgar would have likely defeated Obama and could have changed the course of history.

What Obama couldn't get done in Illinois prior to moving on to the U.S. Senate in 2007, we all know he later accomplished as President with a national version of healthcare coverage called Obamacare. That debate goes on as portions of Obamacare have been found unconstitutional and candidates for President are still proposing various national health care plans.

Back in 2007, the effort in Illinois to expand state-supported healthcare was left up to Blagojevich. Remember, Senator Mike Jacobs was the Senate sponsor of the Local Retail Sales Tax Option legislation (SB835). In a heated meeting with Blagojevich, Jacobs informed the governor that he was not going to support the health care expansion proposal. According to reports from those in the room, including Jacobs, things got nasty and the governor verbally threatened Jacobs and poked him in the chest. Whatever happened for sure, nobody but Jacobs and Blagojevich knows. There are varying accounts. What is for certain is that Jacobs had informed the governor he would not vote in favor of the expansion. In March, the proposal to expand state-sponsored health care in Illinois failed on the Senate floor **by one vote**. Blagojevich felt Jacobs could have gotten the bill out of the Senate by voting for it.

When he declined, Jacobs's perceived betrayal was not forgotten about by-Blagojevich.

This is where the intersection of the Jacobs-Blagojevich feud smashed into our effort to provide a property tax relief option to Illinois residents.

Grudges are hard to overcome. Revenge, as it is said, is a dish best served cold. The grudge Blagojevich held against Jacobs over his no vote on health care expansion was deep. Jacobs was the Senate Chief sponsor of SB835, which established an opportunity for local voters to pass a referendum allowing for up to a 2% retail sales tax to support local school districts. Months after SB835 passed the House and Senate, Blagojevich took revenge. On August 27th, Blagojevich vetoed SB835. It was no real surprise, by then he had vetoed dozens of other bills intending to punish those who had not supported his proposals that year.

Vershoore and I discussed the potential of overriding the veto and after another hard roll call, we were confident we would be able to get the 71 votes required to override this veto. After all, it had received 74 votes in May.

The real concern was if Jacobs could get the necessary votes in the Senate. The measure only received 30 votes in the Senate in May and now Jacobs needed 40 votes to override the veto. On October 10th, Jacobs called the override vote and received an incredible 45 votes in the Senate on a bill that had only garnered 30 votes in May. The disdain for Blagojevich helped Jacob's effort. My Senator, Dale Righter, who had previously voted against the measure, was among those voting yes to override the veto. In the House, a similar result took place as the override vote gathered 79 ayes compared to the original 74 yes votes.

The retail sales tax option became law upon the successful override. Since then, over 50 Counties successfully passed the Local Retail Tax Option. About half the number of local referenda proposed has also been voted down. This is exactly how it is supposed to work; it is supposed to be a local option. Millions of dollars in reductions of property taxes have occurred as local school districts have an alternative funding source.

There are always people who oppose any tax proposal. Some just get angrier than others. One of my constituents from Lawrence County, where the tax was successfully voted in by local voters, called me and quite angrily declared that I had raised taxes in Lawrence County. He surely couldn't be that simple-minded, or could he? His tantrum included moving his business out of Illinois across the river into Indiana and blaming the move partially on what he called the *Eddy Tax*. Oddly, most of the retail purchases made for his business were exempt from the retail sales tax anyway. He would never have a civil or reasonable conversation about the legislation.

Never mind the fact that local taxpayers chose through their right to vote to shift revenue from property to retail sales taxes. A few years later, during an election campaign, he paid for full-page ads in several newspapers to rail against the *Eddy Tax*. I am not going to mention his name in hopes that he has matured a bit since that time.

If someone has a good argument and reasoning behind opposition to any proposal I am happy to listen. When an individual becomes threatening and irrational, I have been known to politely end the conversation and hang up, and move on to better use of my time.

During my third term, I introduced several legislative proposals that were not successful. HB2784 was more of a message bill. The proposal would have added a line to the ballot in Illinois Elections so people would be allowed to choose, "none of the above". The measure was introduced on February 26th, 2007 and referred to Rules Committee where it later died on January 13, 2009 as the 95th General Assembly adjourned Sine Die. I suppose people still have the option of not voting in specific races by leaving the ballot blank and not voting for a specific individual. This is commonly known as an 'under-vote' and does tell a story if the number is very large.

I also introduced a bill that would have required drug testing for any student taking driver's education courses in Illinois' schools. This bill was released from the Rules Committee and assigned a hearing in the Driver's Education and Safety Committee. During the hearing, some committee members indicated they did not like the fact that there was a presumption of guilt of all students by testing all of them. Committee members suggested an amendment to make the proposed testing random. I sensed that if I made the change there would be enough support to get the bill out of committee.

The amended version of the bill did make it to the House floor and all the way to 3rd Reading. Once the proposal advanced to the House floor, there was an immediate and intense media reaction. Like just about anything else of this nature, there were those strongly supporting the idea and those concerned about the cost as well as privacy concerns. Questions arose about the details related to the random selection of students to be tested.

After the ACLU came out strongly opposed, the legislation was in trouble and eventually died on the floor.

As always, I introduced several congratulatory resolutions during the 95th General Assembly. Lincoln Trail College Baseball Coach Mitch Hannahs had been named to the Missouri Valley Conference All-Century team, the Casey High School football team finished second in the State, and the Lady Pirates Volleyball team from Cumberland High school had an outstanding season. All were recognized as well as others.

I learned about a guy from Lawrenceville named Howard Cleff. Howard Cleff was born in 1914 in a dot of a town in southeastern Illinois named Birds. Cleff was hired by the Illinois State Police in 1941 and among other impressive things he accomplished in his career, he apprehended a *Ten Most Wanted* fugitive during the 1960 Cairo riots. Cleff retired from the State Police in 1973 after 32 years of service. Cleff was the first person to suggest painting a white line on the side of Illinois highways so that drivers could visually distinguish where the shoulder started. For that suggestion, he won a $100 War Bond. One man, from Lawrenceville, Illinois, born in Birds, made a significant contribution to public safety. To honor him, HJR108 was passed unanimously by the House and Senate and a portion of Illinois Highway 50, near Lawrenceville was dedicated to his memory. On a portion of the highway where he patrolled, there is now a sign designating it as *The Howard Cleff Memorial Highway.*

I also introduced House Joint Resolution 36. This Resolution created a task force to look at issues beginning to boil related to Dual Credit in Illinois. At the time, there was a developing controversy about how students in high school courses were earning dual credit. In other words, they received both credits for a particular class toward their high school graduation as well as college credit. It was a very popular concept and had expanded substantially in recent years.

The concerns of the higher education community regarding the quality of the credits earned in some of the courses threatened the very existence of dual credit in Illinois.

The task force was supposed to look at issues related to the practice and report back to the General Assembly regarding findings and potential public policy solutions to any identified problems. Little did I know at the time that this Task Force would take lots of time and energy in 2009 during the 96th General Assembly. There will be much more on this issue and how it was resolved later in this book.

While members of the House were working on legislation important to them, Governor Blagojevich was busy with his agenda for his second term. By this time, even though he had defeated Judy Barr Topinka by 11% in November of 2006, there was a steady stream of news reports linking his inner-circle to federal investigations. He had become the first Democrat since Otto Kerner since 1964 to win two consecutive terms as Illinois Governor but his reputation was taking daily hits. By the time he was sworn in to begin his second term as Illinois Governor in January of 2007, just two months after winning re-election in November of 2006, his approval rating was terrible.

Even though during their speeches that Inauguration Day, fellow elected Democrats Dan Hynes (Comptroller), Alexi Giannoulias (Treasurer) and Jesse White (Secretary of State) all mentioned the need for cleaning up Illinois government, during his Inaugural Speech, Blagojevich never hinted that there were any ethical issues to face. Blagojevich was silent on the issue. Instead, he bragged about the Illinois I-PASS tollway system's success and once again zeroed in on the expansion of health care coverage. After the speech, Blagojevich refused to answer any questions from the press and sequestered himself in the Governor's Mansion. The Inaugural Ball held that evening was nothing like the one four years earlier.

The 2007 Budget and State of the State Address were not delivered until March 7th. Blagojevich asked for an extension of time from the usual delivery dates for these speeches and asked that the speeches be combined. He claimed to need more time to analyze the issues facing Illinois.

Blagojevich began this speech by recognizing wounded Illinois war veteran Tammy Duckworth. He then used most of the speech to explain why important it was to expand healthcare services to Illinois residents. He railed against Illinois fixed income tax as regressive and called for changes to end what he labeled an, "Archaic tax system in Illinois." He proposed that the current system of taxation in Illinois be changed. According to Blagojevich, Illinois should adopt a Gross Receipts TAX (GRT). For example after example, he outlined how education funding, pension funding, healthcare funding and other state programs important to the middle class required funding.

According to Blagojevich, the choice had to be made between underfunded programs, increasing the already regressive taxes (sales and income taxes) which would further burden the working class, or adopt a tax which would be much fairer. Require wealthy corporations to pay their fair share. Multiple times, he repeated the phrase, "The choice is simple, we can ignore (fill in the blank with any program related to education or health care) or have corporations pay their fair share."

He then outlined his plan to increase education spending by $10 billion over the next four years. His plan would spend more money on classrooms and teachers, expand early childhood education and build more schools. These would be coupled with real reforms like cutting administrative waste and consolidation of schools. Using quotes from Martin Luther King about the need to end inequalities in health care, Blagojevich called for universal health care in Illinois. He encouraged Members of the General Assembly to be bold and not wait for Washington, DC to do what needs to be done. He provided several stories about people who need health insurance and were suffering. A plan was proposed that would provide all Illinois citizens with high-quality government-run health care. The plan was called *Illinois Covered.* This type of plan was affordable if major corporations started to pay their fair share.

His, "Tax Fairness Plan", as he went on to outline, contained several provisions.

One of the plan components was to lease or sell the Illinois Lottery system. According to his estimate, this move would provide $10 billion for education to be invested over the next four years. The funds would be used to pay teachers and provide the poorest schools in the state money which would support equity in funding. There would also be money for building and repairing schools, allowing for full-day kindergarten and preschool for all three and four-year olds in Illinois. Part of this would be accomplished by reducing administrative costs and consolidation of schools. He had kept his promise once again to Senator Meeks by proposing the sale of the lottery.

Another pillar of the plan was to revisit bonding (aka borrowing) more of Illinois' huge pension debt. His proposal would have added tens of billions of dollars of support to the pension systems by issuing bonds with proceeds going directly into the State's five pension funds to make up for years of underfunded payments. Low bond rates made this sound attractive, but it was more debt for Illinois.

The centerpiece of his proposal was the aforementioned expansion of health care coverage. This was red meat to his fellow democrats. The party had long held as part of the national and state platform that health care was a basic human right and should be provided by the government. The expanded proposal he entitled, Illinois Covered, came with a high price tag. Based on most estimates it would cost the state over $5 billion.

He was hitting all of the high notes with his speech as far as Democrats were concerned.

Public education spending and universal health care are key cornerstones of the party faithful.

The issue was the same, how the health care expansion would be paid for?

He did propose how education funding increases could be paid for- the Illinois Lottery lease or sale could provide the money for public education. The revenue from the lottery was already part of the budget and was already thought to be used to support education. If the lottery was sold or leased, the result was either losing the annual recurring revenue from the lottery with a one-time infusion of dollars or a lease payment that would not add significantly to the revenue already going to education. The truth is that a dollar cannot be spent twice. There was almost audible laughter when the lottery idea was uttered. The idea of selling or leasing the Illinois Lottery was dead on arrival.

The significance of the lottery proposal was to once again show that his promise to Meeks was kept. Later in the speech, Blagojevich again suggested that Illinois could sell or lease the Thompson Center in Chicago for revenue. The State is still trying to figure out a way to sell the Thompson Center. Whenever it, IF-ever that sale takes place, this is *one-time* revenue and cannot be used for sustaining on-going expenses.

What about the massive health care expansion? How would he propose paying for this multi-billion dollar expense? That is where, Blagojevich, claiming to have found the answer to the revenue problems facing the state proposed a Gross Receipts Tax (GRT). According to his calculations, the implementation of a GRT in Illinois would result in an additional $7.6 billion in new recurring revenue to fund the health care expansion plus provide money for a major capital infrastructure program.

In this March 7th combined budget and State of the State Address, he railed against giant corporations declaring that these corporations do not pay their fair share. He proclaimed that several hundred of the largest, most profitable corporation in America, doing business in Illinois, paid zero income taxes. He repeated that phrase, "Zero, nota, bupkis." This was new…it was the first time I heard the governor use Yiddish in one of his speeches.

Over and over again during the speech he stated that there was a choice to be made; you can side with giant corporations that do not pay their fair share or you could side with the hard-working people of Illinois. He manipulated all kinds of facts and figures to support his plan.

The corporate share of Illinois taxes had reduced from 21% to 12% over the last decade. The CEO's of Fortune 500 Companies make outlandish salaries, as much as four hundred times the average workers' pay. He, Blagojevich, was going to side with the 88% of working people who were footing the bill and stand up for the people stating, **"I will work hard for the people who play by the rules."** When he said that, I turned to Senator Righter, sitting next to me during the speech and said, "Did he just say that?" Audible laughter was heard throughout the entire Assembly and balcony after that line. The House was packed full; as Senators joined House Members for these speeches which were delivered on the House floor. The upper deck House gallery was also packed; so the level of laughter was quite something.

Toward the end of the speech, he once again warned everyone that he would not support any proposal to increase income taxes or sales tax. He would not place any additional burden on hard-working people when corporations were not paying their fair share. Blagojevich returned to the style reminiscent of his first few years as an enemy was identified. Large corporations were the villain this time around and he shot multiple times at his new target.

So, just what was a Gross Receipts Tax? Many, actually I would say most, of the members of the General Assembly, really didn't know much about the tax. To those embracing the possibility that all of Illinois' problems could be solved with this silver bullet, it seemed like maybe a good idea. According to Blagojevich, we could fund education fully so all kids could have an equitable opportunity for high-quality education, have free preschool education for all 3-4-year-olds, kindergarten for all and new or updated facilities in which to educate children. Plus, the plan included universal healthcare for every citizen? And all of this could be accomplished by taxing wealthy corporations. Magic! This all sounded too good to be true, and it was.

Blagojevich was certainly right about one thing he said during this speech. When he said there would be opposition to the plan, it was an understatement. Almost immediately information was provided to members of the General Assembly describing what the Gross Receipts Tax (GRT) was and how it works. By definition a GRT is a broad-based, low rate (usually around 1%) tax on all income received by a business without any deductions for the cost of doing business. A GRT is not based on a company's profit or loss but owed on all income even if the business is not profitable. Corporate income tax is levied against income *after* consideration of expenses. GRT is quite the opposite.

The information provided to members of the General Assembly, much of it very negative, immediately came from all corners. It was not simply the wealthy corporations who would oppose the idea. Chicago's well-respected Center for Tax and Budget Accountability (CTBA) came out strongly against the idea. In a well-researched and extremely well-written fact sheet regarding the GRT, the CTBA stated several reasons why GRT was not a good solution for Illinois. Among those reasons quoted:

- GRT does not treat all taxpayers fairly and new firms pay a higher effective tax rate than established firms in all industries. New firms did not have the advantage of subtracting start-up costs from gross income for example.

150

- GRT is, much like the flat income tax, a regressive tax. Low-profit margin and start-up businesses would pay a higher effective tax rate than established high-profit margin businesses making it very regressive.
- GRT, in the end, would be regressive for consumers because the tax would be passed on at the point of sale. Besides, the GRT is imposed at every phase of the product sale from the raw material stage to the manufacturer, to wholesaler, to the retailer and then the customer also pays a regressive sales tax upon purchase. This was described as the pyramid effect of the GRT. Often, to avoid the manufacturing part of the GRT pyramid, some manufacturing, and ultimately jobs, would move out of the State to avoid the GRT. There was also fear that the GRT would result in lower wages to offset the cost of the tax.

The CTBA, along with countless other credible organizations, concluded that the implementation of the GRT was not the answer for Illinois but more likely a disaster. Even though at the time, five other states, including Texas, Ohio and Washington, had implemented the GRT, the consensus in Illinois was that this proposal was dead on arrival.

In addition to the clear evidence regarding the flaws of the GRT, Blagojevich himself had very little, if any credibility when it came to offering real solutions for the fiscal problems that plagued Illinois. His first four budget addresses were so full of gimmicks like pension bonds schemes, fund raids and other borrowing that just about any proposal would have been met with immediate skepticism. Without a strong, credible governor to work with, GRT was seen as the latest in a series of stunts. When Speaker Madigan made it known that he was not going to support the GRT as a source of revenue, the idea was dead and everyone knew it. Well, *almost everyone* could figure it out.

Rod Blagojevich went after the Speaker full throttle for undermining his efforts to pass the GRT and provide education and health care funding. He accused the Speaker of not giving the idea a chance and burying it without a fair hearing. He was quoted as saying the Speaker wanted an income tax increase and was forcing the income tax as the only alternative without giving his idea a fair shake. He demanded that the Speaker allow a hearing in Committee about the proposal. Well, Rod, be careful what you wish for.

Madigan not only allowed for a public hearing on GRT, but he also scheduled the House to meet as a Committee of the Whole. There was very little support beyond witnesses from the Governor's staff. Even though there was no support, the Speaker engineered a committee vote so the measure could move to the House floor for a vote. He called the move an attempt to give the Governor's proposal a fair vote. Representative Jay Hoffman was in the unenviable position of carrying the legislative and presenting the GRT legislation for the governor.

(Signs like this were all over the Senate and House Chambers and throughout the Capital Campus)

On the floor of the House, during a rousing debate, the GRT was roundly rejected by speaker after speaker. The potential effects of the implementation of such a tax were described as devastating. At the end of the debate, the plan was voted down by an unbelievable 107-0 no vote. Not one Representative, not even the House sponsor Jay Hoffman, voted for the revenue plan. Media reports of the debacle were not kind toward the governor.

For his part, Blagojevich continued to play the part of the man who was trying to save the people from the evil conspiracy in the General Assembly, led by Madigan, to raise their income taxes. By this time, media reports of the Blagojevich campaign corruption enterprise were very widespread. Daily accounts of allegations that countless donations were made to curry favor made even the governors most ardent supporters take notice. There were numerous on-going investigations into all aspects of the Blagojevich operations. Time after time, he dismissed all of this as a conspiracy against him because he would not support an income tax increase.

The fact was that there was not an agreement on a sustainable and reliable source of revenue to even fill the existing budget shortfall (some estimated close to $5 billion or more), let alone add any expansion of education spending or universal health care. This meant that all of the spending proposals made by him in that rosy State of the State Address were also dead. When the legislation mentioned earlier which contained the language for *Illinois Covered* was defeated by a single vote in the Senate, the universal health care plan was dead.

The scheme to sell or lease the Illinois Lottery was rejected as a revenue source; all of the increases in education spending were also out of the question.

Door after door was being slammed in the face of the governor.

It mid-May of 2007, it appeared that the only way to pass any state budget for FY08 was to make deeper cuts to existing programs. The fiscal problems for FY08 were further exasperated by a growing pension payment that was due to spike as the result of a pension plan passed in 1994. The plan, credited to former Governor Jim Edgar, established a payment ramp that allowed for lower payments during the first 15 years of the 50-year plan. In FY08 the payment was scheduled to increase by billions of dollars as the ramp became very steep.

All of the inadequate state payments and other gimmicks related to pension funding were also increasing the unfunded liability. Just to make the scheduled increase in the pension payment would mean cuts to other programs. This set those collecting state-sponsored pensions up in future years to be the bad guys. Through no fault of their own, starting in 2007, and continuing thereafter, hard-working state workers and teachers became a constant target. These individuals did not create the pension system, never voted on any of the laws establishing the system and ALWAYS had made the payment required of them. Current law required most State workers to join and contribute to one of the systems. Yet, they were the problem according to some. They might have been an easy target, but they were not the problem.

The FY08 budget stalemate lasted until August when the General Assembly passed a budget over the governor's veto. It was a painful plan with major cuts to many services. The governor, always looking for a fight, decided to reduce spending even more by removing $463 million in projects known as 'Member Initiatives.' These were pet projects inserted by members of the majority party.

It was during the summer of 2007 when this then historic budget stalemate was happening; the die was cast for Blagojevich. Each day of the endless and fruitless special session he had called was costing the taxpayers $22,215 per day. He had lost all credibility, the state was in a fiscal free-fall and the numerous investigations continued to reveal an astonishing pattern of campaign finance abuse and many other questions regarding hiring practices. He had issued executive orders that were clearly beyond his power as governor. He implemented programs expanding health care by Executive Order even after the expansion had been rejected by the General Assembly.

Several things became very clear in 2007. Blagojevich had little support in Springfield. He was the target of an active federal investigation and a completely ineffective governor. I, along with Representative Mike Bost called for Impeachment investigations to begin back in July of 2006. Some people viewed this as partisan rancor. In my heart and mind, I knew we were dealing with someone who thought he was above the law. I also knew that until he was gone, Illinois would not begin to address the fiscal problems we faced. How could we possibly continue or recover with Blagojevich as governor? The fiasco in 2007 was just the first year of a new four year term. How could this craziness continue? Something had to be done.

"Fools said I, you do not know; silence like a cancer grows. But my words, like silent raindrops fell, and echoed in the wells of silence."
Simon and Garfunkel from *The Sound of Silence.*

This popular song had been released by Simon and Garfunkel in the early 1960s. In 2007, it very much seemed like it applied to my life.

In October of 2007 there were calls for a *recall* of the Governor although the Illinois Constitution contained no such provision. A poll conducted in November of 2007 revealed that even 46% of Democrats favored a recall. In my mind, to enact legislation to allow a recall would take too long. It was well beyond the time to act.

As 2007 came to a close, on December 14th, another member of the Blagojevich inner circle directly related to his campaign and administration, Chris Kelly was indicted and charged with tax fraud.

For sure 2007 had been a memorable year in Illinois and the nation. A gallon of gas became even more expensive as the average price ballooned to $3.38 a gallon. On April 16th that year, tragedy struck at Virginia Tech University when 30 students were murdered in a campus killing spree. A bridge on Interstate 35 in Minneapolis collapsed and 13 people were killed. NASA's New Horizon flew past Jupiter in February about a month after something called the I-phone had been introduced by Apple in January, at a price of $599. Major league baseball released a report that there was widespread use of anabolic steroids in the national pastime along with the use of human growth hormones. This was the year the housing bubble began to burst and also the year Nancy Pelosi was elected the first-ever female speaker of the United States House of Representatives.

In primary elections for their party's nomination for President of the United States, the GOP saw names like Mitt Romney, Rudy Giuliani, Mike Huckabee and John Mc Cain enter the fray. The Democrats saw the likes of John Edwards, Joe Biden, Hillary Clinton and a fella named Barack Obama from Illinois vie for the nomination. John Mc Cain eventually defeated Romney soundly by a delegate margin of 1,575 to 271 to win the Republican nomination and this guy from Illinois named Barack Obama narrowly defeated Hilary Clinton 2,272 to 1,978 to become the Democratic candidate for the nation's highest office. The move by Madigan that changed the Illinois Primary date was part of the reason Obama was successful.

Sequels dominated the box office in 2007 as Spider Man 3, Shrek the third, and Oceans Thirteen were released. Hollywood also produced The Simpson Movie and the Best Movie of the year was The Departed. Maroon 5, Ludacris, Jennifer Lopez, Fergie, and Justin Timberlake were all becoming stars.

At the end of 2007, In Illinois, one thing was for certain, 2008 promised to be an interesting year. The antics of an out of control often described as corrupt governor would be the backdrop while one of Illinois' own ran for the nation's highest office.

Chapter Thirteen
...*The Secret to Survival*

It was 2008 and the 95th General Assembly was about to begin the second year of a two year cycle. The previous year's antics of Rod Blagojevich resulted in a record-long session of the General Assembly, including a record number of special sessions being called. It took until almost the end of August for a State Budget to be enacted, and then to get a final budget, it took an override of Governor Blagojevich's veto. It was a painful budget. Cuts to state programs meant less money for schools. These were the same schools and state service providers that were already often waiting more than six months to receive funding. General State Aid (GSA) and mandated categorical payments to schools were way behind and schools were borrowing record amounts of money by issuing tax anticipant warrants and working cash bonds. All of this debt would have to be paid back, with interest.

The fiscal problems plaguing Illinois were affecting the every-day lives of millions of people. Prekindergarten programs, which had been established during the expansion of Universal Pre-K, could no longer remain open due to debt incurred waiting for state funding. Parents no longer had a place to take their young children as early childhood programs closed due to a lack of funding. The expansion of Early Childhood was a failure because there was not money to pay for it. Some had to quit their jobs. Patients relying on existing state health care plans, many of which had been expanded, were being denied health care services because the state was no longer making anything close to timely payments. Those who had supported a governor who established and expanded these programs now knew that these programs were suffering irreparable harm because the Governor was refusing to compromise on how the expansions could be funded.

I recall the countless number of calls to my legislative offices in both Springfield and Hutsonville during 2007 and 2008 with people expressing outrage at the deadbeat status of Illinois. After all, they had paid their taxes, and were demanding to know what was going on. All we could do was try to explain that the State was basically broke, and in many ways broken. To top it all off, Illinois, like the rest of the nation, was in the initial stages of the worst economic downturn in modern history. Unemployment was creeping up and the climate was ugly.

When Blagojevich delivered another combined Budget and State of the State Address in February of 2008, the outlook and attitude of those in the House Chamber watching the speech live were at best subdued. By this time, the practice of Blagojevich delivering one speech instead of two was no longer questioned. The importance of the speech was the Budget Address as it was meant to satisfy the Constitutional requirement that the governor presents a budget to the General Assembly.

In previous years, he often asked for delays to deliver this speech and now he resorted to just one combined speech. Once again, nobody minded. By this time, the less we saw of Blagojevich, the better.

There was very little good news to be heard and the message was being delivered by a governor who had seen public support vanish and long ago lost the support of even his most ardent supporters in the General Assembly. Any speech he made resulted in stinging political attacks against him and any Democrat that might still follow along. If they did, follow along, they deserved the negative response they too would receive. Illinois Senators once again joined House Members in the House Chamber as was the custom and Blagojevich delivered his message.

He began this speech with a moment of silence in remembrance of six college students who had been killed in a campus shooting at Northern Illinois University in De Kalb, Illinois two weeks earlier on February 14th, 2008. The tragedy was still fresh on everyone's mind.

Because I was an alumnus of NIU, the shooting hit home. In my mind, I could still picture Cole Hall on NIU's campus and imagined the sheer horror that these young people experienced when Steven Kazmierczak opened fire with a shotgun and three pistols, killing six and wounding another 17 young people before shooting himself. Reports were that he simply entered room 101 of Cole Hall and started shooting. The incident lasted six minutes but lives were shattered forever. The campus had been shut down for two weeks and the media was still covering the aftermath.

The mood in the House Chamber, already somber, was now tearful as members of the General Assembly silently prayed for those suffering.

Once the moment had passed, Blagojevich acknowledged what everyone already knew when he stated, "Times are tough, and people are worried." Illinois had created most of its fiscal mess the previous five years under a Democrat-controlled General Assembly and an out of control governor. Multiple, consecutive unbalanced budgets implemented by using questionable tactics relying on revenue from fund raids, pension bonding schemes, reckless borrowing and delayed state payments had all but ruined Illinois. Spending increased without sustainable and reliable revenue. The only thing that might have been worse was the unethical behavior of the governor coupled with the lack of response shown by Madigan to begin the process of removing Blagojevich from office. People were very slowly waking up to those facts as well.

The national recession gave Blagojevich an excuse and another target. He strongly suggested that it was the national recession that was negatively affecting Illinois. Blagojevich reasoned it was the national economy getting in the way of all of the great things his administration had accomplished. According to Blagojevich, the State of Illinois had done great things during his time in office. He recounted the two minimum wage increases that had taken place, the expansion of health care for children, expansion of Early Childhood Education and record education funding increases as victories. All of this had been accomplished without raising taxes according to his self-accolades. In early January, Blagojevich had ordered free rides on all public transportation systems for senior citizens too. His speech praised that new free ride policy. How could any of this be his fault or the fault of the majority party?

He outlined his FY09 Budget proposal. The plan was based on three goals:

1. Strengthening the economy by implementing a capital infrastructure plan to put more money in the pockets of those in the trades plus tax cuts for businesses.

2. For families, he proposed a $300 tax credit to match the federal tax credit recently passed in Washington, DC. This would put money into the hands of people and that money would churn through the economy while helping them during these hard times. He challenged the General Assembly to pass this tax credit right away and put aside partisan bickering to help people just the way Republican President George W. Bush and a Democrat majority in the U.S. Congress had set aside their partisan differences to pass a federal tax credit.

3. He proposed to provide relief for small and medium-sized businesses, after acknowledging the defeat of the GRT the previous year

by quoting an old Hank Williams song, "I'm so lonesome I could cry". Do you recall the 107-0 vote against the proposal? Blagojevich once again decried the fact that large corporations do not pay their fair share and proposed a 20% tax cut for small businesses to stimulate job growth during a looming recession. Later it was revealed the plan was to increase taxes on large corporations to cut taxes on smaller businesses.

The most aggressive part of the three-part plan was to pass and implement a capital bill to invest in Illinois' decaying infrastructure. Such an investment would provide desperately needed good-paying jobs. Construction projects would restore the aging transportation infrastructure in Illinois which was necessary to support commerce. He urged the members to pass a public works project that he estimated would create seven-hundred thousand jobs. Using the historic public works projects implemented by Franklin Roosevelt as an example, Blagojevich declared that, "With a Democratic House, a Democratic Senate and a Democratic governor it should happen."

The infrastructure investment outlined was massive. He proposed almost $15 billion for highways and around $5 billion to build schools. Additional projects brought the total to almost $25 billion. Part of that money would be to assist with Chicago's attempt to lure the 2016 Summer Olympics to the city by investing in infrastructure to help in that effort.

He further proposed that the effort to pass this massive public works proposal be led by leaders from both parties and must be a bi-partisan effort.

Later that spring this part of the proposal resulted in a committee led by former Democrat Illinois Congressman Glenn Poshard and former GOP Congressman and Speaker of the U.S. House, Dennis Hastert. Both were, at the time, well-respected party leaders. Hastert hailed from the same Illinois town as then GOP House Leader Tom Cross and was riding the celebrity of having been Speaker of the U.S. House. All House GOP members were presented a signed copy of Hastert's book, *Mr. Speaker,* courtesy of Leader Cross.

Hastert's public disgrace would follow in the coming years with the revelation he sexually abused high school students while a wrestling coach. For years Hastert had been paying hush money to the victim to keep his lurid past under wraps. He was exposed when caught lying about cash withdrawals made to pay the accuser. At the time of this capital plan proposal though, he was the right person to get the GOP on board.

Poshard was well-liked by Democrats and had been the Democrat nominee for governor in 1998, eventually losing to later disgraced George Ryan by a 51-47 margin. He appealed to all as an honest person and good public servant having served ten years in the U.S. House of Representatives. I was surprised to some extent that Poshard would have anything to do with Blagojevich. He was needed, though, for the plan to have any chance of success. Under more normal circumstances, the idea of having these two lead the effort was pretty good. These were not normal circumstances.

The result of the special committee formed with Poshard and Hastert as co-chairs was a proposal that became a $30 billion spending plan. There were numerous pet projects added to the plan to get enough votes to pass it. This seems to always be the case whenever any spending plan is hatched.

Back to the Budget Address- To end the combined FY09 Budget and State of the State Speech, Blagojevich outlined how this massive capital plan would be paid for. For funding, he went back to his reliable source of fictional revenue, his dream of privatization of the Illinois Lottery system. He estimated that the sale or lease would bring in as much as $12 billion. The plan called for Illinois to retain a 20% ownership. Of the estimated $12 billion, $7 billion would be dedicated to infrastructure projects and the remainder to pay back bills and future spending. When he mentioned this as the potential revenue source for his budget plan, this time, instead of laughter, there was an audible groan in the House Chamber. Really, again with the lottery? How was the lottery revenue, already used to fund education, going to be replaced while also using proceeds to fund a capital plan? You can only spend a dollar once.

In addition, he proposed a 3% across the board cut to other state-supported programs, except for health care, education and public safety. Everyone recognized that once health care, education and public safety spending was eliminated from the proposed 3% cuts, there would be little savings. Closing state parks and other facilities would not even begin to yield enough in savings from the proposed reduction in state spending. It was then that Blagojevich made one final push for universal health care, referencing the popular presidential candidate Barack Obama's rallying cry for expansion of public health care. Even referencing Illinois' own Obama and the popular notion among

Democrats to support health care expansion could not save the budget speech from instant dismissal by anyone capable of adding and subtracting.

Little did anyone know, but this would be his last Budget and State of the State Address. His final speech to a joint body of the General Assembly was typical Blagojevich. The oration was full of over-promising populist themes, outlandish unachievable revenue proposals and identification of a culprit. This time, the culprit was once again huge corporations who do not pay their fair share of taxes. The act had worn thin.

There was growing support for a capital plan for sure, and that was the one part of the plan that did garner some attention throughout the spring session. Poshard and Hastert helped the credibility of that idea. But, this proposal would also die later in the spring because an agreed-upon, reliable revenue source was never found. Plus, there were many people concerned that a $25-30 billion State spending plan under this administration would be fertile ground for kickbacks and pay to play. There were few willing to hand this type of responsibility to the Blagojevich administration even if a funding source was identified and agreed upon.

The same was true for another proposal made by Blagojevich that spring of 2008. The plan was to issue an additional $16 Billion in pension obligation bonds. It immediately reminded everyone of the mistake made in 2003 when $10 billion in pension bonds were issued, the pension payments were skipped and the system ended up with a greater unfunded liability than before the bonds were sold. This time, the Governor's office pointed out that real money could be saved by retiring bonds that had interest rates of as much as 8.5% and replacing the debt with new bonds for perhaps as low as 6% or lower, which could eventually save the state millions.

According to Blagojevich, h had learned from the past mistake of 2003, this time declared that all of the bond proceeds from this sale would be deposited into the five systems. The result of the cash infusion would allow a recalculation of the unfunded liability calculated using the reduced bond rate and therefore reduce the amount of the payment which would provide budget relief. Some folks thought that the plan might yield real savings. However, the system was so underfunded that any reduction resulting in the payment made to the pension systems seemed preposterous. The bottom line was that nobody trusted him or the plan.

Causing further concern and possibly the most concern was the fact that the Teacher's Retirement System had recently been publically mentioned in scandalous media reports involving Stu Levine. Levine was a former TRS board member and well-known Blagojevich operative and fundraiser. It was common knowledge there had been attempts to shake down investors in exchange for the TRS business. There were by this time new reports involving William (Bill) Cellini, another Springfield insider, being linked to nefarious activity in the potential sale of State bonds. In that climate, the idea of any new bond sale was impossible.

As the spring session calendar entered the budget month of May, there was growing concern that the General Assembly was heading to another overtime session. There was not enough support for the governor's proposal for Madigan to even humor the program with hearings or votes.

2008 was also an election year for House Members and the Speaker was not about to let his members be subject to voting for or against these types of poisonous and politically charged proposals. Portions of the Governor's plan received mild Senate consideration but did not gain enough traction to go anywhere. The tax credit proposed by the governor was estimated to reduce revenue by $900 million and the proposed cuts in business taxes another $300 million. Illinois could not afford a $1.2 billion reduction in revenue. How could anyone support the Governor's proposal of another $500 million in fund raids? And the idea that House Members, especially Democrats, were going to vote to cut 3% across the board from state programs in an election year wasn't realistic. But when did Blagojevich ever offer anything realistic or well thought out?

On May 3rd, a fellow Democrat, Senator Larry Bomke from Springfield, **finally** publically called for the impeachment of Blagojevich. This was the first time a fellow Democrat had *publically* called for the investigation to begin impeachment proceedings.

The impeachment inquiry call from Bomke in May of 2008 was about 20 months after Representative Bost and I had mentioned the need in July of 2006.

In my mind, there had been plenty of evidence in July of 2006 or even 2007 to start an investigation. When Bomke mentioned Impeachment, now nearly two years later, the evidence was overwhelming. But, there was no movement by Madigan to start proceedings in the spring of 2008 either. That fact was frustrating beyond words. Why was Madigan so slow in fulfilling his duty?

162

Amidst growing media reports of scandals involving the Democratic Governor, and now calls for his impeachment from members of his own party, it became more and more apparent that the Speaker just wanted to get out of Springfield for the year and reduce accessibility to media coverage concerning the fiasco that was thrusting Illinois into a negative light nationally.

The budget was a hot mess; the Democratic Speaker had no good answers now that he had let things get this bad. By supporting a series of unbalanced, irresponsible budgets the previous six years he had helped lead Illinois' economy into a deep ditch.

But, the Illinois Constitution required a budget be passed by the General Assembly which was to be enacted to allow appropriations to flow starting in FY09 in July. That was supposed to mean July 1st. The result was that the Democrat majorities in both the House and Senate, led by the Speaker, literally decided to punt. Facing fourth down and no way to complete a real budget, the Speaker engineered the passage of what most referred to as a *fake budget.* It was just *faker* than the previous six, and maybe the *fakest.*

On the final day of the scheduled adjournment of the spring session, with only Democrat votes in the House and Senate, and only a couple of hours before a midnight May 31st, deadline, a FY09 budget was passed and sent to the Governor. Speaker Madigan simply justified the out of balance budget sent to the governor by stating that the General Assembly had done their job and passed a budget and it was the governor's job to manage the budget and make the necessary spending cuts. The Speaker had, once again, cornered Blagojevich. He could either sign a budget that contained none of his proposals or be responsible for cutting expenses himself.

Everyone knew we would be called back when the governor eventually vetoed the Speaker's plan and Blagojevich obliged, vetoing the FY09 with line-item cuts.

Several weeks after Madigan sent the fake budget to Blagojevich, on July 17th, the General Assembly reconvened in yet another special session. This special session was to act on the vetoes that Blagojevich made to the clearly out of balance, **fake** FY09 budget passed by Madigan and the Democrats. In his vetoes, the Governor, trying to one-up Madigan, made massive cuts to important state programs. He was attempting to show how disastrous and fake the General Assembly and Speaker Madigan's budget was to the state.

This was yet another pathetic move by Blagojevich to demonize both the Speaker and General Assembly. His credibility in Illinois was shot by this time and his public rants about the Speaker and the General Assembly fell on deaf ears. Both the House and Senate used 33 separate motions on July 17th to override many of the line-item vetoes made by Blagojevich. Most of the override votes restored spending to a level within which agencies could at least operate. The final override action did not result in a balanced budget. It was still a **fake** budget.

Illinois was facing a perfect storm as the national recession deepened. Illinois was over $10 billion behind in scheduled payments and falling behind further by the day while facing additional reductions in revenue and higher unemployment as the nation plummeted into the worst economic downfall since the Great Depression.

On May 31st, 2008, the Speaker had also attempted to distance his party from the growing scandals related to Blagojevich by proposing and passing another series of additional ethic reforms that were aimed specifically at the kind of campaign contributions made by those receiving state awarded contracts. The $25K donation club was still a concern. On August 25th, the Governor vetoed the new ethic reforms legislation but the General Assembly overrode that veto in yet another special session on September 12th. Later, it was discovered that part of the reason for the veto by Blagojevich was that he and his minions were in the middle of shaking down individuals for campaign contributions and this particular legislation would have made the attempt to raise money impossible.

The rest of the summer and early fall was filled with fuel for the growing desire for the Illinois House to take immediate action to start an inquiry into the impeachment of Blagojevich. Many of the federal investigations and indictments were now coming to a head and by the day the public was becoming increasingly aware of the gross misconduct and potentially illegal actions of Blagojevich. Media across Illinois was now fully engaged. The Chicago Tribune ran article after article revealing the corrupt activities, as did the Springfield Journal. Still, crickets from Madigan.

On June 4th, 2008, Blagojevich insider and fundraiser Tony Rezko were convicted of money laundering and bribery by a federal grand jury. In October, Bill Cellini, another Blagojevich operative was indicted along with Rezko on charges of conspiring to shake down an investment firm for donations to the Blagojevich campaign fund. When I heard that news I recalled the proposals by Blagojevich during the spring to pass a pension bonding bill and a massive capital plan. Both of these would have required the type of bond sales and borrowing Cellini was allegedly involved in attempted shakedowns.

Even toward the end, with law enforcement actively watching every move, this type of illegal activity was taking place almost daily, spearheaded by Blagojevich. The public was also fed up by this time. A Chicago Tribune poll conducted in October of 2018 revealed that only 13% of Illinois trusted Blagojevich. The only thing surprising to me about that was how could 13% of the people in Illinois be so out of touch? I, along with many others by this time, publically, loudly and repeatedly renewed my desire to see the House begin impeachment proceedings. With only 13% of the population trusting the governor, I couldn't believe that this would be allowed to continue. This time, the mounting calls for the removal of Blagojevich were not rebuked as they were in July of 2006. Even fellow members of my GOP House Caucus, including Minority Leader Tom Cross, who had stood against the idea of impeachment in 2006, were now calling for the governor to face an investigation. Better late than never, I suppose. I often wonder just how much better off everyone would have been in the call for an investigation made in 2006 had been heeded. Earlier action might have saved Blagojevich from prison time.

The lack of action outraged many. I firmly believe the only reason that action was not taken sooner was that it was an election year. Even though the facts were in plain sight, the Speaker once again failed to begin proceedings to end the madness because of politics and protecting his power base. There was no way he was about to allow a public impeachment process to get near any of his party's candidates. It was just too messy to start an investigation before the fall election. With the amount of mud flying, dirt could get on anyone.

This was especially true for his prize candidate for President of the United States. After all, it was Madigan who had promoted and passed special legislation moving the Illinois Primary to February instead of March to help thrust Barack Obama into a better position in the Democrat Presidential Primaries. It was obvious, short of something dramatic, that Madigan was not going to act until the November 4th election was over. I am convinced that politics became more important than fulfilling his duties as Speaker. Illinois suffered greatly due to his neglect and lack of action to fulfill his Constitutional duty.

In the fall of 2008, Barack Obama was the Democratic nominee for President after defeating Hillary Clinton in the spring. Madigan must have determined there was no reason to have the House of Representatives in Illinois involved in the high profile activity of investigating a Democrat governor from Obama's home state.

The national recession was worsening, property prices in the U.S. continued to plummet and gas was now at an average of $3.39 per gallon.

Bank of America took over Countrywide Financial in an attempt to prop up the mortgages of millions of U.S. citizens and Citigroup, the nation's largest bank was about to report a $9.8 billion loss for the fourth quarter of 2008. General Motors reported a record loss of $38.7 billion for the previous year. The U.S. Congress was forced to pass a $150 billion stimulus package initially in the spring of 2008 and later another $700 billion in the *Emergency Economic Stabilization Act of 2008*, and the FED dropped the prime rate to 2.25%.

The Democrats were riding high on the epic failure of the U.S. economy and far be it for the Speaker of the Illinois House, the home State of Obama, to initiate any impeachment proceedings against the governor of his party; especially one that might be tied to Obama. He had been an Illinois Senate Member who had carried Blagojevich's health care expansion proposals and had even endorsed Blagojevich for re-election. Who knew what else could be linked between Blagojevich and Obama.

It was only after Illinois Senator Barack Obama defeated GOP Senator John Mc Cain on November 4th, 2008 by a popular vote of 53-47%, and Electoral College vote of 365-173 to be elected the 44th President of the United States would any action to remove Blagojevich be considered. And that is how it happened.

Finally, weeks after the Presidential Election, Rod Blagojevich was arrested by federal authorities at his Chicago home in that early morning raid on December 9th, 2008. Only then did Speaker Madigan called a special session of the House to take action. It took the arrest of the governor before Madigan finally fulfilled his duty as Speaker to allow other Members of the House to fulfill their Constitutional duty. Keep in mind, the bar set by the Illinois Constitution to investigate malfeasance does not require a crime to be committed or an arrest to be made. The standard is simply referred to as *cause.* There is absolutely no doubt that the same *cause* existed far before December 9th, 2008. However, a set of handcuffs on the wrists of the Governor is what it took for the Speaker to act.

The special session to determine whether the House would take action was scheduled for December 15th, 2008. Rod Blagojevich had turned 52 on December 10th, just a day after he was arrested. Now, less than a week after that arrest, the Illinois House was to meet to discuss whether action should be initiated to determine his removal from office.

In sharp contrast, Democrats in Washington D.C. started talking about the impeachment of Donald Trump even before he was sworn in as President. It took years for the Illinois House Democrats to begin impeachment proceedings against a governor who was involved in corrupt activities for a long time. Much of the evidence presented to the Investigative Committee and Illinois Senate used to impeach and remove Blagojevich from office dated back many years and had been widely reported for at least two years. The standard for impeachment in the United States Constitution involves high crimes and misdemeanors. The standard to begin an impeachment inquiry in the Illinois Constitution is simply, *"cause".* When folks try to compare the Trump impeachment to the Blagojevich impeachment, I have to laugh.

Being summoned into a special session just a couple of weeks before Christmas would normally be upsetting. It was especially busy at Hutsonville Schools as final exams approached and there were numerous Christmas programs, gatherings and events on the schedule.

I was not upset though, not in the least. Finally, almost two and a half years after Mike Bost and I had first mentioned the possibility of an impeachment inquiry, the idea was on everyone's lips. I was excited about the possibility of justice for the people of Illinois. The very thought of a public investigation of the activities surrounding Blagojevich seemed like an early Christmas present to the people of Illinois.

The year 2008 would be remembered for many things. It was the year that the FDA approved the marketing of food from cloned animals, the U.S. government auctioned off radio spectrum licenses to grow the wireless broadband industry (Verizon purchased much of the available spectrum), and Apple introduced the Air-Book. Fidel Castro stepped down in 2008 after 50 years of rule in Cuba, and the TV and motion picture industry endured a 3 month strike eliminating most popular TV shows.

Amid all of those events, I will always remember 2008 because of how it ended. Rod Blagojevich was going to finally be investigated and held to account for almost six years of heading one of the most corrupt administrations in history.

Chapter Fourteen
High Stakes Indeed

When the morning of December 15th arrived, it was like early Christmas to me. Not even a week after Governor Rod Blagojevich had been arrested at his home on federal racketeering charges, the Illinois House was being called into a Special Session.

The December 2008 winter in central Illinois was colder than normal by a few degrees and snowfall was about 2" above normal for December. As a few flurries filled the air that morning during my trip to Springfield, I was not at all affected by the cold temperatures.

I was thrilled that the oath of office I had taken was finally going to be fulfilled and allow me to be part of the removal of an ultra-corrupt governor. At this point I had no idea of the level to which my involvement would rise.

The session was scheduled to begin at 3:00 PM. On that same day, House Resolution (HR) 1650 had been introduced by Speaker Madigan and GOP Leader Tom Cross was listed as the first Chief Co-sponsor.

As per routine, the House Republican Caucus met before the start of session. We were provided with an informational packet regarding the process of impeachment. That is all I can or should say about the caucus meeting. The rule is, "What is said in caucus stays in caucus." It reminds me of an Executive Session of a school board where the discussion is supposed to remain private. Unfortunately, there were too many times that rule was broken in the GOP caucus. I even recall times when caucus discussion points were posted in the popular statewide political blog CapitolFax before the caucus had ended.

As someone who followed the request of caucus confidence, I will not reveal any of the details of the discussion. I will say that there was not an air of joy; this was a sad day for Illinois.

It was the first time in Illinois history that a governor faced impeachment. We knew everything we did would become a precedent for any future action of this kind. The entire nation would be watching and our work might direct impeachment inquiries across the nation in the future.

A little after 3:00 PM, on December 15th, 2008 the special session was called to order and HR1650 was read into the record and voted on. By a vote of 113-0, the Illinois House created a *Special Investigative Committee* for the purpose of, "(I) investigating allegations of misfeasance, malfeasance, nonfeasance, and other misconduct of Governor Rod R. Blagojevich and (II) making a recommendation as to whether cause exists for impeachment;" HR1650 further defined the structure of the Special Investigative Committee on Impeachment **(SICIM)** to consist of 21 legislative members, with 12 members of the House of Representatives appointed by the Speaker of the House of Representatives and 9 members appointed by the Minority Leader of the House of Representatives. HR1650 also allowed the Speaker to name a chairperson and the Minority Leader to designate a minority spokesperson.

The Committee was empowered to establish and adopt rules to ensure due process and fundamental fairness to the governor. In addition, the Committee was provided the power to administer oaths and compel witnesses to testify. Subpoena powers were provided to the Committee in case testimony, and documents or other evidence was necessary to fulfill duties. Punishment, although not defined specifically, was mentioned in the Resolution for anyone not cooperating with a subpoena. Finally, HR1650 called for the Committee to present the House a full report **before the expiration of the 95th General Assembly**. Completing the work prior to the end of the 95th General Assembly would mean that the Committee would be facing a difficult deadline.

The 95th General Assembly was to expire in mid-January. Remember, in addition to the recent Presidential Election, 2008 was an election year for Illinois House and some Senate Members. Members of the 96th General Assembly were going to be inaugurated soon.

I had been reelected on November 4th to my fourth term receiving 41,070 votes as an unopposed candidate. Any action regarding impeachment was to take place before the 96th General Assembly being sworn in based on the deadline in HR1650.

There was a great deal of speculation regarding who would serve on the Special Investigative Committee. The Speaker chose Representative Barbara Flynn Currie as the Chair and Minority Leader Cross selected Representative Jim Durkin to be Minority Spokesperson. Oher

Democrats chosen to serve on SICIM were Eddie Acevedo, Monique Davis, Mary Flowers, Jack Franks, John Fritchey, Julie Hamos, Gary Hannig, Constance (Connie) Howard, Lou Lang, Frank Mautino, and Art Turner. Barbara Flynn Currie was a terrific choice as the Chairperson. She was experienced, well respected and fearless. I found her to be one of the most intelligent members of the House. I also expected that she would keep the proceedings moving along and without theatrics.

The Democrats also had a couple of very capable legal minds on the committee in Julie Hamos and Lou Lang. Lang, along with a couple of other committee members, Franks and Fritchey, had been vocal critics of Blagojevich for some time. None of them had gone so far as to call for impeachment, until recently when everyone discussed it, but they had publically criticized the governor on multiple occasions. The Speaker ran a pretty tight ship and until he was quite ready to start the impeachment, his members were not mumbling much about the possibility. Hannig and Mautino were downstate Representatives and balanced out the mostly Chicago-centric members Turner, Flowers, Davis, Howard and Acevedo.

House Minority Leader Tom Cross selected eight GOP Members to join Minority Spokesperson Jim Durkin: Suzanne (Suzzi) Bassi, Patricia (Patti) Bellock, Bill Black, Mike Bost, Chapin Rose, Jim Sacia, Jil Tracy and **Roger Eddy.** I was a bit surprised that Leader Cross had selected me. We did not always see eye to eye on issues and I had been strongly rebuked by him back in July of 2006 when Mike Bost and I first brought up the possibility of impeachment. But, both Bost and I were selected to be on SICIM.

(These lanyards were provided to members of the Special Investigative Committee- I was number 16. Photo by Roger Eddy)

Other GOP members consisted of experienced law enforcement people. Jim Sacia was a retired FBI agent, Chapin Rose was a bright young prosecutor from the Champaign-Urbana area, and although a relative newcomer to the House, Jil Tracy was also a very well respected attorney. Bellock and Bassi were suburban Reps and Bill Black was the well-known House Republican floor leader. If you recall, it had been Black's job back in July of 2006 to quickly stand and speak against any thought of impeachment at that time. Jim Durkin was a highly respected legal mind and just the right person to lead our GOP team. When Cross retired from the General Assembly, Durkin followed him as House Minority Leader, a post he retains to this day in 2020.

We had a great team assembled and I was thrilled to be part of it. To a former History and Government teacher, the reality of being part of the first impeachment of an Illinois Governor in the history of the state was exhilarating. To this day, being appointed to this select committee remains one of the highlights of my time as a State Representative.

The decision to run, way back in 2001, followed by a difficult primary election, negative attacks by my first general election opponent Jim Lane and all of the long days, performing both jobs as superintendent and State Rep and after nearly eight years of service, I now had a seat at this table and it was high stakes.

The first SICIM meeting was scheduled for December 17th, two days after the creation of the committee by HR1650. Before the initial meeting took place, on the morning of December 15th, David Ellis, Chief Legal Counsel to the Speaker, sent a letter to Sheldon Sorosky via FAX. It was intended to be a heads up. Sorosky was believed to be the retained legal counsel of the governor. The letter informed him that the House was considering the formation of a Special Investigative Committee and that this committee was likely to be formed and begin meeting soon. He informed the attorney for Blagojevich that the Governor could be present at these hearings and have legal counsel present. The letter ended by stating that if the House took action and created the committee, he would be informed.

On that same day, after the passage of HR1650, Chairperson Currie sent a letter via FAX to Governor Blagojevich himself, informing him that HR1650 had passed. She attached a copy of HR1650 to the correspondence. Blagojevich was informed that the committee would meet on December 16th at 10:00 AM to adopt rules of procedure.

On behalf of the Governor, Sheldon Sorosky responded. He claimed that the notice given was too short for the governor to appear before the committee and that the Governor's rights of due process were being violated. Sorosky pointed to a press release from the Speaker's office in which the Speaker stated that the governor's due process rights would not be sacrificed for expediency. He called those comments of the Speaker, "Empty promises", and said the committee should not meet until reasonable notice was provided to the Governor. Sorosky also asked for copies of any rules adopted by the committee.

Another initial early reply to Ellis contained an interesting thought. One of Blagojevich's attorneys was Ed (Eddy) Genson. Genson was a well-known defense lawyer who was famous for some of the individuals he represented. He once defended R. Kelly and Conrad Black as well as members of organized crime. He was famous for once stating, "I have no aversion to organized crime." Genson was considered by many to be a brilliant defense attorney. He recently passed away in April of 2020 at age 78 after a battle with cancer. Blagojevich was now counting on him to defend the Governor in the impeachment investigation. Genson would eventually grow tired of Blagojevich and quit as his attorney. Asked to discuss why he quit, Genson said politely. "I don't require my clients to do everything I ask, but they do have to at least listen."

Genson informed Ellis that the Attorney General Act charged the Attorney General (AG) with the responsibility of representing the Governor under *15ILcs 205/4*. He then claimed AG Lisa Madigan was conflicted because she had recently filed an action in the Illinois Supreme Court to have Blagojevich removed from office due to disability. It was not mentioned by Genson but everyone also knew that Lisa Madigan is the daughter of Speaker Madigan. The word conflicted was an interesting choice of words. Genson called for the committee to first decide if the AG should recuse herself as a potential counsel to the Governor before taking any substantive action. His letter also insinuated that the alternate defense, other than the AG, be provided to the Governor, **and be paid for at taxpayer's expense.**

On December 17th, in a letter to David Ellis, Chief Counsel to the Speaker, Attorney General Lisa Madigan's office responded to Genson's contention that the AG was conflicted and that other counsel should be made available to the Governor. The letter from the AG's Office was not signed by Lisa Madigan; rather it was signed by her Chief of Staff, Ann Spillane. In that letter, Spillane responded to the letter from Genson. Remember that letter from Genson not only requested the AG recuse herself due to the "conflict" but also that the State of Illinois pay for alternate attorneys to represent the Governor both in response to federal criminal charges, the Illinois Supreme Court petition by Madigan to have him removed for disability and the impeachment proceedings. In other words, according to Genson, the taxpayers should pay entirely for the defense of Blagojevich for any proceedings brought against him.

Spillane, on behalf of AG Madigan, responded by first stating that Section 4 of the Attorney General Act, *15 ILCS 5/4 (2006)*, does not apply to the House impeachment investigation. She quoted Section 4 as to the duty of the Attorney General is to "defend all actions and proceedings against any State officer, in his official capacity, in any of the

174

courts of this State or the United States." She informed Genson that SICIM was neither a court, court proceeding nor a suit or any other type proceeding against the governor in his *official capacity*. Spillane went on to state that any assertion that the AG has a disqualifying conflict of interest in the Supreme Court motion to remove the Governor was, "Meritless." Genson's final request, that the state was somehow responsible to pay for defending the Governor against federal criminal charges, was not even addressed and simply dismissed out of hand.

As a member of the committee, I was receiving all of this correspondence. It was interesting that Lisa Madigan was attempting to have the Governor removed from office based on disability. The disability was cited as pending legal actions against the governor. The claim was that these pending legal actions made it impossible for the Governor to perform the functions of his job. Was this yet another attempt by the Democrats to avoid impeachment of the Governor of their own party by having another branch of government remove him? Some people wondered if this might be an effort to avoid a lot of embarrassment for many people, including the Democratic Party.

The committee convened for organizational purposes for the first time on December 16th, 2008. Possibly due to the request by Sorosky and the governor's legal team, there was no action taken regarding the adoption of committee rules that day. It was also possible that since the request by Lisa Madigan to simply remove Blagojevich from office due to disability was being heard on December 17th by the Illinois Supreme Court, the entire process could be considered moot if he was quickly removed from office by the Court.

The Democrats insisted that the impeachment proceedings would continue either way. We will never know for sure though, as AG Madigan's request was rejected by the Supreme Court on December 17th. They were not about to get involved in the fulfillment of the legislative branch of their Constitutional duties under the separation of powers. Now, impeachment was the only avenue left to remove the governor.

The committee adopted rules to govern itself on December 17th. Those rules included a 24-hour notice requirement for any committee hearing and permitted the governor's legal counsel to be present and ask questions of any witnesses. Most of the rules were an effort to provide due process to the Governor and be as transparent as possible with proceedings. Also, the Governor's request to have seven days to gather witnesses and present testimony in his defense was honored. Rule #16 disallowed any committee member to communicate with Blagojevich.

The committee was also made aware of how it needed to be cognizant of the on-going federal criminal investigation of the governor. Committee members unanimously agreed that no witnesses would be called or any lines of inquiry would take place which would interfere with the federal investigation of Blagojevich.

However, there was disagreement by GOP Committee Members to several Rules that were designed to allow for majority party control of the entire process. Much like the rules that governed the House of Representatives, the presiding officer, in this case, Barbara Flynn Currie, was *almost* all-powerful. Nothing could happen without the approval of either Currie or the Speaker's Counsel. The Rules to govern SICIM further stated that, "The authority given to the Chairperson was subject to the approval of the Speaker..." It was made clear Speaker Madigan was in charge even if he was not present or a member of the committee.

While the specific rules governing the functioning of the committee were otherwise well written and fair, the fact that the minority party was not allowed to do anything without the approval of the majority, and the ultimate consent of the Speaker, was unacceptable. It was classic Mike Madigan; he was going to control the proceedings with complete power over Deputy Leader Currie. This was no different than the rules governing the day to day activities of the Illinois House of Representatives. Whether Madigan was physically present or not, he insisted on complete control of all proceedings. Any subpoena request made by the Committee was issued by the Speaker. A simple vote of the majority of the Committee, although still likely to yield the same result since the Democrats had a 12-9 advantage, was not enough to issue a subpoena. Madigan reserved that power for himself.

House GOP Members voted against the Rules governing the House containing this type of dictatorial control when the Rules were presented for a vote at the start of every General Assembly convening and this was no different. The final vote to adopt the Committee Rules was 12-9 along party lines. The result was, after December 17th, whether we liked them or not, we had the same type of dictatorial rules to follow in the committee.

There were a couple of other important aspects to the Rules that bear mentioning. If an individual refused to appear before the Committee after a subpoena had been issued or refused to answer questions, the person was subject to a contempt citation if 11 Committee Members voted to issue a citation. Again, Republicans with only 9 members could not do this alone while the Democrats could. This was another clear example that the Rules favored the majority party in every way.

Importantly, the Committee Rules did contain language that allowed Blagojevich or his legal counsel to call and question witnesses *after* any questions asked by committee members.

Further, the questions by Blagojevich or his legal counsel were limited to, "Clarification of witness testimony."

After the first three meetings of the committee (December 17, 18 and 19), Blagojevich Attorney Ed Genson attempted to use one of the rules in a letter sent to Chairperson Currie. The letter, now identified as Exhibit 20, asked that subpoenas be issued by the committee for certain witnesses to appear on December 29th, 2008. Genson wanted Valarie Jarrett, Congressman Jesse Jackson Jr., Rahm Emanuel, and Nils Larsen to appear before the committee in person. Jarrett and Jackson had been rumored to have been involved in an attempt by Blagojevich to leverage the replacement of now President-elect Obama's vacant U.S. Senate seat for personal gain or campaign cash. Genson claimed Jarrett and Jackson would refute those claims in testimony to the committee. The Governor's lawyer wanted Rahm Emanuel, who had recently been named as Chief of Staff (COS) for President-elect Obama, to appear before the committee to testify that as Chief of Staff, Emanuel was never approached by either Blagojevich or any of Blagojevich's agents in his capacity as COS and was not promised anything in return for an appointment to the Senate seat vacated by President-Elect Obama. Finally, he requested Nils Larsen testify that he was not approached by the Governor, or any of his agents, asking Larsen to fire anyone at the Chicago Tribune in exchange for any benefit for Blagojevich. Larsen worked at the Chicago Tribune as Executive Vice-President.

Another widespread known accusation against Blagojevich was that he was angry with certain reporters at the Chicago Tribune about the investigative articles and accusations being written and wanted certain people at the Chicago Tribune fired. There would be much more information forthcoming to the committee about this accusation later. On December 29th, Ed Genson was attempting to show the Committee Members that these folks were willing to testify against these accusations.

The letter sent to Currie by Genson on December 23rd also asked that the committee to, "Subpoena approximately 14 individuals who benefitted from Governor Blagojevich's programs and policies." He promised names of those, "Approximate 14 individuals," later in the day.

Chairperson Currie immediately returned a FAX to Genson in reply stating that while the committee was certainly open to receiving the list of potential witnesses, it was important to remember that the witnesses were to testify to work being investigated by the committee related to "Misfeasance, malfeasance, nonfeasance, or other misconduct of Governor Blagojevich." She warned him that any testimony by the witnesses would be limited to the scope of the committee's work or in response to evidence that the committee had received to date. She informed Genson that the witness list was originally expected by December 23rd, but she would accept a list, along with a summary of their proposed testimony until 10:00 AM, December 26th. After that, the testimony would not be permitted. She finished by informing Genson that there're would be no subpoenas issued to compel the testimony of the 14 but the committee would be happy to hear *relevant* testimony from individuals mentioned.

In other words, no subpoenas, only testimony she deemed relevant and no testimony intended to show support for the Governor's programs and policies. His policies were not on trial and the hearing was not going to turn into a political show of support for the Governor.

As to the request to hear from Jarrett, Jackson, Emanuel and Larsen, Currie simply stated that she would get back to him later. Both Currie and Minority Spokesperson Jim Durkin signed the reply to Genson. This was a very high profile request and the Committee had already made known by unanimous vote it was not interested in any activity that could potentially interfere with the ongoing criminal investigation of the Governor.

On December 18th, Chairperson Currie, on behalf of the entire committee and signed by all SICIM members, sent a letter to federal lead prosecutor Patrick Fitzgerald. Fitzgerald was the lead prosecutor in the federal criminal case against Blagojevich. The letter sent to Fitzgerald requested various detailed information. She made it clear that the inquiry of SICIM would not interfere with the federal investigation while allowing committee members access to certain evidence and witnesses. Among the information requested was:

Copies of all electronic surveillance and supporting affidavits supporting the federal criminal complaint against Blagojevich, the identities of all individuals in the affidavit who are identified by title and only a descriptive letter such as, "Lobbyist 1", or "Public Official A." The letter went on to request oral interceptions (wire-taps) from the campaign office of the governor and documents like the targeted fundraising list of friends of Blagojevich. Several current and former members of the Governor's staff were also the topics of the letter from Currie and committee members. Committee members wanted any information relevant to the role of John Harris (former Chief of Staff), John Wyman (former Congressional Chief of Staff and current lobbyist), Lon Monk (former Chief of staff and lobbyist), Chris Kelly (special advisor), Bradley Tusk (former Deputy Governor) as well as a host of others. Specifically, the letter requested that individuals who pled guilty regarding detailed allegations against them or who have been convicted of allegations related to the inquiry be allowed to testify. Individuals previously convicted that the committee wanted to hear from included Ali Ata, Stuart Levine, Joseph Cari, Tony Rezko and Steven Loren.

The letter SICIM sent also contained a long list of other names that the committee wanted to talk to regarding other issues like the Governor's expansion of *FamilyCare* and his refusal to recognize the authority of the House Joint Committee on Rules (J-CAR). Other topics of interest to SICIM were audits conducted by the Illinois Auditor General, fraud in the Governor's firing and hiring of state workers and his refusal to comply with the Freedom of Information Act. The complete letter containing all information requested to be released or allowed to be part of the proceedings is listed as Exhibit #10 in the official records and final report of the committee.

The breadth of the request and the number of issues that were of concern were breathtaking. The sheer number of allegations for which we were requesting information released was stunning. **Many of the inquiries related to incidents and requested information that began shortly after or even before Blagojevich started his first term in office.** It was further evidence to me and reminded me we had waited far too long to start these proceedings. As I read the letter before signing it, I remember uttering, "How in the world did he get away with this so long?" The truth is that he did not do this alone. I blame many others for turning a blind eye and not beginning an inquiry sooner. The requests made of Fitzgerald in Exhibit #10 is clear proof that the evidence necessary to satisfy an impeachment inquiry under the Illinois Constitution had been met much earlier in the administration of Rod Blagojevich than the Speaker was willing to act.

In response to the inquiry made by Currie and the committee, the United States Department of Justice, in a letter signed by Patrick Fitzgerald, responded on December 22nd. The response came a day before Genson made his request to have Jarrett, Jackson Jr., Emanuel and Larsen testify and was unknown to Genson at that time. The response from U.S. Attorney Patrick Fitzgerald was very instructive to the committee. He started by thanking the Committee for the consideration and then went on to be very specific regarding potential evidence and testimony. Remember, in the original request by the committee, there was an enumerated list of items or documents requested:

(1) Copies of all electronic surveillance applications and supporting affidavits referenced in paragraph 14 of the affidavit of Special Agent Cain in support of the criminal complaint in *United States v. Blagojevich.*
**It is important to note here that the affidavit referred to in this request was already available to the committee and contained in Exhibit 3 as evidence for SICIM. Exhibit 3 was a copy of the two-count Federal Indictment returned against Blagojevich by the Northern U.S. District Court Illinois, Eastern Division. These Indictments were the basis of the Federal Arrest warrant and the court proceeding and contained the testimony of Agent Joseph Cain referenced above in the Currie request. The specifics of this testimony by Cain were critically important to SICIM and will be discussed later in more detail.
(2) The identities of all individuals referenced in the Affidavit who are only identified by a descriptive title and a letter and/or number (e.g., "Lobbyist 1," "Advisor A," etc.).

(3) The identities of all witnesses who have information about the alleged criminal activity of Governor Blagojevich who have been granted immunity or have a cooperation agreement with the federal government that would allow them to testify before the committee.

(4) Documents described in the Cain Affidavit (e.g. the "Targeted fundraising list", on page 32 of the Affidavit).

In his reply to the request made by Currie regarding these first four items, Fitzgerald, "After careful consideration", concluded that "Producing these items at this time could significantly compromise the ongoing criminal investigation." So, all four of these requests were denied.

As far as the Committee's request to get the transcripts or recordings of the wiretaps on Blagojevich's personal and campaign phone and any other intercepts, Fitzgerald informed Currie that, "The request for wiretaps was still under consideration." The committee would have to wait a long time for any final decision regarding the wiretaps. Eventually, but not until December 29th, Fitzgerald and the federal government did file a motion to disclose redacted versions of portions of four wiretap recordings. The oral and wire communications were obtained after the feds originally requested authority for a 30 day period which started October 29th, 2008. An additional 30-day extension was made to the original request on November 26th, 2008. The intercept of a lobbyist cellphone was also approved in November of 2008. This particular period, covering about two months, proved to be critical in both the consideration of impeachment and the eventual criminal trial against Blagojevich.

The timing of the request made to release these intercepts for committee consideration came too late. It took several hearings in court for the decision to be made to release some redacted portions of the wiretaps and SICIM was moving too fast to wait for the transcripts. The wiretaps were later introduced as evidence in the Senate trial after portions of the redacted wiretaps were released by court order.

Fitzgerald went on to respond to Currie's request for guidance regarding hearing testimony from any potential witnesses. Any testimony from witnesses potentially involved with the alleged criminal proceedings against Governor Blagojevich or his staff should be off-limits because that could harm the federal criminal case. This included testimony from present or former members of the Governor's staff. A specific list of names of former staff members was thus eliminated as witness possibilities. These included, but were not limited to Lon Monk, Bradley Tusk, Joh Harris and Chris Kelly. The complete list of names is contained in Exhibit 10 (the Currie request letter) and are identified under the heading lettered "A".

As far as other potential allowable witnesses, Fitzgerald identified names of certain people to be avoided as listed in items B through E of the original request for possible testimony before the Committee. Items B through E included the names of Ali Ata, Joseph Cari, Stuart Levine, Tony Rezko and Steve Loren. Those individuals had already pled guilty in exchange to cooperate with the Federal Government. Any individuals referenced in the Affidavit by descriptive title should also not appear to the investigative committee.

Currie request even listed several names of people that by title or description could be identified as Patrick Magoon of Children's Memorial Hospital, Nils Larsen from the aforementioned Chicago Tribune, as well as a list of registered lobbyists from the horse racing industry. The federal prosecutor also did not want testimony provided in front of the Committee by certain State Board or Commission members that could be identified by descriptions in the Affidavit. The names specifically requested were known to be members of the Health Facilities Planning Board.

It was clear that Fitzgerald was not interested in seeing any witness appear that might harm his case. Denying access to all of these witnesses was both puzzling and very troubling. It was also clear that the requests by Ed Genson to have Jarrett, Jackson Jr., Emanuel or Nelsen testify would not be allowed by the Democrats. Nils Larsen was the only person specifically mentioned by name in the request letter by Currie to Fitzgerald.

I was among those who felt that Emanuel, Jackson Jr., and Jarett should be subject to subpoena. In fact, in an article written on December 27th during a phone interview with Bloomberg News, I joined many others by publically calling for the subpoenas. I felt that if Fitzgerald did not want these high profile individuals to testify that he would have requested by name that they not be called. Plus, the accusation or assumption was that Blagojevich had made direct quid pro quo offers to appoint these individuals to the vacated Illinois Senate seat. Why not just subpoena them, swear them in, and ask them? Well, because there was no way the Democrats were going to allow the subpoena of so many from their party, especially those with connections to President-elect Obama. I knew that. The sole power to subpoena was the Chairpersons', **with the consent of the Speaker,** of course.

There little good news in the Fitzgerald response. Fitzgerald indicated that he specifically did not have a problem with some of the requests for guidance made by Currie on behalf of the Committee. In response, Fitzgerald indicated that he had no issue with Currie's list of items labeled as, "I (F) or II (A) through (D)." The item I (F) was a request to hear from individuals identified in a Chicago Tribune article from April 27, 2008 Entitled, "The Governor's $25,000 Club."

Also, any items related to the Governor's expansion of the *FamilyCare* program and refusal to recognize the Joint Committee on Rules (J-CAR) was fair game. Any audits conducted by the Illinois Auditor General would be allowable, investigation of state hiring practices at the IDES relating to hiring and firing of state workers, and the Governor's refusal to comply with the Freedom of Information Act could also be investigated.

The first few meetings of the Committee proved that the pace was going to be hectic.

Already, inside of just a few days, the Committee Rules had been adopted, and agreed to letter of inquiry had been sent to and then returned by the U.S. Attorney's Office and Ed Genson had made some headlines requesting that the AG recuse herself from a case before the Illinois Supreme Court.

It was disappointing that the requested wiretaps were not released in time for consideration. It was also disappointing that we would be so extremely limited in hearing from potential witnesses. But, much of the actual transcript of the conversations and incriminating statements were already in possession of SICIM in the form of the 78 page Cain Affidavit (Exhibit #3). This exhibit was entered into evidence early on in the committee hearings. The exhibit contained the Federal Indictments and a lengthy Affidavit which contained sworn testimony from key federal witnesses. This indictment against Blagojevich and John Harris, a high ranking administration official, came on December 7th and contained two counts:

"Count One

From on or about 2002 to present, in Cook County, in the Northern District of Illinois, defendants did, conspire with each other and with others to devise and participate in a scheme to defraud the State of Illinois and the people of the State of Illinois of the honest services of ROD R. BLAGOJEVICH and JOHN HARRIS, in furtherance of which the mails and interstate wire communications would be used, in violation of Title18, United States Code, Sections 1341,1343, and 1346; all in violation of Title 18 United States Code, Section 1349.

Count Two

Beginning no later than November 2008 to the present, in Cook County, in the Northern District of Illinois, defendants ROD R. BLAGOJEVICH and JOHN HARRIS, being agents of the State of Illinois, a State government which during one year, beginning January 1, 2008, and continuing to the present, received federal benefits in access of $10,000, corruptly solicited and demanded a thing of value, namely, the firing of certain Chicago Tribune editorial members responsible for widely-circulated editorials critical of ROD R. BLAGOJEVICH, intending to be influenced and rewarded in connection with business and transactions of the State of Illinois involving a thing of value of $5,000 or more, namely, the provision of millions of dollars in financial assistance by the State of Illinois, including through the Illinois Finance Authority, an agency of the State of Illinois, to the Tribune Company involving the Wrigley Field baseball stadium; in violation of Title 18, United States Code. Sections 666(a)(1)(B) and 2."

The Counts were legal language mostly, but the Affidavit that accompanied the Indictment as proof of wrongdoing was stunning. This document contained much of the evidence that was being used in the criminal proceeding and came directly from wiretaps. We were not allowed to hear the wiretaps, but the Affidavit was an adequate substitute for the actual wiretaps. It was the *sworn statement* of Daniel Cain, a Special Agent with the FBI who worked out of the Chicago, Illinois Field Division. His sworn testimony included a mountain of evidence against Blagojevich. A couple of examples of the testimony delivered by Cain in the Affidavit include:

"b. Defendants ROD BLAGOJEVICH and JOHN HARRIS, together, with others, offered to, and threatened to withhold from, the Tribune Company substantial state financial assistance in connection with Wrigley Field, which assistance ROD BLAGOJEVICH believed to be worth at least $100 million to the Tribune Company, for the private purpose of inducing the controlling shareholder of the Tribune Company to fire members of the editorial board of the Chicago Tribune, a newspaper owned by the Tribune Company, who were responsible for editorials critical of ROD BLAGOJEVICH;

c. Defendants ROD BLAGOJEVICH and JOHN HARRIS, together with others, attempted to use ROD BLAGOJEVICH's authority to appoint a

United States Senator to obtain personal benefits for ROD BLAGOJEVICH, including, among other things, appointment as Secretary of Health & Human Services in the President-elect's administration, and alternatively, a lucrative job which they schemed to induce a union to provide ROD BLAGOJEVICH in exchange for appointing as senator an individual whom ROD BLAGOJEVICH and JOHN HARRIS believed to be favored by union officials and their associates."

These facts, according to Cain, were the basis for the request for the wiretaps. Judge James F. Holderman agreed to the wiretapping of Blagojevich's phones beginning in October of 2008. However, even before the authorization to wiretap, Cain recounts that there was evidence that Blagojevich and his operatives solicited and obtained campaign contributions in exchange for official actions as Governor.

The first example of Blagojevich attempting to secure campaign contributions used in the Affidavit to support the indictment involved Ali Ata. Ata had earlier entered into a negotiated plea agreement to reduce his federal sentences related to lying to the FBI and tax fraud. Back in 2002, Ata admitted that after conversations with Blagojevich, he was hoping for a high-level appointment for himself in state government. In the direction of Tony Rezko, Ata provided a list of three state agencies to which he would be interested in being appointed. After Ata held a fundraising event held for Blagojevich in 2002 which eventually netted $25K in campaign contributions, he was approached by Rezko to provide additional monetary support for Blagojevich. After another $25K was raised, Blagojevich himself asked Rezko if he had talked to Ata about positions in state government. Then, in early 2003, once Blagojevich was in office as governor, Rezko informed Ata that he was going to be named the head of the State Capital Development Board. That position was later given to someone else and Rezko then discussed an opportunity with the Illinois Finance Authority (IFA) with Ata. In July of 2003, Rezko asked Ata to raise an additional $50K in contributions. Ata agreed to another $25K and that check was delivered around the end of July in 2003. Ata was soon thereafter named head of the IFA.

In addition to the Ata incident, Cain's Affidavit included detailed information regarding the sworn testimony of Joseph Cari, who was now a government informant, due to a written plea agreement reducing his sentence. In his testimony, Cari testified that he had conversations with

Rod Blagojevich in which Blagojevich informed Cari of ways he could use his power as governor to generate campaign contributions. Cari had similar conversations with Tony Rezko and Chris Kelly. Joseph Cari was a significant fundraiser for the national Democratic Party. In particular, Cari served as the national finance chair for Al Gore when Gore ran for President in 2000. Cari could be very valuable in efforts to raise campaign money for Blagojevich.

According to the sworn testimony by Cari, in October of 2003, he along with Blagojevich, Kelly, and Stuart Levine rode in an airplane provided by Levine to a fundraiser in New York. During that plane ride, Cari had a conversation with Blagojevich in which Cari described his background as a national fundraiser. Blagojevich then informed Cari that he was interested in running for President of the United States. During that same conversation, according to Cari, Blagojevich told Cari that it **was easier for governors to solicit campaign contributions because governors could award grants, give legal work, consulting work, and investment banking work to campaign contributors.** He then, once again according to Cari and included in the sworn Affidavit, told Cari that Rezko and Kelly were his point people in raising campaign contributions. **Cari testified that Blagojevich told him directly that the State of Illinois contracts and other State of Illinois work could be given to contributors who helped Blagojevich.** In separate conversations with Rezko, Cari was later informed that the Blagojevich administration would be financially helpful to Cari's business interests in exchange for raising assistance.

As early as March of 2004, the conversation was followed up on by Kelly in a meeting between Cari and Kelly. Eventually Cari becomes involved in what he admitted was the attempted extortion of JER, a real estate investment firm that was seeking an investment from TRS. On the inside was Stu Levine, who was assisting JER in obtaining investment business from TRS. Levine had previously been named to the TRS Board by Blagojevich. According to Cari, he was informed that to make the transaction work, JER would need to hire a consultant. However, the governor and his people would pick the consultant to be used in a particular deal. Cari informed JER that if the proper consultant was not hired, JER would not receive the investment money they were seeking from the State of Illinois. The affidavit goes on to report that JER actually threatened to expose the attempted extortion and then received the investment money. But, it was crystal clear that the Blagojevich fundraising team had attempted to shake down JER.

This was just one of the multiple examples cited in the Affidavit of influence peddling at the TRS Board involving Rezko, Kelly and the Governor. In another instance, a proposal to consolidate TRS with two other pension boards was nixed after Bill Cellini and Levine approached Kelly and informed them they were opposed to this consolidation. Since Blagojevich was promoting the elimination and consolidation of state boards to save taxpayers money, he had to be convinced that the pension boards should not be consolidated. The governor asked why he should listen to Kelly rather than a senior state official who had made the consolidation recommendation. Ultimately, for whatever reason, Blagojevich became convinced that the consolidation of these particular state pension boards was a bad idea. The Affidavit further reveals there would need to be payback to political contributors by helping those contributors get investments from TRS. There were times when, according to Levine, Rezko or Kelly would provide names of funds or individuals to help those funds or individuals receive the TRS business.

Now it became even clearer why any type of new pension bond plan was not under consideration as part of the FY08 Blagojevich Budget proposal. One of the more infamous attempts by Levine, Cellini, Kelly, and Rezko involved an attempt to extort campaign money from a company named Capri Capital. As described in the sworn Affidavit, this case involved an individual named Thomas Rosenberg who was representing Capri Capital. Rosenberg was informed by Bill Cellini that to receive $220 million of TRS money for Capri Capital to take under management, Rosenberg was going to have to make a $1.5 million campaign donation to Friends of Blagojevich or pay Levine and Rezko a 1% fee. Rosenberg threatened to expose the extortion to law enforcement and Cellini backed off on the threats after Rezko instructed Cellini to go ahead with the $220 million this one time, but no further business was to be given to Capri Capital. It was also revealed in the affidavit that allegedly Blagojevich himself was aware of the attempted extortion. In sworn testimony, it was stated that Rosenberg meant nothing to, "The big guy." It was after that when Blagojevich agreed that no further business should be conducted with Rosenberg. If you don't pay, you don't play!

In yet another example cited in the affidavit, **back in 2003**, the FBI began an investigation involving Stuart Levine, related to the Illinois

Health Facilities Planning Board. Levine served on two state boards after appointments made by Blagojevich. In addition to the TRS Board, Levine served on the Health Facilities Planning Board. This Board, among other things, is responsible for approving applications for health care facility expansion. The allegation was that Levine was soliciting bribes in exchange for state contracts or appointments. Information, obtained after receiving court authorization to record multiple phone lines used by Levine, revealed that he was part of a scheme to shake down medical facilities that might be looking to expand service facilities, in exchange for campaign contributions.

Levine was indicted in May of 2005 on 28 counts of mail and wire fraud, extortion, bribery and money laundering. Faced with overwhelming evidence against him, Levine entered a plea agreement with the federal government and some charges were dropped and he received a reduced sentence and then later testified against Blagojevich's top dealmaker, Tony Rezko. The escapades of the Health Facilities Planning Board were revealed as part of the deal with Levine.

Just one example of the scheme at the planning board involved a particular hospital expansion. As a member of the Planning Board, Levine was involved with a proposal for expansion made by Mercy Hospital to build an additional hospital in Illinois. After Rezko was supposedly promised that Mercy Hospital would arrange for a substantial campaign contribution to Blagojevich, plans were made to influence the Planning Board, through Levine, to issue a permit, known as a Certificate of Need (CON). That certificate would allow for the expansion to begin and was required for the project to move forward.

The Affidavit revealed that Levine, along with planning board members Thomas Beck and Imad Almanaseer, received instructions directly from Rezko as to which applications for permits should be approved. For whatever reason, the contribution that was to be arranged by Mercy Hospital was not made. In a back and forth, Levine was informed that since Mercy hospital was not making the requested contribution, they would not be receiving the CON permit. At that point, Levine, who had a relationship with the contractor that was intended to build the hospital, asked Rezko if the CON could be obtained *if the contractor* made the campaign contribution. According to testimony, Rezko indicated that such a contribution could change his mind about the requested CON. Ultimately the CON application by Mercy Hospital was resurrected for a vote during a highly controversial Planning Board meeting. At that meeting after having been talked to by Levine, and in what has been described as a highly controversial and irregular vote of the Planning Board, Imad Almanaseer and Beck voted in favor of the CON for Mercy Hospital, and by a 5-4 vote, the permit was approved.

Another very disturbing example of attempts to obtain campaign contributions, in exchange for official acts, involved a different medical facility. This example was also described in the Affidavit that the members of the Special Investigative Committee were provided. According to the evidence presented in the Affidavit, on October 8, 2008, just two months before the governor was arrested, a recorded discussion between Blagojevich and others in his administration related to Children's Memorial Hospital. In that discussion, Blagojevich was quoted as saying words to the effect of, "I'm going to do $8 million for them and I want to get [Hospital Executive 1] for 50." It was a direct attempt to get the CEO of Children's Memorial Hospital to donate $50K to the Blagojevich campaign in exchange for $8 million of state money which would come from pediatric care reimbursements. Later, recorded phone calls revealed that Blagojevich was considering rescinding the promise of state funds to Children's Memorial because the hospital executive had yet to contribute.

Several other recorded conversations directly quoted in the affidavit revealed multiple attempts by Rezko, Kelly and Blagojevich to obtain campaign funds in exchange for state funds. Besides medical facilities, state highway contractors, as well as the gaming industry were also a prime target for campaign cash requests quid pro quo.

Specifically, the horse racing industry was the focus of efforts to obtain money. Because there was a specific bill filed directing a percentage of casino revenue to go to the horse racing industry, they became a fundraising target. This was just another opportunity to make money for the Blagojevich team. As previously mentioned, in phone calls intercepted by the FBI, testimony in the Affidavit revealed Chief of Staff John Harris, along with others associated with Blagojevich, attempted to exert financial pressure on the owners of the Tribune to get some people fired who had written or allowed the publishing of negative stories about the Governor.

At the time, the Tribune Company also owned the Chicago Cubs and in the fall of 2008 was attempting to sell the team. As a part of the attempt to sell the Cubs, the Tribune Company had explored the possibility of obtaining financial assistance from the Illinois Finance

Authority (IFA). Rod Blagojevich directed John Harris to inform the Tribune owner and other top Tribune officials that financial assistance from IFA would not be forthcoming unless members of the Chicago Tribune Editorial Board were fired. The Editorial Board approved and published several editorials favoring the formation of a committee to investigate the possibility of the impeachment of Blagojevich.

It actually took a little over two years after impeachment was first mentioned in July of 2006 for the Chicago Tribune to get on board full throttle with the idea of impeachment. But, once they did get on board, the newspaper was relentless with editorials that were extremely damaging to Blagojevich. Multiple phone calls are recounted in the Affidavit making it crystal clear that the quid pro quo offer from Blagojevich through Harris to the Tribune was real.

Perhaps the allegation in the Affidavit that captured the attention of everyone in Illinois, was the most dramatic and captured the attention of the nation was the section which described activities concerning efforts by Blagojevich to obtain personal benefits in return for the appointment of a United States Senator.

When Barack Obama was elected President his senate seat was vacated. The duty of naming a replacement for Obama prompted Blagojevich to attempt to gain personal benefits in return for the appointment of certain individuals to the US Senate seat. This unreal allegation was captivating and made national headlines almost immediately.

The evidence contained in the Affidavit included testimony that "Intercepted phone calls demonstrated that **Rod Blagojevich and others have engaged and are engaged in efforts to obtain personal gain, including financial gain, for the benefit of Rod Blagojevich and his family through the corrupt use of Rod Blagojevich's authority as Governor of the State of Illinois to fill the vacant United States Senate seat previously held by the President-elect."** The Affidavit references the fact that by law the Illinois Governor has the legal authority to name a successor to the vacant seat. As of November 16, 2008, when Obama vacated the seat, Blagojevich indeed had that exclusive authority and sworn testimony was very clear that he attempted to use that authority illegally.

In some of the intercepted communications, it was also clear that an attempt was made to exchange the Senate appointment for Blagojevich to become the United States Secretary of Health and Human Services. In

190

addition, recorded evidence proved attempts were made to have the Governor's wife, Patti Blagojevich, placed on paid corporate boards or placed at a private foundation with a substantial salary. There were other intercepts in which Rod Blagojevich himself would potentially be employed by a multi-million dollar funded non-profit with a substantial salary.

On November 3rd, 2008 Blagojevich was recorded in a phone conversation with Deputy Governor A in which he informed Deputy Governor A that if Blagojevich was not going to get anything of value for the seat that he may as well take it. Later that same day, it became known that a high profile advisor to President-elect Obama was interested in the Senate appointment.

The Affidavit described that high-level advisor as, "Senate Candidate 1", later identified as Valarie Jarrett. During a call later in the day, once the information became known that the President-elect supported the appointment of Jarrett, Blagojevich made these statements: **"Unless I get something real good for [Senate Candidate 1], shit, I'll just send myself, you know what I'm saying?"** Later in the same conversation, **"I'm going to keep this Senate option for me a real possibility, you know, and therefore I can drive a hard bargain.**

And if I don't get what I want and I'm not satisfied with it, then I'll just take the Senate seat myself." Later, he made a statement that became perhaps the most well-known and the statement that defined the entire episode of attempting to auction off the Senate seat when he stated, **"It is a f****** valuable thing, you just don't give it away for nothing."**

On November 4th, Blagojevich was recorded in other calls with advisors, including John Harris discussing the importance of making a list of things that Blagojevich would accept in exchange for the seat. None of it was to be in writing and according to the transcript, in a phone conversation with John Harris, Blagojevich said the "Trick is how to conduct indirectly...a negotiation"... for the Senate seat. Blagojevich used the analogy of a sports agent shopping for free agents when he stated, "How much are you offering, [President-elect]?

What are you offering [Senate Candidate 2}...Can always go to [Senate Candidate 3]." His instruction was to end the negotiations with something like, "[President-elect], you want it? Fine. But, its' got to be good or I could always take [the Senate seat]."

Additional recorded conversations took place on November 5th, 6th and 7th ranging for trading the seat in exchange for a variety of personal benefits. In one of the conversations, Blagojevich states that he is, "Financially hurting." Harris said they were looking at options that would help the financial security of the Blagojevich family while keeping Blagojevich, "Politically viable." Blagojevich replied that he "Wanted to make money."

The conversation continued regarding the attempt to gain something in exchange for the Senate seat on November 8th and 10th. Those discussions included how Patti Blagojevich could also gain financially by being named to positions with a substantial salary. Blagojevich asked if the President-elect could help in the private sector to get these things done. In one of those calls, Blagojevich said he was struggling financially and, "Does not want to be Governor for the next two years." It was during this series of calls that some advisors told Blagojevich that he might have to just, "Suck it up for the next two years and do nothing and give the President-elect his senator." Blagojevich's response, according to the Affidavit was, "F*** him. For nothing? F*** him." Then stated that he would put [Senate Candidate 4] in the seat, "Before I just give f****** [Senate Candidate 1] a f****** Senate seat and I don't get anything." The Affidavit notes that Senate Candidate 4 was a Deputy Governor of the State of Illinois.

Another candidate, Senate Candidate 5, was also discussed that day in recorded calls and Blagojevich instructed that someone should leak a story to the Chicago Sun-Times that Blagojevich was considering Senate Candidate 5 to pressure the President-elect to come up with a deal if he wanted someone else. Current Illinois governor, JB Pritzker, was also recorded on these calls discussing the possibility of various appointments, including the Senate seat and the position of Illinois Attorney General. Pritzker is a billionaire who also made contributions to Blagojevich.

On November 11th, intercepted communications included the idea that perhaps someone like Warren Buffet and others could come up with $10, $12, or $15 million to start a *501(c)(4)* non-profit organization to employ Blagojevich and/or his wife in substantial positions with high salaries if the President-elect would encourage them. They later discussed Senate Candidate 6, another wealthy individual from Illinois and discussed whether that person might fund such a non-profit organization in exchange for the seat. There is widespread speculation as to who that wealthy individual was. It was all intended to be a clear message to Obama. If the President-elect wanted the person he supported to be the next U.S. Senator from Illinois, something had to be done which benefitted Blagojevich.

Then on November 12, 2008, CNN reported that Senate Candidate 1 was no longer interested in the open seat. While his advisors suggested that this was just a tactic being used by the President-elect, Blagojevich, by this time, was now focused on attempting to get wealthy individuals to fund a non-profit to employ him and perhaps his wife. He still felt the President-elect could help make that happen. Different strategies were discussed including going straight to Senate Candidate 1 and explaining that if there was interest in the seat they could help get the non-profit funded and simply go around the President-elect. In a conversation that same day, Blagojevich clearly states to John Harris, on a recorded line, that his decision about the vacant Senate seat would be made based on three criteria in the following order of importance: "Our legal situation, our personal situation, my political situation. This decision, like every other one, needs to be based upon that. Legal. Personal. Political." According to the sworn Affidavit these types of conversations continued throughout November.

The issue of the Senate seat was foremost in the Governor's mind throughout November and into early December. On December 4th additional recorded conversations reveal that Blagojevich was focused on how he could leverage Senate Candidate 5 in exchange for something of value. By this time, there were widely circulated stories in the media that Blagojevich was involved in scurrilous activities surrounding the naming of a Senate replacement. In one of the December 4th conversations that were recorded, just days before being arrested, Blagojevich said, **"You gotta be careful how you express that and assume everybody's listening, the whole world is listening. You hear me?"** That statement was indeed prophetic.

The most remarkable evidence came from a thorough reading of the Affidavit and left little doubt that Blagojevich was deeply involved in multiple schemes involving pay to play on a quid pro quo level on steroids. What else was on the wiretaps, would we have a chance to listen to the entirety of the recordings? Even without full access to the entire suite of recordings the evidence seemed overwhelming and damning. In most everyone's mind, the standard of *cause* necessary to move forward with a recommendation had been met.

How would the governor respond to all of the evidence and negative media coverage? Everyone soon found out. On December 19th Blagojevich, true to form, called a press conference *to proclaim his innocence.* According to him, he had done nothing wrong; the charges were being levied by the Speaker and the Republican members of the House for political reasons. He claimed that he had fought the entrenched powerbrokers in Illinois and was being impeached because he dared to fight for the people.

In response to this claim of complete innocence by Blagojevich, Currie and Durkin sent Blagojevich a letter, on behalf of the committee, re-invited Blagojevich to testify before SICIM. Referencing the December 19th Press Conference by Blagojevich, in what become Exhibit #15, co-signed by both Currie and Durkin, they encouraged Blagojevich to appear before the Committee. He was welcome to appear to prove he, "Had done nothing wrong", and that he was not going to be quit, "...because of false accusations." To nobody's surprise, he did not show up. Looking back, I can only think about how great it would have been for him to show up.

The Committee adjourned on December 22nd and was scheduled to resume on December 29th, 2008. I had some time to return home, prepare for and enjoy Christmas with my family and research the dozens of questions I had. I was interested in many things and as I drove home to Hutsonville December 23rd. My mind was swimming.

For one thing, I wanted more information about the history of impeachment, and anything else the Illinois Constitution had to say about the subject. What about other states? A million thoughts were on my mind on the two and a half-hour drive back to my home in Hutsonville. The Special Investigative Committee was not scheduled to meet again until December 29th.

What I wanted most of all was a few days with my family to enjoy Christmas.

Chapter Fifteen
Know When to Hold 'Em

The 2008 Christmas holiday season seemed shorter to me. I arrived in Hutsonville mid-afternoon on December 23rd after the first few meetings of the Special Investigation Committee were in the books. We had only met for a few days but the amount of information reminded me of the old saying about trying to drink water from a fire hose. I tried hard to put the events of the past week completely out of my mind for at least a few days upon returning home. It was, after all, Christmas.

With five children and our first grandchild coming to visit, it was time to set this aside and enjoy the holiday with those dearest to me. Bella, our first grandchild, was born just a few weeks earlier in mid-November. As with all firstborn grandchildren, she had a profound effect on the way I looked at life. The pure joy of having grandchildren is an emotion that cannot be adequately described. There are only a few times in life that the depth and intensity of emotion one feels is almost overwhelming. Joy and sadness are polar opposites in these experiences. I felt those types of intense emotions when my children were born, when my grandchildren were born and when my parents passed away.

I did my best to discard my thoughts about impeachment activities, but that was almost impossible. Even on Christmas Eve, I received phone calls from reporters and emails from people wondering about the proceedings. Many of the inquiries came from friends and supporters as they wanted to know everything. They had heard this or that and wondered what was true or false. What could I share? Some of the facts were so egregious surrounding the now known behavior of the Governor, folks could hardly believe what they were hearing.

I, along with other members of SICIM was warned that some of the information the committee had been provided was not to be shared. So, I really could not tell them *everything* I knew, but I tried to be as forthcoming as possible. I do vividly recall warning some of my Democrat friends who had claimed the entire episode was political that they might want to refrain from defending the Governor. In this case, I told them they just had to trust me.

I answered some of the calls and emails and was, at times, clearly distracted from my family. Despite all of the distractions, we had a great Christmas. I think it was finally the traditional Eddy Christmas Eve Celebration of the Birth of Jesus that cleared my head and re-focused my attention on my family. Each year, on Christmas Eve, we had a family dinner and Birthday Cake for Jesus. That tradition was still alive in 2008. Around that table, as we read the story of the birth of our Savior, I was reminded of the most important things.

The day after Christmas, I decided to take a deeper dive into the topic of Impeachment and what the Illinois Constitution had to say on the topic. The current Illinois Constitution was the result of a Constitutional Convention and ratification in 1970. Thanks to the internet, it was easy to find a lot of information about the Convention, including discussions and rationale of those delegates who helped construct the Constitution. I learned that, Michael Madigan, current House Speaker, was a delegate to that convention.

As I read Article IV, Section 14 of the Illinois Constitution over and over again, I was struck by the simplicity and flexibility of the passage. It reads as follows: **"The House of Representatives has the sole power to conduct legislative investigations to determine the existence of cause for impeachment and, by a majority of the members elected, to impeach Executive and Judicial officers. Impeachments shall be tried by the Senate."**

The United States Constitution, in Article I, Section 2 similarly provides that the House of Representatives "Shall have the sole power of impeachment." And in Article I, Section 3, in clauses 6 & 7 provides that, "The Senate shall have the sole Power to try all Impeachments."

The U.S. Constitution then goes on to provide details related to conducting the Senate trial which follows Impeachment by the House. We all watched this process unfold recently with the impeachment of President Donald Trump. The process was about all that was similar though.

Beyond having the sole power to Impeach, the United States Constitution, in Article Two, Section 4 contains more *specific language* as to the *causes* for which this exclusive power can be implemented: **"The President, Vice-President and all civil Officers of the United States, shall be removed from Office on Impeachment for,**

196

and <u>Conviction of, Treason, Bribery, or other high crimes and misdemeanors.</u>"

When contrasting the language of the Illinois Constitution with the United States Constitution regarding impeachment, the first thing that jumped out was the fact that the Illinois Constitution does not contain the same specific language related to causes. "Treason, Bribery, or other high crimes and misdemeanors," are specifically listed in the United States Constitution while the Illinois version simply states, "The existence of **cause** for impeachment." To understand the difference, it took a little more research.

As mentioned, the current Constitution for Illinois had been ratified in 1970. Previously, the Illinois Constitution, written in 1870, had different language regarding impeachment. In the 1870 version, in Article V, the language provided for Impeachment of an Executive or Judicial Officer for any, "Misdemeanor in office." So, even in the 1870 version, there was not only a noteworthy difference between the United States and Illinois version of the language, but there was also a difference between the 1870 and 1970 Illinois versions regarding the topic.

After some study, I determined that the reason for the elimination of the term misdemeanor likely had to do with the variance in the popular understanding of what the word meant in 1870 compared to 1970. In 1870, the term *misdemeanor* referred more generally to misconduct. By 1970, the term was commonly associated with a more petty offense. So, the Framers of the 1970 Illinois Constitution did not want to simply transfer the language using the term misdemeanor and create the assumption that impeachment should be for something minor or petty as the term was now popularly known. The new language allowed for the current determination of **cause** to reflect **current times**. It was intended to allow wide discretion to members of the House of Representatives who were selected to investigate whether **cause** existed. As I studied, the gravity of being selected to serve on that Investigative Committee became more solemn and somewhat surreal. We, the SICIM, collectively, were the sole determiners of **cause.** The committee would be establishing the first definition of what **cause** would mean.

The Illinois Constitution does offer some further guidance in Article V Section 10 under the heading, "Removals." The section is contained in the part of the Illinois Constitution enumerating the powers of the Governor. The text of Section 10 states, "The Governor may remove for incompetence, neglect of duty, or malfeasance in office any officer who may be appointed by the governor." Although this passage is contained in a portion of the Illinois Constitution dealing with executive branch powers, it is generally at least a bit more of an indication of how the framers viewed reasons for removal. I remember thinking as I read the passage that if the Governor could remove someone for this standard, then what was good for the goose was good for the gander. Clearly though, even after reading this passage related to gubernatorial power, the fact remained that *cause* was to be determined by the Committee that I was chosen to serve upon.

Just exactly what level of behavior should meet that bar? The Special Investigative Committee's work was establishing that precedent in this specific instance since there had never been Impeachment proceedings brought against an Illinois governor in the nearly 200-year history of the State of Illinois. It was critical that as this committee performed this work that we make sure that the bar was set high enough to avoid impeachment being used as a political tool.

Recently, in the Impeachment of President Donald Trump, many feel that the impeachment was simply a political activity. Public opinion polls indicate that many people thought the entire impeachment was political in nature. The fact is that the vote in the impeachment of Trump was totally and completely partisan with only Democrats voting in favor of impeachment. Some Democrats voted against the impeachment of the President.

I sat on a bi-partisan Impeachment Committee, although the Democrats held a clear majority of committee appointments. Besides, during the impeachment of Blagojevich, there was a Democrat-controlled House, under the control of Democrat Speaker Madigan, which had initiated the proceedings. The fact that it took so long for Madigan to be convinced to begin the proceedings had, in my opinion, been politically motivated. It was important to me that the work of the committee be fact-based and not become political.

I believed that *cause* should be set at a very high bar as we made our determination. After my research, I was convinced that the framers of the 1970 Illinois Constitution did intend for *cause* to indeed be a high bar. First of all, by removing the term, "Misdemeanor", the clear message was that impeachment should not be for minor offenses. Whether any member of the committee liked or disliked the governor, the fact remained that he had twice been elected by a majority of the citizens voting in two general elections. The second election of Blagojevich had been relatively recent. Whether or not I agreed or disagreed with the policies brought forth by his administration, and there were many disagreements, these could not and should not be the basis of a recommendation to impeach the governor.

The impeachment of an Illinois Governor must be based on the Constitution of Illinois.

Even so, it was helpful to look at the use of impeachment powers in other states and the national level. Research further revealed there are very few examples of impeachments at the state level across the United States. However, one did catch my attention. The Texas Supreme Court, in a 1924 case called Ferguson V. Maddox, referred to impeachable offenses as, "Official wrongs that need not be statutory offenses or common-law offenses, or even offenses against any positive law." That statement, along with the fact that the 1970 framers did not specifically refer to felonies or conviction of high crimes, did seem to support that the decision we made regarding Blagojevich did not need to rise to the level of conviction of any crime. I felt very comfortable that the definition of *cause* for which we were setting a precedent did not have to meet such a level.

This was important because the Governor's legal counsel, as part of his defense, would attempt to use the argument that we should wait for results of the criminal trial to act in the impeachment committee proceedings. Blagojevich had not been convicted of a crime. Any trial that might eventually determine criminal convictions of the Governor would likely take years. I was quickly convinced that *cause,* as a precedent to be applied in Illinois for this and future consideration was not intended to meet a criminal conviction level. The impeachment proceedings were also providing Blagojevich adequate due process. The guarantee of due process should always be applied. Being denied due process rights are protected by the United States Constitution and must be provided in all circumstances.

In an impeachment case in Connecticut, and during the time leading up to the probability of the impeachment of Nixon during the Watergate scandal, the notion that a pattern of misbehavior could be applied as the basis for impeachment was discussed. In other words, while one particular act or misbehavior might not rise to the level of impeachable cause, perhaps a clear pattern of multiple, perhaps even less severe misbehaviors could be considered.

This concept of a pattern of behavior was also mentioned in the recent Trump impeachment.

Without clear evidence of a crime being committed or lacking the fact that someone is convicted of a crime, could a pattern of misbehavior establish the necessary level of *cause* to warrant a recommendation to impeach? Good question.

In the case of a Connecticut impeachment inquiry of Judge James Kinsella in 1984, the special counsel in that proceeding stated that "Each element by itself need not justify impeachment." In my mind, this meant that if there was not a criminal conviction and not a single act of misconduct rising to the level of *cause* to recommend impeachment, then certainly if a pattern of misbehavior existed, the Special Investigative Committee could use the pattern of misbehavior standard in our deliberations. Remember, at this time, the committee had been presented multiple examples of questionable behaviors that were revealed in the Affidavit.

I found one Illinois case to study. While there had not been a governor undergo impeachment proceeding in Illinois, there had been an impeachment investigation at the judicial level in Illinois.

In 1990 James Heiple was elected to the Illinois Supreme Court. In 1996 there were inquiries and investigations into complaints that Heiple abused his position as a Justice during several traffic stops in which he allegedly disobeyed police. At that time, some believed that these charges stemmed from a controversial opinion Heiple issued in an adoption case known as the Baby Richard Case. In other words, while there was evidence brought forward that Heiple potentially abused his power; many thought the charges were politically motivated. Heiple was the Chief Justice of the Illinois Supreme Court at the time.

In April of 1997, the controversy surrounding Heiple led to what was at that time the first judicial impeachment proceedings in 145 years in Illinois. In the Heiple case, a ten-member panel investigating cause voted not to impeach Heiple based on the evidence brought forward. Heiple was later formally censured by the Illinois Supreme Court and resigned from his post as the Chief Justice. He served out his term on the Court which ended in 2000. In other words, the accusations, even if found to be true, did not rise to the necessary level to recommend impeachment.

We were in unchartered territory as far as what *cause* for Impeachment should be. However, there was some standard we could use based on historical precedent. I continued to come back to the same conclusion. The committee members of SICIM were the ones establishing the definition. That made the evidence and level of wrongdoing even more important. What evidence did we have that Blagojevich committed behaviors that were, if not criminal, rose to the level of misconduct and displayed a pattern of such misconduct? While there was a criminal trial unfolding, and media reports seemed to support the prevailing belief that crimes were committed. We needed to rely on the evidence we had, and determine if the evidence was reliable, sufficient and not politically motivated.

So far, the evidence that had been submitted in the proceedings related to Blagojevich was serious, including 78 pages in the Affidavit containing multiple allegations. In addition, the plea agreements from Ali Ata and Joseph Cari had also been introduced into evidence. In both of these plea agreements, Ata and Cari specifically recalled meetings that took place either with Blagojevich or with Blagojevich and Rezko when cash contributions to the Blagojevich campaign committee were made, or discussed, in exchange for certain appointments or other official acts of the governor. These plea agreements completely backed up the claims made in the Affidavit referenced in detail previously. It was necessary to keep in mind that these plea agreements were made in exchange for lighter sentences for Ata and Cari.

In addition to the Affidavit, the committee had been provided other written documentation introduced as evidence, including a report by Auditor General William Holland detailing improper hiring practices by the administration. It was revealed that the administration routinely ignored laws related to hiring, including ignoring the Veteran's hiring preference rules.

There was also evidence introduced in which Barry Maram, Director of Healthcare and Family Services (HFS), provided the committee documentation related to the purchase of flu vaccine. The documents expose that after the purchase was deemed illegal by the federal government, Blagojevich ordered the purchase anyway.

Documents revealed Blagojevich knowingly ignored JCAR. In the case of the extension of state health care coverage to additional Illinois families (*FamilyCare*), the Joint Committee on Rules (JCAR) had voted against the emergency rule ordered by Blagojevich which initiated the expansion of coverage. This proposed expansion of state-provided health care had been defeated in the General Assembly as legislation and then the governor implemented the program anyway by emergency rule through HFS under Maram's purview. When the Joint Senate-House Committee, charged with the responsibility to approve such an emergency rule, voted against the emergency rule expansion, Blagojevich ignored the ruling of JCAR, calling the JCAR ruling, 'advisory'. Several court battles and millions of dollars later, the court sided against Blagojevich's attempt to by-pass JCAR and upheld the authority of JCAR to approve or disapprove rules made by state agencies.

The amount of evidence seemed overwhelming against the Governor and when we returned for the next scheduled meeting of the Committee on December 29th, we knew there was much more evidence to come. None the less, it was important to attempt to stay away from a conclusion until we heard all sides. We had not yet heard from the Governor or his counsel to any large degree. Blagojevich had relied on denials through media outlets or the press conference as his defense. Perhaps after we returned, the Governor and his lawyers would provide witnesses to dispute some of the evidence that had been presented. The break could be used to mount a defense. Even though the evidence to this point had been very strong, I was interested in allowing extreme levels of due process to the Governor.

There had been some precedent regarding due process as applied to other impeachment proceedings. In the Arizona impeachment inquiry of Governor Evan Meacham, the Arizona Supreme Court ruled that the concept of due process does not protect the right of the governor to hold office. According to that proceeding, the rights of a person accused of a crime are not the same as a governor's right to hold office. The United States Supreme Court has refused to get involved in imposing limitations on impeachment proceedings as well. Due process was not likely subject to limitations or specifics that would be imposed by a court. However, to me, a high level of due process needed to be afforded the governor. Since we were establishing precedent, it was even more important. Thus far, I felt the Committee had provided the Governor with due process opportunities that far exceeded any reasonable or historical expectation.

The real question was whether or not Blagojevich would seize his opportunity for due process. On December 29th, when the Special Investigative Committee reconvened to continue the Impeachment inquiry, we wondered what type of defense the Governor and his counsel would provide against the charges and seemingly overwhelming evidence.

Prior to the Christmas break, the Governor's lawyer Edward Genson, sent a letter to the Chair of SICIM, Barbara Currie, requesting that a list of witnesses including Valerie Jarrett, Jesse Jackson Jr, and Rahm Emmanuel appear before the committee as witnesses. The committee had previously agreed to abide by federal prosecutor Patrick Fitzgerald's desire regarding testimony from witnesses related to the Governor that he felt might harm the ongoing federal investigation. Fitzgerald, in a letter dated December 26th, indicated that testimony from the witnesses requested by Genson would harm the case and therefore we should not interview them.

Since these witnesses' requests were denied, on December 27th, Genson sent a letter to Currie requesting that certain exhibits be included for the Committee to consider upon the December 29th reconvening of the Committee. Those documents included a copy of a memo from Greg Craig to President-elect Obama dated December 23rd, 2008 regarding, "Transition Staff Contacts with the Governor's Office," plus a copy of a tape and the pertinent excerpts from Jesse Jackson Jr.'s December 10th press conference.

The memo Genson referenced was admitted in evidence and is listed as Exhibit 26.

In that memo, Greg Craig, an Obama transition staff contact, did confirm that he could not find any accounts of any inappropriate discussions with Blagojevich or anyone from his office about a deal or a quid pro quo arrangement in which he would receive any personal benefit in return for any specific appointment to fill the vacancy.

In that memo, Craig stated that while he personally did not have any such contacts, Rahm Emmanuel did have contacts of the type covered by the request. He further stated that David Axelrod and Valarie Jarrett, also members of the transition team, did not have any such contacts. The memo went on to state that Obama himself had no contact or communication with Blagojevich or members of his staff about the Senate seat. Craig did state that in some conversations, the President-elect did express his preference that Jarrett work with him at the White House but would not stand in her way if she wanted to pursue the Senate seat.

Jarrett subsequently decided on November 9th not to pursue the seat. Jarrett did subsequently work in the Obama White House as a senior advisor.

According to the memo, Obama did have conversations with Axelrod and Emmanuel about his successor and those candidates included Jan

Schakowsky, Jesse Jackson Jr., Dan Hynes and Tammy Duckworth. According to the memo, Obama simply understood that Emmanuel would provide the names to Blagojevich to add to the pool, but there was never any discussion or suggestion that the Governor expected a personal benefit or favor in return for making this appointment to the Senate.

The memo detailed the involvement of Emmanuel and Jarrett in any discussions related to the Senate appointment. He confirmed that Emmanuel had contacted Blagojevich in early November to inform him that he (Emmanuel) was going to resign his seat in Congress to become Chief of Staff for Obama. They spoke about potential candidates to replace Emmanuel as Congressman. It was at that time he had a brief discussion with the Governor about the Senate seat. He also stated that there was not a discussion about a cabinet position for Blagojevich during those conversations or any 501(C) (4) established to benefit the governor.

In early conversations, Emmanuel did recommend Valarie Jarrett, but this was before he knew about Obama ruling out the preference of any particular candidate and before he knew that Jarrett was going to take a position in the White House as a senior advisor instead of pursuing the Senate seat. He admitted to having several conversations with John Harris about the Senate seat but that those conversations did not include any type of quid pro quo.

According to Genson, this memo refuted evidence that one of the claims in the Affidavit was not entirely factual; therefore other aspects of the Affidavit were also false or misleading. But, that memo did not completely dispel the notion that the Affidavit revealed, based on the intercepted wiretaps, that Blagojevich was involved in a quid pro quo attempt. The scheme to extort favors from individuals in exchange for naming them to the Senate seat was revealed in the quotations from the wiretaps that were contained in the Affidavit.

Did the memo create doubt that some of the rest of the Affidavit, including testimony from those who had entered plea agreements, was truthful? The wiretaps still contained the most damaging evidence that there was a clear attempt to leverage favor in exchange for personal benefit. However, I did find the evidence presented by Genson a creative defense.

The other request made by Genson was to allow for a portion of a comment made by Jesse Jackson Jr. during a December 10th press conference to be put into evidence.

At that press conference, Jesse Jackson Jr. stated, "I want to make this fact plain. I reject pay to play politics and have no involvement whatsoever in wrongdoing. I did not invite or authorize anyone at any time to promise anything to Governor Blagojevich on my behalf." Once again, at least some contradictory evidence regarding one charge had been introduced.

As to the question of the standard to be used when considering Impeachment, Genson introduced evidence on December 29th urging the Committee to use a standard that he claims was used in the case of Judge Heiple. Before the holiday break, SICIM member Representative Chapin Rose asked Genson whether the use of a totality of evidence approach was appropriate.

At that time, Genson, in his response, stated that SICIM should indeed use the totality of evidence standard. In evidence he entered as Exhibit 35 on December 29th, Genson made it clear that while the totality of evidence standard was important, it was also important that the evidence itself used in compiling the totality of evidence also meet the high legal bar of clear and convincing. In other words, he wanted to make certain that the Committee considers that the evidence of wrongdoing meets a higher standard like used in criminal proceedings. His opinion conflicted with the fact the Illinois Constitution does not require that standard.

Combined with other evidence, the strategy used by Genson was to question the criminal standard of the evidence as clear and convincing. Genson was arguing that since SICIM was not allowed to hear most of the wiretaps, or subpoena several key witnesses due to the ongoing federal criminal case, there was not a clear and convincing standard being met, even if there was the appearance of a totality of evidence based on the sheer amount of testimony covering multiple examples of malfeasant behaviors by Blagojevich.

That was summed up the attempt by Genson to counter the charges and defend Blagojevich. There was not much he could do and Blagojevich did not show up to provide testimony or answer to the charges.

On December 29th, the Committee adjourned without a clear date as to when we would reconvene. I figured we would meet shortly after the start of the New Year. It appeared as if we might complete our work by the end of the first week of January of 2009 and a vote could take place as to the recommendation of the Committee to the House of Representatives regarding impeachment.

On December 30th one burning question was answered. Even though Blagojevich's image had been severely damaged by the overwhelming evidence already presented to SICIM, despite the fact Democrat State Treasurer Alexi Giannoulias had written a letter on December 23rd in which he informed the General Assembly Members that the governor's legal issues were contributing to further financial hardship in Illinois because bond sales were delayed due to the governor's arrest and surrounding circumstances, and although in early December, the United States Department of Homeland Security had revoked Blagojevich's security clearance, Blagojevich remained defiant. On December 30th, he named Roland Burris as the replacement for Barack Obama as U.S. Senator for Illinois.

The move, I suppose, was to dispel the fact that previously entered evidence.

The fact that no person mentioned in the Affidavit was chosen to be the U.S. Senator was supposed to convince the committee that nothing happened. Once again, this was an attempt to discredit the Affidavit which contained quotes from various wiretaps regarding the bartering that took place for the Senate seat. If he now named someone like Burris, who had never been mentioned in any of the conversations, he could claim he did not commit any quid pro quo for the seat. Genson later referred to all of the evidence in the affidavit of the wiretap quotes revealing the quid pro quo for the Senate seat, as nothing more than, "Chatter."

The choice of Roland Burris to replace Obama was interesting. Burris was generally well-liked and had an extensive record of public service. If sworn in, he would replace Obama as the only African American U.S. Senator at that time. Burris had actually lost to Blagojevich in the primary election back in 2002. He had once made headlines by designing an elaborate monument at his cemetery plot which included the engraving of the words, "Trail Blazer", on the back of the monument. Under that inscription, it reads, "The First African-American in Illinois to Become"… What follows that pronouncement on the monument is a list of his accomplishments. Included in the list are being elected to the Statewide offices of Comptroller in 1979, and Attorney General in 1991. There is another section of the monument which lists, "Other Major Accomplishments." For this elaborate monument, Burris had been tagged with the nickname, "Tombstone."

(*Wikipedia* 2008 by Eric Allix Rogers)

Any choice made by Blagojevich at this point came with a mountain of suspicion and skepticism. According to practice and precedent, the choice was to be approved by Secretary of State Jesse White for the selection to be officially conveyed to the United States Senate. On December 30th, White refused to sign the paperwork. Eventually, but not until January 9th, the Illinois Supreme Court ruled that the signature of White was not necessary for the Governor to carry out his constitutional authority to name a replacement.

After the appointment and the start of the New Year, on January 2nd, 2009 Currie sent a subpoena to Burris ordering him to appear before the Special Investigative Committee on January 7th.

On January 5th, in response to the subpoena, Burris's legal counsel sent Currie a letter in which he informed Currie that Burris was not available to appear since he was supposed to be in Washington DC preparing to be sworn in at noon on January 6th, 2009 as Illinois next U.S. Senator. His legal counsel informed Currie that other meetings scheduled for Burris on January 7th would not allow him to return to testify.

Attached to that letter was a signed Affidavit from Burris which included the timeline of the events leading up to Burris being named to replace Obama. In that Affidavit, Burris stated that it was Friday, December 26th, 2008 when he was first contacted by an attorney, Samuel Adams, representing Blagojevich to question whether or not Burris had an interest in the Senate seat. According to the Burris timeline in that sworn statement, Burris told Adams that he needed a couple of days to

207

discuss the possibility with friends and family and would then be ready to discuss the possibility again.

In that Affidavit, Burris states that on December 30th, Blagojevich's legal counsel contacted him again to see if he had determined whether or not he was interested. It was at that time, according to Burris, that he informed the Governor's legal counsel that if the seat were offered, he would accept the appointment. That same day, at about 4 PM, Burris states that Governor Blagojevich called him, praised his public service and offered to appoint him to the U.S. Senate.

In this signed Affidavit, Burris emphatically went on to state that before December 26th there was absolutely no contact between himself or any of his representatives with Governor Blagojevich regarding the Senate seat. He also added that other than the appointment, he discussed no other topics with the Governor.

It was obvious that Burris was attempting to avoid appearing before the committee hoping that the Affidavit would suffice. Burris was clearly in hopes that if the committee accepted the Affidavit instead of an official appearance and testimony that the existing schedule to be sworn into the Senate could occur. But, it did not suffice. The committee wanted to speak with Burris as a witness, in person.

There was so much controversy surrounding the appointment of Burris, the U.S. Senate would delay the swearing-in until Burris could appear before the House Investigative Committee. On January 8th, in what would be one of the most televised and documented moments of the committee hearings, Burris did appear and did provide testimony.

I was among those quizzing Burris from my seat in the front row. Among the final SICIM Members to ask questions, I wanted to make sure I understood two things. First, I wanted to know if Burris had made any type of quid pro quo arrangement with Blagojevich. Second, I wanted to know why Samuel Adams, someone previously identified as the Governor's criminal defense attorney, was the person who had made contact with Burris about the Senate appointment rather than an administration official.

Ed Genson countered that neither he nor Adams was the Governor's criminal defense attorney. Genson stated, "Mr. Adams Jr., does not, has not, and will not represent Governor Blagojevich in the criminal case." I had struck a nerve for sure. Genson likely had already decided that once this impeachment committee work was completed that Blagojevich would no longer be his client. I was still curious as to why one of the

Governor's counsel, during the impeachment proceeding was making phone calls regarding the Governor's duty to name a replacement for Obama. Shouldn't that call be made by someone in the administration? So, I rephrased my question, "Let me ask you this, Mr. Burris, when Mr. Adams called you, what capacity did you believe Mr. Adams was acting within? Did you believe he was the Governor's criminal defense attorney?" In response Burris stated, "I know Mr. Adams, he's a good friend of my son. I helped raise Mr. Adams to some extent. Mr. Adams contacted me and indicated, and I had to verify that he was coming from the Governor, that he was delivering a message from the Governor, and I treated it as being a counsel to the Governor, that's how I treated it. I didn't know whether or not he was criminal defense or what defense, as a counsel to the Governor."

I found it peculiar that Burris took at face value that a friend of his son had the authority to call him and discuss such an important appointment and for Burris not to at least ask more questions regarding the authority of the caller. It was clear that Adams was representing the Governor in some capacity beyond his duties related to the impeachment proceeding and as a representative of the Governor's administration to replace Obama in the effort to name a new U.S. Senator from Illinois. To me this was a conflict intended to use the office of the Governor to assist with his impeachment defense. I asked Burris if Mr. Adam's discussion with him included any discussion regarding the criminal case. My specific question was, "So there is nothing related to the criminal case that is related to the Senate appointment?" Burris responded that there was never any such discussion.

I believed him, in this instance, I do not think there was any quid pro quo in the seating of Burris as a replacement for Obama. I did not like the fact that the Governor was using the same counsel who had appeared in his defense in the impeachment committee to make official contact as someone representing the administration. This was all designed to create the appearance that although there was chatter about what Governor Blagojevich could get for the Senate seat, he did not follow through. No harm no foul as far as Blagojevich was concerned.

After initially refusing to seat Roland Burris in early January, U.S. Senate President agreed to seat Burris after his January 8th SICIM testimony.

Finally, on January 15th, 2009, Burris became a United States Senator when sworn in by Vice-President Dick Chaney.

On the afternoon of January 8th, 2008, the Special Investigative Committee convened one final time to review evidence and vote on a recommendation. Blagojevich yet again opted to not appear in front of the Committee to answer questions or attempt to provide any additional defense to his cause.

The final report compiled by the staff, contained a summary of the key findings of the committee including a review of the acts of behavior by Blagojevich which we all felt met the bar of *cause.* It appeared to me that both standards of *cause* and pattern were clearly met. Among the charges against Blagojevich and evidence provided which met, in my mind, both a clear and convincing evidence standard (although not required) and a pattern of abuse or wrongdoings, therefore, creating the *cause* required for impeachment and included the following:

At the top of the list, **the attempt to obtain personal benefits in exchange for an appointment to the U.S. Senate.** Despite the testimony of Burris, which was intended to demonstrate that Blagojevich did not commit a quid pro quo in the final selection, it was very clear from the Affidavit he attempted or instructed others to attempt to make this exchange for his personal benefit on several occasions within various scenarios.

- The amount of time it took to name a replacement coupled with the direct quotes like, "I've got this thing and it's f****** golden, and, uh, uh, I'm not just giving it up for f****** nothing", provided clear and very convincing evidence that Blagojevich, on multiple occasions and in multiple ways, was indeed attempting to gain personally from his power as governor to make the Senate appointment even if it did not end up happening.

There was also evidence that Blagojevich himself knew his conduct was unethical and illegal. On several wiretaps, he mentioned that, "Lists can't be in writing", and, "That you gotta be careful how you express that and assume everybody's listening, the whole world is listening." The Burris testimony, while interesting and hyped, in the end did not convince the Committee that the Governor did not intend to follow through with the quid pro quo. It was only after he found out about the wiretaps that he changed his course and named Burris.

This is not in any way meant to incriminate Burris. His testimony in which he stated that there were never any discussions of quid pro quo with him regarding the seat appeared to be honest testimony to me. I did feel that Blagojevich, by naming Burris, was attempting to distance himself from the quid pro quo, and claim innocence regarding trading the Senate seat by naming Burris. In other words he was claiming, "I didn't do it, I named this guy and there is no recorded proof of quid pro quo." However, multiple conversations did reveal a clear and patterned attempt to make deals related to the naming of a U.S. Senate replacement.

Although none of those earlier attempts were followed through on, the quid pro quo was evident regarding the Senate seat fiasco.

The second in this series of behaviors which revealed a pattern of illegal and unethical behavior was the attempt to condition state financial assistance to the Tribune Company to support the sale of the Chicago Cubs on the firing of Chicago Tribune Editorial Board members who had been critical of the Governor.

Federal agents intercepted several conversations in which the Governor's Chief of Staff John Harris and an unnamed Deputy Governor specifically stated that certain Tribune editorial board members are fired or the Tribune would not receive consideration for public funding for renovations at Wrigley Field.

The Illinois Finance Authority (IFA) would have been of great assistance to the Tribune Company with the potential approval of over one hundred million dollars. Conversations captured on recorded lines revealed Blagojevich was attempting to exchange this financial if certain individuals were fired. These individuals had been highly critical of Blagojevich and written several negative investigative articles. In fact, in one of the recorded conversations, Blagojevich stated simply, "Maybe we can't do this now. Fire those f******", about IFA funding. In later conversations, Blagojevich even suggested that the funding did not just depend on the end of negative articles and stated that Harris should also tell the Tribune ownership, "…We sure would like to have some editorial support from your paper." This was a clear attempt to tie taxpayer-supported funding to a personal favor for the Governor. Another very clear quid pro quo.

Next was the charge of attempting to trade other official acts for campaign contributions. Some of the examples of this behavior came from wiretaps but there was even other evidence that Blagojevich had indeed been involved directly in a pay to play scheme. Some of those involved with Blagojevich in carrying out this scheme provided testimony against the governor to reduce sentences for their participation. The accusations revealed this type of behavior began in the early years of the Blagojevich administration and continued throughout the entire time he was Governor.

The examples in the final report of the Investigative Committee are not all-inclusive. One of the cited examples is typical, and to me, the most disturbing. In October of 2008, around $8 million in pediatric care reimbursements were the subject of negotiations between the governor's office and the CEO of Children's Memorial Hospital. In a conversation with a witness cooperating with federal agents, the witness testified that Blagojevich said, "I'm going to do $8 million for them. I want to get ["Hospital Executive 1"] for 50." Six years earlier, in 2002, a similar deal was made with Ali Ata who had made two separate $25K donations to the Blagojevich campaign coffers and became the head of the Illinois Finance Authority.

Then there were the cases of Joseph Cari and Stu Levin involving the TRS and Health Facility Planning Committee shakedowns back in 2004 and 2005. Once again, very specific eye witness testimony from Tony Rezko, Stuart Levine, Joseph Cari and William Cellini was included. When those individuals faced charges themselves, they sang like songbirds in exchange for lighter sentences. The clear pattern of pay to play presented to SICIM involving large donations to the Blagojevich campaign fund were multiple, well documented and one quid pro quo after another was revealed, it was truly never-ending!

There is an excellent book written by Elizabeth Brackett which reveals in greater detail the incredible pay to play culture f the Blagojevich administration. The book, entitled, *Pay to Play: How Rod Blagojevich Turned Political Corruption Into a National Side Show*, is a must-read for those interested in more. Brackett died tragically at age 76 in 2018 from injuries sustained in a bicycle accident while riding along Chicago's 38th street beach.

In addition to the clear evidence of multiple quid pro quos, **a clear pattern of abuse of power** also emerged during the three weeks of testimony and evidence presented to SICIM.

Once again, this pattern dated back to the early years of the Blagojevich administration. **Back in October of 2004**, after the FDA announced a shortage of flu vaccine so the Blagojevich Administration began to look for supplies of flu vaccine from foreign suppliers. The documentation provided to the Investigative Committee showed that the Center for Disease Control found enough flu vaccine for Illinois to ensure that the most vulnerable populations would be served without the proposed purchase. Despite that, and without approval from the FDA, with the direction of Blagojevich, Deputy Governor Bradley Tusk proceeded to purchase over one half a million doses of flu vaccine from unapproved foreign suppliers. The state never was allowed to use the vaccine and the entire episode cost Illinois taxpayers $2.6 million.

The example was in 2003 when the Blagojevich administration initiated the I-Save Rx Program. In this instance, a special advocate was directed by the Governor's Office to explore the possibility of implementing a program that would allow state employees and retirees to get prescription refills from foreign pharmacies at a reduced price.

Without approval from the FDA, the importation of foreign drugs amounts to a federal offense. In **June of 2004**, the FDA wrote a letter to Governor Blagojevich informing him that his proposed Rx program was not legal and the FDA also denied a request for a waiver of the law.

Despite that, evidence was clear that in October of 2004, the Governor implemented the program allowing I-Save RX participants to order refills from pharmacies in Canada and the United Kingdom. In 2005 the program was expanded further to include pharmacies in Australia and New Zealand. Although about 74 foreign pharmacies were approved, only 2 or 3 filled prescriptions. This was a violation of Illinois Law as well. Under the Pharmacy Practice Act, it is illegal for anyone to engage in the practice of pharmacy unless it is authorized by Illinois Law.

None of the pharmacies were authorized even by state Law. Moreover, evidence indicated that the Governor clearly understood that this practice violated the law yet ordered the implementation and the continuation of the program.

There are other examples of brazen abuses of power that were presented to the Investigative Committee. **One of the most concerning examples was when the Governor refused to stop the expansion of the *FamilyCare* program even after J-CAR voted against his emergency rule to expand government healthcare coverage**.

As you recall, Blagojevich, from day one, wanted to expand the Illinois healthcare program (Medicaid) to cover more people. On several occasions throughout his time in office, he proposed expansion in Budget addresses and with legislative proposals. The cost was always too high for implementation and the proposals, although coming very close, did not pass. The most widely publicized attempt was in 2007 when the governor proposed the *IllinoisCovered* expansion which was supposed to be funded by the Gross Receipts Tax (GRT). The GRT was the revenue proposal that was defeated by a vote of 107-0. After this legislative defeat, on November 7th, 2007, the Governor ordered, through the Department of Family Services, the implementation of the expansion of healthcare coverage anyway in an existing program called *FamilyCare*. At the time, under *FamilyCare*, Illinois citizens in families with income levels of between 133% and 185% of the federal poverty level were eligible for State Health Insurance Assistance. The new Rule Blagojevich implemented would raise the federal poverty bar to 400% for eligibility. The 185% level was established by statute. This action greatly expanded the pool of those covered and added millions and millions of dollars to the cost of Medicaid, contrary to existing Illinois law.

In Illinois, as in most states, there exists a quasi-legislative body that has the function of approving or dis-approving rules implemented by state agencies. In Illinois, the authority to approve or disapprove lies with the Joint Committee on Administrative Rules (JCAR). JCAR is a bi-partisan committee that consists of 12 legislators, each of the four caucus leaders appointed these members. On November 13th, this Committee voted 9-2 to suspend the expansion that had been ordered by Blagojevich.

To review, although JCAR suspended implementation of the new rule, Blagojevich and his administration continued to implement the illegal policy and refused to follow the JCAR ruling.

Blagojevich referred to the JCAR as advisory and claimed that he, as Governor, had the authority to implement this rule anyway. Evidence presented to SICIM revealed that the Governor was aware of the history and authority of JCAR and simply chose to ignore it. The matter was settled through the Court system at a huge cost to Illinois taxpayers in legal fees. Lower courts ruled that the JCAR rule was valid but Blagojevich appealed the lower court decisions all the way to the Illinois Supreme Court. In a case known as Baise/Gidwitz vs Blagojevich, the court made the final ruling against the governor. It was not until April of 2008, after thousands of families signed up for the initial emergency expansion, that a lower court ruled that all new enrollees must end. Then almost 11 months after the Blagojevich initial emergency rule, on October 15th another Court ordered that no additional state funds could be expended for *FamilyCare*. Then, finally on December 10, 2008, the Illinois Supreme Court made a final ruling and upheld JCAR's authority in this matter.

Another damning example of the abusive behavior of Blagojevich was a myriad of evidence that his administration regularly by-passed laws related to hiring practices. In a very detailed report presented as evidence to SICIM, the Office of Executive Inspector General (OEIG), back in 2004, reported that Illinois Department of Employment Security (IDES) by-passed state hiring practices and intentionally and illegally ignored hiring mandates. In that report there were eight instances of improper hiring cited. The report further revealed that a, "Veteran's preference," rule was routinely ignored. In many cases, a paper trail was evident back to supporters of Blagojevich which had requested either the job or the placement of someone in the job.

Unbelievably, there were even more instances than these that I have outlined. So, when the Committee met the afternoon of January 8th to review all of this evidence and vote on a recommendation, there was little doubt as to what our recommendation would be.

(After each committee member had a chance to state the reasons for their individual conclusions regarding the final recommendation, a vote was taken.
Roger Eddy Photo from T.V.- *C-Span*)

Unlike the recent vote to Impeach Donald Trump, this Special Investigative Committee vote was unanimous and bi-partisan. By a 21-0 Vote, the Committee recommended that the Illinois House of Representatives Impeach Rod Blagojevich.

Chapter Sixteen
Know When to Fold 'Em

January 8, 2009 was a historic day in Illinois and a media event for sure. That morning, the Special Investigative Committee had heard from Roland Burris and that afternoon the Committee voted unanimously, for the first time in the near 200 year history of Illinois to recommend to the full House that a Governor be impeached.

All of the committee members pointed to the overwhelming evidence of the patterns of abuse and attempts by the governor to enrich himself by using the powers of his office. The evidence was also clear that this pattern started very early in his first administration and continued throughout his time as Governor until the very end.

I am still astonished that Blagojevich was allowed to continue as Governor for as long as he was. Suggestions that an investigation start earlier were ignored by those in leadership positions, especially by the majority party. Unlike the case against Donald Trump, which began after an anonymous whistleblower was concerned about a single phone conversation; the repeated pattern of abuse and corruption by Blagojevich was widespread, well known and spanned years. The Impeachment of Trump was on the minds of Democrats from the first days he took office, or even before. Many people believe impeachment discussions started on election night. The subsequent investigation and impeachment was a completely partisan effort, with only Democrats voting in favor.

When I consider the work of the Special Investigative Committee of the House in the case of Rod Blagojevich, I am very proud of the fact that the vote was bi-partisan and the evidence overwhelming. These types of proceedings such as in the case of the Trump Impeachment can potentially become nothing more than a political show.

The framers of both the United States and Illinois Constitutions had a clear standard for which they felt Impeachment would be the remedy. In my view SICIM met and surpassed that standard.

So, on January 9th, when the Illinois House was called to order to act on the recommendation made by SICIM and led in prayer by Reverend Milton Bost of the Chatham Baptist Church, I was satisfied with the work we had done, albeit very long overdue.

There were 115 members of the Illinois House initially responding to the roll call.

Speaker Madigan began these with these words, "On page 5 of the Calendar, on the order of Resolutions, there appears House Resolution 1671." He then recognized the sponsor of HR1671, Representative Barbra Currie. Currie, as you recall, served as chairperson of the Special Investigative Committee.

Currie started her remarks, "Thank you, Speaker and Members, of the House. We stand here today because of the perfidy of one man, Rod Blagojevich." Perfidy, what a seldom-used but appropriate word, yet perfect to describe Blagojevich.

The word, among other things, is used to mean dishonesty, betrayal, treachery, and disloyalty. All appropriate.

Currie continued, "Exactly one month ago, the Governor was arrested by federal agents.

The House permitted him a week to do the right thing, to do what should have been readily apparent that he should have done and that is to resign his office." Those words bothered me because they revealed that right up until the end, there was not going to be any action taken by the Speaker unless there had been an arrest. The Illinois Constitution did not require an arrest to be made to begin an investigation to determine *cause* for Impeachment. Currie's words indicated to me that the Speaker only took these necessary steps after the arrest. Even after the arrest, there was a preference given to simply a resignation.

Currie went on to state that instead of resigning, the governor stated that he would "Fight, fight, fight and he castigated us as nothing more than a political lynch mob." She disputed the idea that a political lynch mob existed by describing the efforts made to allow Blagojevich to defend himself.

In a clear departure from the recent events surrounding the Trump Impeachment, she made it clear that, in her words, "The cornerstone of our Democracy is the fair, free and open election. To overturn the results of an election is not something that should be undertaken lightly."

She pointed out that even though the Illinois Constitution gives the Illinois House of Representatives great latitude in determining the *cause* for impeachment proceedings, the power should not be taken lightly: "It's not supposed to give us the latitude to impeach someone because we don't like his policies, because we don't like his style of governance, because we don't like the way he brushes his hair." That line lightened the mood and brought some chuckles. Blagojevich had a well-known infatuation with his hair.

Currie continued. "Impeachment is reserved...this power is reserved for cases of allegations of serious infractions, serious betrayals." She then went on to provide specific examples of a large number of betrayals committed by Blagojevich. As part of her conclusion, Currie described his actions this way, **"They show a public servant who is prepared to turn public service into an avenue for private benefit. They show a public servant who has betrayed his oath of office, who has betrayed the public trust, who is not fit to govern the State of Illinois....The totality of evidence shows that Governor Blagojevich has forfeited his right to hold office; and should be impeached."**

When Currie finished, Speaker Madigan recognized Minority Leader Tom Cross to speak. Cross thanked the Investigative Committee members from both sides of the aisle and then recounted more specific instances in which the governor betrayed his oath. This was a tough day for Cross. Sadness was evident in his face. Once again, I believe Cross waited way too long to begin beating the drum for the removal of Blagojevich.

Cross was followed by GOP Investigative Committee Member and vice-chair, Jim Durkin.

Durkin also thanked everyone involved and highlighted, even more, the overwhelming evidence against Blagojevich. Jim had done a terrific job as Minority Spokesperson on SICIM.

There were a few questions by Democrat House members asked of Currie as to why we were acting before the Governor being convicted in Court. Currie and Durkin responded to these questions by revealing what the Illinois Constitution standard was and that criminal conviction was not the necessary standard to Impeach. A few more Representatives made additional comments and observations. As I recall, one Representative even referred to Watergate and drew comparisons to the initial proceedings against Nixon. Nobody came remotely close to making any statement defending the governor. As comments became repetitive and began to appear political, it was evident no more words were necessary. It was time to vote on HR1671.

Currie was called upon to make a closing statement before the vote. Her final closing remarks were well said, **"My heart is heavy but my responsibility is clear. The evidence we gathered makes it clear that this governor tramples on the legislative prerogative; he breaks state and federal laws. In his own words, he expresses a willingness to barter state official acts and state taxpayer money for personal and political gain, the Governor has violated his oath of office. The Governor has breached the public trust. This Governor must be impeached. And I urge you aye vote"**.

Madigan then called HR1671 for a vote, "The question is, Shall the House adopt House Resolution 1671?" Moments later, Madigan ordered the Clerk to, "Take the record." Then came these historic words from Madigan, "On this question, there are 114 people voting 'aye' and 1 person voting 'no'. The House does adopt House Resolution 1671 and Governor Blagojevich is hereby impeached."

People often ask me who voted against the impeachment. Below is a photo of the recorded roll call on the board located on the floor of the House. It reveals that Debbie Mell was the lone present vote. It was not a 'no' vote as Madigan stated in the House transcript of the vote. It was not a vote against impeachment per se. A 'present' vote is sometimes made when a person is not convinced either way. Debbie is the sister of Rod's wife, Patti Blagojevich. It was an option she chose to use. Nobody was overly critical of the 'present' vote. Who would want to be in those shoes?

(Roger Eddy personal photo from House floor)

We had done our work; the Impeachment was the first-ever of a Governor in the History of Illinois.

Reaction to the Impeachment was swift. This was not simply an Illinois media story. In the entire United States there had been very few Impeachments of any kind.

It was noted by some media outlets that back in 2007 both Mike Bost and I were the first lawmakers to publicly mention possible impeachment proceedings against Blagojevich. After the vote to impeach, Bost's comment was, "Rod was just bizarre, I'm ready to move on." My official statement was, "I think justice is served today, he became a self-servant rather than a public servant." I think most Members of the House, like Bost, were ready to move on. Of course, this story was not going away very soon.

The Senate Trial followed. Very similar to the recent Trump Impeachment, The House of Representatives selects a House Prosecutor to make the case for removal of the impeached individual in the Senate. The House Persecutor was named- David Ellis. Ellis had served as the Speaker's Counsel during the Special Investigative Committee phase. Below and on the following pages is a portion of the evidence that Ellis introduced to the Senate. The text comes from the official documents of the Senate trial.

IN THE HONORABLE SENATE OF THE STATE OF ILLINOIS FOR THE NINETY-SIXTH GENERAL ASSEMBLY SITTING AS AN IMPEACHMENT TRIBUNAL (Impeachment of Governor ROD R. BLAGOJEVICH) HOUSE PROSECUTOR'S MODIFIED MOTION FOR ADDITIONAL DOCUMENTS OR MATERIALS House Prosecutor David W. Ellis, pursuant to Senate Impeachment Rule 15(b)(2), moves for the admission of additional documents into evidence and, in support thereof, states as follows:

1. In the event that the Honorable Senate grants the House Prosecutor's requests to call Special Agent Daniel Cain and the modified list of witnesses, the House Prosecutor will be withdrawing all motions for additional documents filed on January 21, 2009. Instead, the House Prosecutor will seek to admit this modified motion for additional documents or materials.

2. The House Prosecutor seeks to admit a flowchart detailing the process of obtaining authority to intercept oral and wire communications at the Impeachment Trial. A copy of this document is attached to this Motion. This document is relevant and material because it demonstrates the process for Obtaining court authorization to intercept oral and wire communications. The Affidavit of Special Agent Daniel Cain (Exhibit 3) includes content contained in four court-authorized intercepts, which provide grounds for multiple paragraphs of the Article of Impeachment. This document will be used for demonstrative purposes during live testimony and is not redundant because it is not in the House Impeachment Record.

3. The House Prosecutor seeks to admit an excerpt of Exhibit 44, namely, the remarks of Chief Judge James F. Holderman regarding the legality of the federal government's interception of oral and wire communications regarding the Governor at the Impeachment Trial. A copy of this document is attached to this Motion. This document is relevant and material because it demonstrates the lawfulness of the wiretaps that were used by the federal government as referenced in the Affidavit of Special Agent Daniel Cain (Exhibit 3). This document will be used for demonstrative purposes during live testimony and is not redundant because it does not exist in the proposed form.

4. The House Prosecutor seeks to admit excerpts from Exhibit 3, the Affidavit of Special Agent Daniel Cain for demonstrative purposes at the Impeachment Trial. Copies of these documents are attached to this Motion. These excerpts are relevant and material because they provide evidence of the Governor's abuse of power. These excerpts will be used for demonstrative purposes during live testimony and are not redundant because they do not exist in the proposed forms.

5. The House Prosecutor seeks to admit a document detailing the purpose and function of an organization known as "Change to Win" at the Impeachment Trial to illustrate the Governor's interest in trading a Senate appointment for a position that with the organization. A copy of this document is attached to this Motion. This document is not redundant because it is not in the House Impeachment Record.

6. The House Prosecutor seeks to admit the December 5, 2008, front page of the Chicago Tribune at the Impeachment Trial. A copy of this document is attached to this Motion. This document is relevant and material because it demonstrates Governor Blagojevich's discovery that the federal government was listening to his conversations regarding his plot to obtain a personal benefit in exchange for his appointment to fill the vacant seat in the United States Senate and reversed his actions upon that discovery. This document is not redundant because it is not in the House Impeachment Record.

7. The House Prosecutor seeks to admit Chicago Tribune editorials critical of Governor Rod Blagojevich from July 2, 2007, to December 5, 2008, and a list of all such articles at the Impeachment Trial. A copy of these documents is attached· to this Motion. These documents are relevant and material because they display the Chicago Tribune editorials that led to the Governor's plot to condition the awarding of State financial assistance to the Tribune 2 Company on the firing of members of the Chicago Tribune editorial board. These documents are not redundant because they are not in the House Impeachment Record.

8. The House Prosecutor seeks to admit an excerpt from Exhibit 7, pages 41-42, at the Impeachment Trial. A copy of this document is attached to this Motion. This document will be used for demonstrative purposes during live testimony and is not redundant because it does not exist in the proposed form.

9. The House Prosecutor seeks to admit a timeline detailing Ali Ata's appointment to the position of Executive Director of the Illinois Finance Authority and contributions Ali Ata made to Governor Rod Blagojevich's campaign at the Impeachment Trial. A copy of this document is attached to this Motion. This document is relevant and material because it demonstrates the Governor's plot to trade official acts in exchange for campaign contributions. This document is not redundant because it is not in the House Impeachment Record.

10. The House Prosecutor seeks to admit an excerpt from Exhibit 8, pages 30-31, at the Impeachment Trial. A copy of this document is attached to this Motion. This document will be used for demonstrative

purposes during live testimony and is not redundant because it does not exist in the proposed form.

11. The House Prosecutor seeks to admit the bill status of House Bill 4758 of the 95th General Assembly at the Impeachment Trial. A copy of this document is attached to this Motion. This document is a public record. This document is not redundant because it is not in the House Impeachment Record.

12. The House Prosecutor seeks to admit a letter from Governor Rod Blagojevich to Tommy Thompson, Secretary of Health and Human Services at the Impeachment Trial. A copy of this document is attached to this Motion. This document is relevant and material because it demonstrates the Governor's action concerning, and responsibility for, the I-SAVE RX Program. This document is not redundant because it is not in the House Impeachment Record.

13. The House Prosecutor seeks to admit a letter from Lester Crawford, Acting Commissioner of the Food and Drug Administration, to Governor Rod Blagojevich at the Impeachment Trial. A copy of this document is attached to this Motion. This document is relevant and material because it demonstrates the Governor's action with regard to, and responsibility for, the I-SAVE RX Program. This document is not redundant because it is not in the House Impeachment Record.

14. The House Prosecutor seeks to admit various newspaper articles and a press release dated September 16, 2006, relating to the creation and expansion of the I-SAVE RX Program at the Impeachment Trial. Copies of these documents are attached to this Motion. These documents are relevant and material because they demonstrate the Governor's actions with regard to, and responsibility for, the I-SAVE RX Program. These documents are not redundant because it is not in the House Impeachment Record.

15. The House Prosecutor seeks to admit a copy of a document included in Exhibit 6, namely the timeline detailing the events that transpired during the procurement of the flu vaccine, at the Impeachment Trial. A copy of this document is attached to this Motion. This document is relevant and material because it demonstrates the Governor's action with regard to, and responsibility for, the procurement of the flu vaccines. This document will be used for demonstrative purposes during live testimony and is not redundant because it does not exist in the proposed form.

16. The House Prosecutor seeks to admit a copy of a document included in Exhibit 6, namely the timeline detailing the events that transpired before and after the Governor launched the I-SAVE RX Program at the Impeachment Trial. A copy of this document is attached to this Motion. This document is relevant and material because it demonstrates the Governor's action with regard to, and responsibility for, the I-SAVE RX Program. This document will be used for demonstrative purposes during live testimony and is not redundant because it does not exist in the proposed form.

17. The House Prosecutor seeks to admit the Joint Committee on Administrative Rules' Statement of Objection to and Suspension of Peremptory Rule issued on November 19, 2008 at the Impeachment Trial. A copy of this document is attached to this Motion.

There were twenty items total listed in the official filings, but I am sure you get the idea. The evidence was entirely overwhelming and Ellis did a masterful job of presentation.

A sharp contrast to the political theatre performed by Adam Schiff and his counterparts in the recent Trump Impeachment hearings held before the United States Senate.

During the days before January 26th when the Senate Trial started, and after the Inauguration of a new General Assembly, Blagojevich went on a media tour proclaiming his innocence. He made appearances on *The View, Good Morning America*, and *The Today Show*, to name a few. In his mind, somehow he thought he could influence the outcome by proclaiming his innocence that way. The media tour had no effect and after a few days, on January 30th, 2009, the Senate voted to remove him from office and also took away his right to ever again hold public office in Illinois. The Senate vote was unanimous. As one of my colleagues put it, "Elvis has left the building."

Later that day, on January 30th, Lt. Governor, Pat Quinn was sworn in as Governor to replace Blagojevich. The impeachment and removal of Blagojevich was certainly not the end of the struggles Illinois faced. But, it was an important first step.

As mentioned, impeachment and removal from office was not the end of the Rod Blagojevich story. Not even close. This book is not meant to be about the criminal trial or other future events. However, a brief review is warranted.

On April 2, 2009, Blagojevich was indicted along with his brother Robert, Chief of Staff John Harris, Chris Kelly, William Cellini and former Chief of Staff, Alonzo (Lon) Monk. Blagojevich, along with the others pled not guilty.

Even if he was out of jail during the on-going federal criminal investigation, federal authorities were tightening the case against him. In July of 2009, John Harris changed his plea to guilty and agreed to testify against Blagojevich. It was not until June of 2010 that Blagojevich, along with his brother Robert went to trial in a federal courtroom in Chicago.

The first trial of Blagojevich ended with a deadlocked jury with a lone holdout not convinced of Blagojevich's guilt. In August of 2010, Federal Judge James Zagel declared a mistrial and announced that a new trial would take place.

After another round of media tours, this one including a now-famous appearance on Donald Trump's show called *The Apprentice* in March of 2011, a new trial began in April of 2011. This time, federal prosecutors dropped charges against Blagojevich's brother, Robert, and focused completely on the case against Rod.

There were over twenty counts brought against Blagojevich in the new trial and on June 27th, 2011, a different jury found Blagojevich guilty on 17 of those charges. Blagojevich's reaction was classic. When asked about the guilty verdicts, Blagojevich said, "I frankly, am stunned."

According to records, a key part of the evidence that resulted in the unanimous verdict was the attempt by Blagojevich to obtain a Cabinet position in the Obama Administration in exchange for naming Valarie Jarrett to the U.S. Senate to replace Obama.

After more appeals and other legal filings, the inevitable occurred. On December 7th, 2011, Blagojevich was sentenced to 14 years in federal prison. It had been almost three since the time he was arrested outside of his home in Chicago. Blagojevich was finally sentenced. It was not until March 15th of 2012 that he reported to prison in Englewood Colorado to begin serving his sentence.

Blagojevich then began a series of appeals, the first on December 13th, 2013.

The initial appeal was denied but on July 21, 2015, during another appeal, five of the counts against him were thrown out. The fact that several of the convictions were overturned did not result in a reduced sentence. Sentencing was a separate matter. The final appeal as to the remaining counts which had not been dismissed continued until they reached the U.S. Supreme Court. In March of 2016, the U.S. Supreme Court refused to hear the case. The conviction on the remaining counts was sustained.

After the convictions on the remaining counts were upheld, there were also appeals regarding the length of the 14-year sentence. The original sentencing judge, James Zagel, would also be the judge to hear the initial appeal to reduce the sentence length based on the fact some of the counts had been dismissed. Zagel, not to anyone's surprise, refused to reduce the 14-year sentence. In August of 2016, the 14-year sentence was maintained by Zagel. In April of 2017, Blagojevich's legal team filed an appeal of the decision to maintain the 14-year sentence in a further effort to get the sentence reduced. These appeals also went all the way to the United States Supreme Court. The U.S. Supreme Court refused to hear that appeal. It appeared as if the fourteen-year sentence would have to be served.

There was, however, one final chance though for that to change. Power to make any change to the conviction or the sentence would require action by the President of The United States. Obama was not about to consider any leniency for Blagojevich.

When Donald Trump took office, Blagojevich supporters, led by his wife Patti, encouraged the President to review the case and consider pardoning Blagojevich.

Trump tweeted about the case back in May of 2018 and that single tweet set off a firestorm in Illinois among Republicans and Democrats.

In June of 2018, lawyers for Blagojevich officially filed paperwork for leniency.

In August of 2019, Trump announced he would consider commuting Blagojevich's sentence to time served. Members of the Illinois GOP Congressional delegation advised trump against any leniency.

Despite that request, on February 18, 2020, Trump issued a Presidential Commutation of the remaining years of the sentence. More on that later. On February 19th, 2020, after 8 years in federal prison, Blagojevich walked out of a Colorado federal prison a free man.

Chapter Seventeen
A Brand New Deck

In addition to the Presidential Election which resulted in Barack Obama becoming the first-ever African-American President of the United States, 2008 was an election year for the Illinois House and Senate. I won re-election without opposition in November of 2008. It was the fourth time I had been elected. The 95th General Assembly had been a memorable one for certain. When the gavel came down on January 13th, 2009 and the motion was made by Representative Barbara Currie to end the session Sine Die, history had been made with the impeachment of Blagojevich.

Due to timing issues related to the Sine Die of the 95th General Assembly, the decision was made that since a new Senate and House was being established when Members took their oath, it was necessary for the incoming House to once again pass an Impeachment Resolution. An Impeachment Resolution coming from the House of Representatives of the 96th General Assembly could then be acted on with a trail by the incoming Senate which would soon be sworn in and compose the 96th General Assembly.

On January 14th, 2009, a day after the adjournment of the 95th General Assembly Sine Die the Inauguration of House Members of the 96th General Assembly took place. Once again, the Inauguration took place at the University of Illinois in Springfield and it was once again Secretary of State Jesse White who stepped to the podium. "The House of Representatives of the 96th General Assembly of the State of Illinois will come to order", blasted through the sound system of the auditorium. White asked that the House be led in prayer by Pastor Thomas Cross. Thomas Cross is the father of Tom Cross, House GOP Minority Leader. After the prayer, Speaker Madigan led the Members in the Pledge of Allegiance. Roll call was taken, it was reported that 118 Representative-elects answered the roll call.

Judge Alan J. Grieman, a retired Illinois Appellate Judge, led the 118 individuals in reciting the oath of office. Each of the 118 then signed two copies of a written version of the oath that was to be turned in later in the day. The new 96th House of Representatives for the State of Illinois was sworn in and ready to conduct business.

Representative Barbara Currie led the nomination of Michael Madigan as Speaker on behalf of the Democrats. Legendary State representative Bill Black of Danville, Illinois then led the nomination of Tom Cross as Speaker for the GOP. I say these two led the nominations because several other State Reps from each party seconded the nominations. There was no doubt which of the two would prevail as Speaker. After a roll call vote along party lines, Madigan was once again elected as Speaker by a 70-48 margin. The Democrats held a firm majority, just one vote shy of veto-proof in the 96th General Assembly. Cross was once again elected Minority Leader. GOP Representatives were abandoning the tradition of everyone voting unanimously for the Speaker.

After being sworn in as Speaker, Madigan delivered his acceptance speech and during that speech reminded everyone of the fact that Illinois Government operated within a *separation of powers* structure. Madigan highlighted that the House of Representatives holds the power to impeach. Those powers can be used, if necessary to impeach Executive and Judicial officers. He went on to say that the power was rarely used and that until recently the Illinois House had never impeached a Governor. The last time that a Supreme Court justice was successfully impeached was 1833. Describing the evidence against Blagojevich as, "Crystal clear," he congratulated House Members on carrying out their duties under these powers. The recent impeachment was the centerpiece of Madigan's message that day.

In his acceptance speech as Minority Leader, Tom Cross spoke about the need for the House to continue to work together. "There are huge problems that we have to work together on and, Mr. Speaker, and to those on your side of the aisle, we want to work together and rebuild that trust to regain the confidence of the voters and just as important, to make sure that those challenges that all we have talked about today are met or at least there is an attempt to solve those problems." The message was appropriate; there was a big question of trust in government from the people of Illinois. The people had just witnessed a Governor who was involved in various dishonest activities spanning many years; too many years in my opinion. Remember, it took handcuffs and a federal indictment to get the Madigan to initiate proceedings to remove Blagojevich from office.

This time, due to unique circumstances, the Inauguration Ceremony had an added feature.

Madigan explained it to the gathered crowd, "The Rules Committee will now meet. If the Members of the Rules Committee will come forward. Ladies and Gentlemen, for those of you who are in the audience, ordinarily we would have finished our proceedings for today, but as we know, we have been living in extraordinary times. The Rules Committee is meeting to approve for consideration two additional Resolutions.

One would be concerned with the recreation of the House Committee on Impeachment which reported to the House where we voted on the Impeachment..."; "The other Resolution would be identical to the Resolution adopted...and it would call for the impeachment of Rod Blagojevich." He went on to explain that this second vote on impeachment was recommended by lawyers for legal purposes to ensure that the impeachment would withstand any challenges due to the fact that the Senate would soon become a newly sworn-in body as part of the 96th General Assembly.

House Rules Committee chair, Barbara Currie then reported to the House Members that House Resolution 4 of the 96th General Assembly simply recreated the Special Investigative Committee. House Resolution 4 was adopted by voice vote. I was once again named to the Investigative Committee.

Currie then introduced House Resolution 5 (HR5). This contained the exact language of the Impeachment Resolution which had passed in the 95th General Assembly and HR5 if successfully passed would impeach Blagojevich, once more. This time the impeachment would be by the 96th House of Representatives. Both Currie and House GOP Member and lead person of the Republicans on the Special Investigative Committee, Jim Durkin, made statements in support of HR5 and then a roll call vote took place. Madigan earlier explained that, in the interest of time, both sides agreed to one person to speak on HR5. This time, the vote was 117-1 with Blagojevich's sister-in-law, Debbie Mell, voting 'no' rather 'present' as she had voted in the 95th General Assembly.

It was now double official and Blagojevich was impeached by both the 95th and 96th General Assemblies. The Senate could then officially begin the Impeachment trial which started on January 26th as previously detailed. The folks attending this Inauguration Ceremony were able to view more than just a typical House Inauguration. They were part of history in the making.

The impeachment and removal from office of Rod Blagojevich in January of 2009 were significant. It was certainly historical, as he was the first-ever Governor in Illinois to be impeached (twice) and later removed from office. It was also significant because it provided everyone an opportunity to start fresh.

The State of Illinois was severely damaged during the 6 years of Blagojevich's time as Governor. It was on the verge of fiscal collapse.

Pat Quinn was sworn into office on January 30th as the new Governor. This was the same night that Blagojevich was removed from office by a unanimous vote of the Illinois Senate. Quinn, along with Members of the 96th General Assembly now faced significant challenges.

People were waiting to see how Pat Quinn was going to handle the new role and the challenges we faced. Quinn was no newcomer to Illinois politics. He served as an aide to Illinois Governor Dan Walker, Illinois 36th Governor from 1973-1977. This is the same Dan Walker who had served time in prison after a 1987 conviction for bank fraud after having served as Governor.

In the late 1970s Quinn earned a reputation as a reformer and political activist when he led the *Illinois Initiative*. The purpose of the *Illinois Initiative* was to increase the use and power of public referendums. He led a successful petition drive to present the idea to voters but the initiative was never voted on because the Illinois Supreme Court ruled that it was unconstitutional.

Quinn started another organization called *The Coalition for Political Honesty* in 1980. This group successfully led a campaign to reduce the size of the Illinois General Assembly from 177 Members in the Illinois House to 118. This time, Quinn was successful in championing an Amendment to the Illinois Constitution. It was known as the 'Cut Back Amendment'.

Admittedly, amending the State Constitution is not an easy thing to do as it takes a super-majority of votes made by the citizens of the State in 1980. His effort to pass the change was helped by the fact that the Illinois House had recently voted itself a 40% pay raise. People were angry and they made that fact known. Quinn gained statewide name recognition with this effort.

He was first elected to statewide office in 1991 as State Treasurer. He got into a public argument with then-Secretary of State George Ryan during his term as Treasurer and decided to run against Ryan in 1994 to oust Ryan and become Secretary of State. He lost that election to Ryan.

Quinn also lost to become the Democrat nominee for the United States Senate in 1996. Senator Paul Simon, a tremendously popular United States Senator from Illinois, had served in the U.S. Senate for 12 years before deciding not to run for re-election in 1996. Quinn decided to jump into that race with the blessing of Simon. However, Quinn lost that primary to Dick Durbin, who later won the General election and became United States Senator. Durbin continues in that role to this day.

Quinn got back into the political arena in 2002 when he won the Democratic Primary for Lt. Governor. Those were the days when the Lt. Governor and Governor ran separately. Today, they are on the same ticket. Quinn won the 2002 Democratic Primary for Lt. Governor and then was elected Lt. Governor of Illinois, along with Rod Blagojevich in November of 2002. He served in that capacity from 2003 until the removal of Blagojevich from the office of Governor. As the Illinois Constitution calls for, he was sworn in as Illinois' 41st governor.

He had always kept a safe distance from Blagojevich. In December of 2008, after the arrest of Blagojevich, when asked about his relationship with Blagojevich, Quinn stated, "Well, he is a bit isolated. I tried to talk to the Governor, but the last time I spoke with him was in August of 2007." Blagojevich, back in 2006, announced that Quinn should not be considered part of his administration.

This clear separation from Blagojevich, coupled with his experience in government made Quinn someone that might be able to heal wounds and move us forward. He was facing significant challenges for sure. I was prepared to give him a chance.

I found his words from the night he was sworn in to be a good start:

"In this moment our hearts are hurt. It is very important that all of us understand that we have a duty, a mission, to restore the faith of the people of Illinois in the integrity of our government and to make sure that all of our elected officials have the confidence of the voters. I think this is our highest calling," he said. "I think that is what we have to do in the coming days."

I was also ready to have the House and Senate function as intended. Maybe there would be a new spirit of cooperation. I was once again operating in the minority, and the House Republicans had only 48 votes. If you understand math at all, when it takes 60 votes to even advance a bill out of the House for consideration in the Senate, you better be willing to work with members on the other side of the aisle. Many great public servants are serving as State Representatives in Springfield today.

Unfortunately, there are also a few 'do-nothings' in the Illinois House today who simply whine, moan and complain. They are self-serving, self-righteous and practice self-praise. Believe it or not, there is currently a group of Representatives in the minority party of the Illinois House who refers to themselves as the, "Magnificent Seven."

The basic math facts, the 'Rule of Sixty' faced me again as I tried to make progress on several issues that I was working on. The focus on Blagojevich, the budget crisis and then impeachment resulted in a negative effect on the last couple of years. It was, in my mind, time to get busy and make up for the lost time. I did have a bigger office in the Stratton building with a window and corner view. My license plate was now 70, I gained another 10 spots in seniority.

My committee assignments in the 96th House continued to be mostly education associated. I was named to the Elementary and Secondary Appropriations Committee, Computer Technology (where I served as Minority Spokesperson), Elementary and Secondary Education (regular non-appropriation related), and Revenue and Finance. In addition, I was named to serve on the Public Policy and Accountability Committee, Infrastructure Committee and became Minority Spokesperson of a new committee called the Education Reform Committee.

In a somewhat rare move, I was named as *co-chair* of the Education Reform Committee. The other Co-chair of the new Education Reform Committee was Democrat Representative Linda Chapa LaVia. Linda was always very hardworking and determined regarding education issues.

She was also a Veteran and was involved in many public policy issues regarding Veterans. I very much enjoyed working with Linda. She was always prepared to listen and consider thoughts of anyone when contemplating public policy issues. I found her to be interested in compromise and solutions. She went on to eventually be named the head of the Illinois Veterans Department.

I say that this was rare because the title of *Co-chair* did not occur very often in the Committee structure of the Illinois House. Normally, the majority party names a Chairman and the Minority party has a Minority Spokesperson. This Sub-committee also had four GOP Members and four Democrats instead of the standard Majority for the Democrats based on the fact that they had a majority of seats in the House. I am not sure of the reason for this change. Maybe it was an attempt to try something new and show a new bi-partisan approach by Madigan after the Blagojevich years.

In previous years, I had gained valuable experience in several areas of public policy. In the 96th General Assembly I had some new assignments. I was no longer on the Gaming, Labor, Higher Education Committees or the Ethanol Committee. I had once served as Minority Spokesperson of the Ethanol Committee, but the Ethanol Committee was no longer a recognized committee in the 96th General Assembly. My standard line was that the Committee did such a great job that it was no longer needed. These types of proposals were now likely being funneled to the Agriculture Committee. All of my previous experiences on several key House Committees during my previous three terms had provided me with experience and knowledge on a wide variety of public policy issues, which proved to be very helpful.

During my fourth term (2009-10), a two year time period, I successfully passed seventeen bills out of the House, through the Senate that were signed into law. I was also the chief House sponsor of five Senate bills that became law. In addition, I passed fourteen House Resolutions.

I worked extremely hard to get all of this done. But, the fact that Rod Blagojevich was gone, and we could concentrate on doing the business of the people was a major reason for the success.

During the recent impeachment of Trump the same type of dynamic was evident. The important work of the United States Congress was set aside due to impeachment proceedings.

I also knew the Rules of the House better than ever before. I knew the system and had learned how to get things done much better than I did in my first few terms. I was never the partisan, self-righteous type of Representative that we see far too much of today. I was able to support public policy proposals which made sense that came from members of either party while maintaining my core values. No question, I was independent-minded and did not always toe the line. That fact did not always sit well with some in the GOP who thought they were in charge of determining the, "Party Platform."

While the Blagojevich criminal case made its way through the Court System, the General Assembly seemed to recover, at least a little bit, from those disastrous years. We would hear some updates about the criminal trial from time to time. It was difficult not to follow the case. The crazy attempts by Blagojevich to use the media to garner public support brought about head shaking and laughter on the House floor. The details of the telephone call transcripts and chronic corruption Blagojevich was involved in were made very public and very few were fooled by his antics.

As mentioned, during the two years of the 96th General Assembly, I was successful in guiding seventeen ideas through the process that became law.

In the first year of the two years of the 96th General Assembly, ten bills passed through the House and Senate that became law.

The same process I detailed earlier was still necessary for an *idea* to become a *law*. Somehow though, the process seemed easier to me. Perhaps it was the years of experience coupled with what seemed to be a new spirit of cooperation in the General Assembly. Previous years were so acrimonious under Blagojevich.

The process was the same, each of these ten bills began in draft form after the Legislative Research Bureau (LRB) was contacted by either me or a staff member with merely an *idea* in the form of a proposal to change or add to existing Illinois public policy. After I received the draft form back from the LRB, I made any necessary changes and sent it back for a final draft to be written. If the changes were made to my satisfaction, the bill was introduced and read into the record by the House Clerk. This *first reading* usually took place during a perfunctory session of the House. Once read into the record by the House Clerk, the proposal would go to Rules Committee and, if it garnered a majority of votes in the Rules Committee, the measure would be assigned to a substantive or standing committee. I would attend the appropriate committee hearing and explain the bill to the committee members. If the bill received a majority in that committee, it went to the House floor where it was placed on *second reading*. Amendments to the language could be made while the bill was on second reading.

The bill was moved to *third reading* after an explanation and approval of the full House membership. Normally this move from second to third was made with a *voice* vote, "In the opinion of the chair, the ayes have it." Sometimes, if the bill was at all controversial, a roll call vote would be taken for the measure to move from second to third reading. Once on third reading, the bill could be called for a final vote.

Once on third reading, the measure could not be amended. This is when the voting takes place. Most of the time, a simple majority vote was all that was needed to pass the bill out of the House on third reading. There are a few exceptions when a supermajority vote is necessary for passage. An example of that is when a proposal affects 'Home

Rule' powers. Larger municipalities retain Home Rule powers unless legislation specifically intends to diminish these powers. The exceptions as to when the supermajority vote is necessary are spelled out in the House Rule handbook with which I had become very familiar.

Once a bill was successfully passed in the House, a Senate sponsor was needed, the measure would need to be filed in the Senate, and the entire process would start again in the Senate. If the bill receives the required majority vote in both the House and Senate, the final step was for the governor to either sign the bill into law (Public Act) or veto the bill. In the case of a veto, the General Assembly can act to override the veto. An override requires a super-majority vote rather than a simple majority. Sometimes, the governor makes only minor changes to the bill and the original sponsor can simply file a motion to accept the changes made by the governor.

I review this process to emphasize that it is a long road, most of the time, for any proposal to become a law. During this process, there are constituents and lobbyists to work with as well. Getting support and finding groups or individuals to work for the proposal is critical. In 2009, I was able to, with the assistance and input of many others, shepherd these ten proposals from the idea phase into law:

- HB613 became Public Act (P.A.) 96-081. This allows for certain public bids accepted by schools to be accepted through an electronic bid process once important requirements are met related to publication and transparency are met.

- HB 942 became P.A. 96-0510 and requires the Secretary of State to provide information regarding E-85 vehicles to all recipients of license plate renewal notices.

- HB944 became P.A. 96-0668 and changed the calculation used by the State Board of Education when determining the financial rating of a school district. The State Board would now be required to consider the amount of the outstanding (late) payments from the State that was due to the school district in the rating. Schools were often classified in lower financial rating categories simply because the State had not made scheduled payments. The late payments made it appear as if the school district was not performing well when the poor finances were due

236

to the lack of payments. If schools were not getting their promised funding, then a new calculation and rating would allow for this fact to be revealed.

- HB999 became P.A. 96-0019 and established some flexibility for school districts in establishing a line of credit at financial institutions other than banks. This was necessary due to the fiscal problems the state was facing and the delay in payments to schools which required so much borrowing by school districts.

- HB1079 became P.A. 96-0194 and was the result of years of work and dealt with the issue of dual credit. I had previously, through a House Joint Resolution (HJR) established a Task Force to study and recommend changes to the practice of students earning dual credit while enrolled in high school. Students, while still enrolled in high school, were enrolled in some classes at their high school that was classified as dual credit courses. That meant in addition to the high school credit, they would also receive college credit through dual enrollment at a local Community College. Today, there are 39 public community college districts composed of 48 community colleges. The system in place allowed for each of these community colleges to establish an understanding with the high schools in their territory. These various agreements served as the template for what would constitute a course eligible for dual credit.

The idea was popular and the enrollment of high school age students into community colleges increased with the infusion of these dual credit students. In my school district we established a written Memo of Understanding with the Illinois Eastern Community College (IECC) District. Together, our administration worked with the IECC to determine which of the courses that we offered locally on our campus should be eligible as dual credit classes.

The K-12 school district was still allowed to claim state aid for the student. It was also advantageous for the community college district because they were allowed to claim state aid for the same student as well. This aid is known as Full-time Equivalency (FTE). If the course were taught at the high school, the local school district typically paid all of the expenses associated with the course offering and the community college would still receive FTE funding. In many instances, because of this, tuition was not charged to the students. The student would earn credit toward college thus reducing the future cost of attending college. Easy to see why the program was very popular all over the State and gaining popularity each passing day.

As the program grew in popularity, there began to be concerns about the quality of the high school coursework being identified as dual credit eligible. There was not much of a question about the courses taught at the community colleges that could also count as high school credit. However, mounting concerns about the overall quality of some of the credits being issued which originated from the high school courses grew to a point that some institutions of higher education at the university level were becoming hesitant to accept any college credits earned on high school campuses. This was a real threat to the future of a program that was not only popular; it was a threat to the entire existence of dual credit. If implemented correctly, dual credit could provide an incentive for young people to attend college once they graduated high school.

The *Dual Credit Quality Task Force* that I established during the 95th General Assembly met three times, once at Governors State University in the northern part of Illinois and twice in Springfield. A final report of the findings and recommendations was released in December of 2008. The recommendations focused on how the program could continue to provide the obvious positive components while addressing the growing concerns of higher education institutions. The Task Force was made up of 28 members representing higher education, teacher unions, community colleges, K-12 education, career centers as well as business and industry. I served as Chair of that Task Force. The legislation we introduced during the 96th General Assembly came as a direct result of the work of that Task Force.

As with the work of any Task Force that included such a wide range of interests, not all of the concerns and desires of all of the participants were completely satisfied. As a group, we were able to agree on several key components.

The first agreement resulted in adopting three stated goals of the Task Force: 1) Ensure quality, 2) Improve access, equity and attainment, and 3) Increased accountability. Each of these three goals later included corresponding recommendations for public policies to be established into law. While, as stated, this does not end the need for future review of the program and likely continual changes, this measure was instrumental in saving dual credit in Illinois at that time. The bill had dozens of co-sponsors in the House and passed both the House and Senate unanimously. For many reasons, it is one of the most important issues that I was involved in during my time in the House.

The remaining success stories in 2009 were:

- HB1108 which became P.A. 96-0568. At the request of Regional Superintendents in Illinois we made changes to the structure and some of the functions of ROE advisory boards.

- HB2619 became P.A. 96-0517 and was special to me because it involved the hard work of an entire community, a committed and talented school superintendent, and bi-partisan spirit and cooperation. More detail on this legislation is necessary to understand how important it was.

    As a result of a devastating flood, the high school in Martinsville, Illinois had been left in shambles. The building would need to be replaced. Working with a very talented and committed school superintendent, we determined that Martinsville was eligible for both state and federal support to help build a new school in Martinsville. We held a joint meeting with staff from the office of Congressman Tim Johnson to determine what could be done. During our meeting, we discovered that there were, in fact, grants available at the state and federal level that could provide a great deal of assistance in the effort to build a new school. Those grants would require some level of matching funds from the Martinsville school tax base to make it happen.

    There was one major problem though. Even though the community was supportive of a bond issue to ensure the necessary local match, existing law did not allow the bonds to be issued without special legislation that would allow the school district, in this particular case, to exceed the existing statutory bond limit.

Using language narrowly defined to allow for the bonding authority to exceed the current statute, and if the Regional Superintendent used existing authority to declare the building closed due to the flood damage, I introduced legislation to allow the local board to exceed the existing limit and issue the bonds necessary to provide the local match.

During this time, I became aware that another school district in Illinois had a similar problem. The Gillespie School District, south of Springfield, was experiencing severe damage to buildings due to mine subsidence. That school district also needed to build a new school and was also not able to issue bonds for the amount that was necessary to pay their portion of the cost to build and repair their buildings. Working with my colleague, Representative Tom Holbrook (he represented the Gillespie area), I amended my proposal to include his need and together we were able to get the bill through the House with 95 votes. It was a great bipartisan show of support by House Members. Often this type of legislation, which allows a local school board to exceed statutory bond limits, also results in a higher tax levy. Many Members will not vote for this type of proposal no matter the circumstances. In fairness, this type of vote often results in attack ads in the next election.

With the tremendous help from Martinsville Superintendent Jill Rogers, and the bi-partisan support shown by Holbrook, a new High School was built in Martinsville now serves a new generation of young people. I smile every time I drive by.

- HB2674 became P.A. 96-0401. This measure made some changes to the existing laws regarding school districts facing difficult fiscal issues. This dealt with the implementation of Financial Oversight Panels (FOP's). The State's fiscal condition coupled with the ongoing recession caused severe financial problems in many Illinois Schools. A much more substantial study of these panels and additional changes would take place in 2010.

- HB2675 turned into P.A. 96-0689. This measure allowed for schools, in the case of school closing related to public health concerns, to collect state aid for the days that school was not in session due to the public health crisis which forced the school to close. It required that schools work with local public health officials to determine if schools should be closed. In circumstances like that, the school would not have to consider fiscal issues or lose any state funding in the event of a serious epidemic. This has assisted schools in multiple instances since the year it was passed into law. This type of public policy flexibility was important during the Corona Virus pandemic in the spring of 2020.

As the year 2009 ended, I felt a sense of satisfaction. The General Assembly was a much more pleasant place to conduct business. Everything was going fine at Hutsonville Schools as well. Despite the difficult economic times, we found a way to balance our budget and improve our programs. Due to the availability of federal stimulus funding, we were able to renovate a building once used for vocational classes into a Special Education center to serve autistic children. The building serves multiple school districts to this day.

Teachers and administrators agreed to a pay freeze and budgets were cut drastically.

We, like most other districts were getting by because of the dedication of the staff. No doubt that our teachers purchased necessary supplies for their classrooms out of their own pockets again that year and got by the best they could. All the while, Julie Kraemer was gaining valuable experience as an 'acting superintendent' during my absence.

The average price of a gallon of gasoline had dropped to $2.73 and the Hubble Telescope was repaired in May of 2009. We all heard about the heroic efforts of a guy named Chesly B. Sullenberger (later became known as just Sully). He was the pilot of U.S. Airways Flight 1549 that made an emergency landing in the Hudson River. On June 25th of 2009, pop star Michael Jackson died of an overdose. Harry Potter was still popular at the box office.

When we returned to Springfield in January of 2010 for the second year spring session of the 96th General Assembly, I was hopeful that the General Assembly would continue to be as pleasant as it was in the previous year.

Whether you were a Democrat or a Republican though, everyone knew there would soon be one major change. Representative Bill Black of Danville decided to retire after 2010. He had served in the House since 1986 and could accurately be described as a legendary icon. He was the GOP floor leader for much of that time. The floor leader is the person responsible for most of the questions asked during floor debate prior to the third reading vote on legislation. Bill was arguably the best ever in that role. He could holler and scream one minute about some horrible bill before us and then minutes later get the entire legislature to belly laugh with his wit, humor and wisdom.

There was at one time, a House ritual that all freshman legislators had to endure when they introduced their first bill to members on the House floor. Members of the House from both sides of the aisle would playfully or painfully, depending on your point of view, question the freshman sponsor about their bill. For that reason, normally a freshman chose a bill that was very minor in nature for their first bill. I know I did.

Bill Black would invariably ask the freshman lawmaker questions there was no way they could answer. Often times, his questions were about the legislative process or some questionable language in the bill, accusing the newbie of bringing forward a proposal that was clearly unconstitutional or worse. I cannot remember the number of times I heard Bill Black say something to the effect that, "This is the single worst bill I have ever seen introduced in all of my years on the House floor!" It was hysterical. In almost every case, he would ask the freshman representative to, "Take the bill out of the record," and have it amended. Later, he along with almost everyone else would vote in favor of the bill. That only came after the initial votes were 'no'. The big boards located at each side of the chamber displayed the votes of Members. The boards were almost entirely red to start with until slowly, ever so slowly turning green.

All freshmen legislators were warned to take the kidding in good spirit and not become too upset. The very few times that Members get upset resulted in an actual red board staying red and the failure of the bill. I can remember that happening only a very few times. They should have chosen a less controversial bill for their first piece of legislation.

A couple of times, Black had to admit that he was serious and that there was a major problem with the legislation.

It was hard to know if he was serious about objections until the last second. I understand that, sometime after I retired from the House, the ritual of freshman bill orientation ended. Some might have claimed this was a form of bullying. I guess by some definition might be. There was never intent to cause harm though. I think it is a shame if the practice has ceased. The practice allowed for levity and some good bi-partisan jostling.

Bill Black often said most of his theatrics were a result of his past life on the stage in various acting roles. He could certainly play many roles. On any particular bill before the House, he could go from angry, to elated, to perplexed, back to outrage several times on the same bill. And then, in an instant, he was often not sure about the proposal. When he was opposed, or he was speaking for the minority opposing a proposal, Bill could silence the entire body with his oratory and booming voice.

He carried our message well. Just when I thought he was going to lose it, or maybe have a heart attack based on his outrage, I would look over and he would be sitting in his chair laughing and joking around with the staff. One night, they removed Bill from the House floor on a stretcher and many thought he had had the big one. It turned out not to be a heart attack after all and both sides of the aisle were relieved.

Much of what Bill did was part of an act. He often said that he did not take himself very seriously. That statement was always followed by a statement that he, "Always take the process seriously." I remember his iconic rants when describing the House Rules. He was hard on the Democrats daily about the way they were proposing budgets and railed against the annual unbalanced budgets, often warning them that a day of reckoning was going to come. Long before most people, he understood that the out of control spending, shorting of pension payments and other fiscal schemes like fund raids would lead to a fiscal crisis for Illinois. He was correct.

When Bill announced his retirement, everyone speculated as to who would replace him as floor leader. The truth was that nobody could really replace him. He finished the 2010 year and retired in early in 2011. When I returned to the House floor after a weekend, early in the 2011 session, I was assigned to a different seat. My nameplate was now occupying the seat where Representative Black had previously sat. When I walked to the new location and stood in front of the microphone, a tear came to my eye. I apparently was chosen to attempt to help fill the shoes of Representative Black. Officially, I was one of several Representatives that Tom Cross had identified to fill the obvious void left by Black. Unofficially, partially due to where I was now seated, and the fact that I worked directly with the team of staff members who had supported Black daily in his time as floor leader, most now considered me to be the new GOP floor leader. It was a huge new responsibility.

(Debating my colleagues on House Floor in my role as floor leader- Roger Eddy personal photo)

Over the next few weeks, I settled into the new role and thoroughly enjoyed it. I read dozens of bills and worked after hours to learn about the legislation we were scheduled to debate the following days and weeks. I was thrilled when one of my former legislative staff was assigned to assist me in the new role.

Laura Roche came to the Statehouse as an intern at my request. I asked then GOP House Chief of Staff, Scott Reimers, to strongly consider her application for an internship in the House. The Internship program was through the University of Illinois at Springfield (UIS). Laura was working on her Master's Degree at UIS at the time and had previously volunteered at my district legislative office in Hutsonville, working with Kathleen Rankin.

After looking over her application, Scott agreed to have Laura in the program and assigned her to my office. With the increased workload and all of the bills I was working on plus the added responsibilities of floor leader; I needed assistance. Laura came highly recommended. Of course, most interns are highly recommended on paper. I knew the recommendations regarding Laura were spot on because in addition to working with Kathleen in my local legislative office, she grew up in

Crawford County and attended Robinson High School. Her father and mother were both teachers.

Laura did a great job as my intern and when I assumed the duties of floor leader, she worked even harder to make sure that my legislative agenda did not fall aside due to the additional duties. Then, when a vacancy occurred on the House floor among staff members who support the floor leader, I requested that Laura fill that position. She excelled in that role as well. I was so fortunate to have her and others assist me.

There was something called the 'bill box' which was located directly behind the floor leader's seat on the House floor. The box contained various research and notes that were relevant to the hundreds of bills filed and potentially up for debate. The use of the bill box was critical to performing the duties of the floor leader. Laura became the person that handled the bill box.

The new duties were a challenge but a welcome one. I had the necessary support to perform the role and still was able to pass several pieces of legislation in 2010. Many of the proposals that passed during the second year of the 96th General Assembly were items I had worked on for several years. Among the successes:

HB4711 became P.A. 96-1441. This was intended to allow school districts some relief from unfunded mandates. It required a school district to identify a mandate that they would like to waive, have a public hearing and then seek permission from the Regional Superintendent of Schools to waive the required statute.

This meant that for most new mandates passed after the effective date of the bill, schools would not be required to enact the mandate unless a separate specific appropriation was made to pay for the mandate. For existing mandates passed into law prior to the effective date of the legislation, the process for waiving the mandate allowed for the local district to request a waiver from the Regional Superintendent. Any such request would have to include a public hearing. The legislation was far more limiting than what I would have liked and involved a lot of unnecessary red tape. It also included some exemptions that I would rather not have included.

Remember my philosophy regarding the perfect not becoming the enemy of good?

This was a start and I was hopeful schools would use the new authority to challenge unfunded mandates in the future. Regretfully, this waiver authority has not been used very often. Mandate relief for public education is still a topic of debate in Illinois.

HB4717 became P.A. 96-1135 and dealt with Electric Vehicle license plates.

HB4879 became P.A. 96-1264 and allowed preschool-aged children to ride regular school bus routes without financial penalty to the school district. Before this public act, any preschool-aged student riding on a regular bus route negatively affected the transportation reimbursement formula for school districts. Sometimes that meant schools would establish a separate bus route for preschool-aged children to avoid the negative affect. Two kids, often relatively the same age and from the same family might be on different busses and bus routes until this law was passed.

I am happy to say that is no longer the case, school districts can now allow these kids on the same bus without harming their transportation aid.

HB 96-1046 is now P.A. 96-1446 and tightened up reporting requirements related to students with disabilities.

HB5511 is now P.A. 96-1046. This proposal addressed an issue regarding the way Illinois Municipal Retirement Funds (IMRF) are calculated, levied and collected by schools for some employee's pension contribution in schools known as Cooperative High Schools. Paris, Illinois is the home of the State's only Cooperative High School existing at this time.

HB5863 is now P.A. 96-1489 and deals with requirements related to substitute teacher criminal background checks and how the records related to those background checks are maintained.

HB6041 is now P.A. 96-1277 and allows Chicago Public Schools (CPS) and all other school districts in Illinois the flexibility to transfer funds between various designated accounts. It specifically allows the transfer of funds from the Working Cash Fund to the fund determined most in need by the Board of Education. I add the fact that Chicago is included in this public act because CPS is covered by a different section of law than all other public schools in the state. Although this might be necessary due to the unique nature of CPS and its' structure, it often allows CPS to escape some of the unfunded mandates thrust upon all other schools. I often offered to amend legislation by including CPS in the mandate. If it was such a great idea for our schools, we should invite CPS to also enjoy the mandate, right? CPS officials would oppose any attempt to include them and I was often unsuccessful with my attempt to amend the mandate bill due to that opposition. In this case, they loved the idea of additional fund flexibility and requested to be included in the law.

Those were the proposals I brought forward that became law in 2010. In addition, as mentioned, I was also the Chief House Sponsor of legislation originating in the Senate regarding additional Financial Oversight Panel regulations for K-12 School Districts. Senator Kimberly Lightford was the Senate sponsor. The legislation is very technical, detailed, and somewhat confusing as it dealt with very specific school finance and funding formulas and accompanying laws. It was negotiated with all K-12 stakeholders and seen as a significant improvement in the financial oversight of public schools in Illinois. It was a sign of respect to me that Senator Lightford, a Democrat, requested that I carry the bill in the House.

Easily the most controversial bill that I dealt with in 2010 in regards to education was one I did not sponsor. A proposal by Senator James Meeks to allow for a private school voucher program to be established in Illinois became a very memorable proposal. As a public school educator, I am and always have been opposed to public funds being provided to students in private schools via vouchers. What I am in favor of is a fair and **equitable** funding formula. I believe that private vouchers and charters divert public funds away from the equitable support for all students. However, I do support **public** charter schools.

Many strongly disagree and that is fine. There are some good arguments to be made for providing an opportunity for what some consider a better education by the use of private vouchers. The issue is that ALL students should benefit from **public** funds. Some argue that vouchers would eventually improve the education of all due to the competition they provide. This is a weak argument that does not compare apples to apples.

In March of 2010, Senator Meeks successfully passed SB2494, a private voucher bill, out of the Senate. It was designed to allow for the diversion of public funds to a private voucher program that would serve students in schools rating poor performing in Chicago only. The original legislation as passed in the Senate was amended in the House before being called for a vote in May. I was strongly opposed to the bill. Many others were also strongly opposed. The State Board of Education confirmed that there would be a fiscal impact on other school districts if the measure passed. The State Board of Education was officially neutral but privately opposed the legislation. They were careful about public opposition due to the politics involved.

After a long and very contentious floor debate, which included the Senate sponsor James Meeks appearing in the House and standing in front of me while almost begging me to not continue speaking against the bill, the measure failed to gain enough votes. It was difficult to ignore Meek's plea. I had worked with Meeks on several proposals before that day and supported many of his ideas related to education reform. Not this one though!

SB2494 was defeated and the sponsor of the Amendment which served as the vehicle for the legislation, Representative Kevin Joyce of Chicago, filed a motion to put the bill on what is called the 'order of postponed consideration.' That meant that he was going to look for additional votes and perhaps try again later in the session. He tried to find additional votes for the proposal but the bill died when the 96th General Assembly ended. The School Choice Act had failed, for the moment.

My vote against the proposal, along with the fact that I revealed the bill was poorly drafted and terribly flawed in many aspects led to some nasty articles from conservative Republican publications. Numerous political threats followed. According to these self-proclaimed experts regarding the GOP platform, real Republicans would never vote against a school choice bill. Although I took much of the heat for the bill failing, at least a dozen other House Republican Members joined me in voting against the proposal. It was truly poorly written and a completely unfair proposal and it didn't take long to shine a light on the flaws.

Never the less, some self-proclaimed party leaders were determined to make me pay for my opposition. Of course, none of the most vocal critics had ever successfully held public office at the State level, although one of them though came in fifth in a seven-person primary for Illinois Governor in February of 2010, losing by over 40,000 votes. I suppose that made him an expert and an authority on the GOP platform? For years, he continued to write an occasional nasty article and post on social media sites in an attempt to discredit my reputation. To this day, I am not sure exactly why he continues to be hateful. Maybe as the young folks say, and as popularized in a song from Taylor Swift, "Haters Gonna Hate."

I sponsored dozens of congratulatory or memorial House Resolutions during 2009 and 2010 as well. One that was very special to me was HR1341 which honored Bev Turkal for her outstanding career upon her retirement. If you recall, Bev had been one of the two individuals who showed up in my office back in 2001 and asked me to initially consider running for State Representative. That, of course, was not why I filed the Resolution to honor her. The Resolution came as the result of dozens of requests from educators from throughout the state to recognize and honor Bev's service to public education. Bev also served on the State Board of Education and also as President of Lincoln Trail College after her retirement.

I also sponsored a Resolution honoring a Veteran named Sammy Davis. Sammy was a Vietnam War Veteran who had received the Congressional Medal of Honor for bravery in battle. He was from a little dot on the map called Flat Rock, Illinois. The character Forrest Gump, played by Tom Hanks in the movie with the same name, was based on the service of Sammy Davis. A plaque is erected on Route 33 near his home to honor him.

The final week of the 96th General Assembly took place in early January of 2011. In November of 2010, another election cycle for the Illinois House and Senate took place. I was re-elected to my fifth term and received 76.5% of the General election vote. My opponent was a truly nice guy by the name of Tim Cyr. We had several very cordial appearances together. Elections do not have to be negative. The House Republicans did gain some seats that election cycle and now had 54 Reps compared to 64 for the Democrats. Not nearly the 60 needed to wrestle away the majority.

The general election was over, but the 96th General Assembly was not yet adjourned and had not yet finished their work. Not by a long shot. Between the fall election and the scheduled end to the two-year cycle of the General Assembly, there are several weeks. During this time, there was a veto session during which Representatives have the opportunity to override any vetoes made by the governor. The veto session came and went without too much fanfare.

However, the veto session was calm before the storm. In January, following election years, and after the veto session, there are often a few days when the General Assembly meets during which legislation can still be passed by the members elected to the exiting General Assembly. Some of those Members of the existing elected General Assembly have chosen retirement or possibly been defeated; the session days added in January are commonly referred to as the *lame-duck session.*

Amid the fiscal crisis in Illinois there was widespread speculation that Speaker Madigan and the Democratic majority were going to attempt to pass an income tax increase during the upcoming January *lame-duck session*. Several retiring and/or otherwise non-returning House Members, commonly referred to as *lame ducks,* could now safely vote in favor of a tax increase and not pay a political price.

As the calendar year, 2010 ended. I remember 2010 as the year gold spiked to $1,237 an ounce during the continued recession and British Petroleum experienced a major oil spill in the Gulf of Mexico. It was also the year that President Obama successfully pushed through the U.S. Congress a national healthcare program that came to be known as, "Obamacare."

What Obama had failed to get done in Illinois, he accomplished at the federal level. Parts of that have been found unconstitutional since then and the debate rages on regarding national healthcare. By the way, 2010 was also the year that a 2008 you-tube video of a kid named Justin Bieber was discovered by a talent agent.

What seemed to be on the mind of Illinoisans at the end of 2010 were the looming lame-duck session and the potential of an income tax increase. On January 11th, 2011, the last day of the 96th General Assembly, that is exactly what happened.

Chapter Eighteen
The Chickens Come Home

I can still see clear visions of Representative Bill Black at the end of at least three legislative cycles standing up as our floor leader admonishing the Democrats for yet another irresponsible and unbalanced budget. Bill, along with many others from the GOP, along with some Democrats warned the Democrats that they were creating a fiscal crisis that would **someday** result in a large income tax increase. Like addicts, the Democrats who were addicted to spending, led by Speaker Madigan, could not help themselves until that day arrived. *Someday* became January 11th, 2011, the last scheduled day of the 96th General Assembly. The *lame-duck session* became the setting and **the Chamber** was certainly full of *lame ducks*. Over a dozen Democrat Members of the house had either announced retirement, made a deal for an appointment as a Department Head or had been defeated in the recent November election. It was fertile ground for this type of vote- a vote they could not be held accountable for.

January 11th was the very last day of session for the 96th General Assembly. One of the first bills Democrat Leader Barbara Currie introduced that day was SB3461. This was an extension to an emergency budget authorization package that passed about six months earlier. The purpose of the package was to allow additional time for the Governor to use some extra-ordinary powers the General Assembly had granted Governor Quinn before the spring session expired. The legislation was necessary at that time, prior to the expiration of the spring session, because certain powers related to the budget were powers the General Assembly statutorily held. The thought at that time to justify these powers being transferred to the governor's purview was that while the General Assembly was not in session during the summer and fall, some additional authority might be needed for the governor to manage a very difficult FY11 State Budget. At that time, there was good reason for the extension of such authority.

251

To extend those powers at this particular time was not necessary. Bill Black had retired and now, as floor leader, it was my job to express why there was strong opposition to the bill. First, I pointed out that it was premature to vote on emergency powers if, as suspected, the Democrats were going to push through an income tax increase. The additional revenue created by an income tax increase would significantly reduce the need to extend these powers.

Secondly, the incoming General Assembly should be considered. If this type of flexibility was necessary, the new House and Senate could handle their responsibilities as intended by the separation of powers. A brand new House and Senate, recently elected by the people would soon be sworn in and they could pass some type of emergency powers if they were indeed necessary. This premature action by an outgoing legislature *with over a dozen lame-duck House Members* unnecessarily permitted those ending their terms to decide what would be allowed in the future, beyond their time as elected officials. This, in my mind, usurped the authority of those recently elected.

Finally, I was absolutely certain that the Democrats only passed authority originally for half the year because they were not sure Quinn was going to be elected Governor. If he had not been elected, they would not be interested in these extra-ordinary powers being given to a new GOP Governor.

Pat Quinn had defeated Republican Bill Brady November 2nd by a slim margin and had not necessarily been a heavy favorite going into the election. Quinn received 46.8% of the vote and Brady 45.9%. Quinn won the election by about 33,000 votes out of a total of almost 3.5 million.

The Democrats made sure that if Brady were elected he would not have the same flexibility to manage the budget. This premature action was a purely political maneuver. However, the Democrats had the votes needed to win this purely political battle.

After some blunt and heated debate, SB3461 passed by a 63-51 margin. The additional flexibility would be allowed for another 6 months. One lame-duck vote completed with much more to come.

Currie then introduced SB44. That proposal would have raised the tax on tobacco products. The additional revenue was supposed to help fund education according to the explanation provided by Leader Currie. I have seen debate when Currie was passionate about passing a bill.

I did not see that passion with SB44. I believe there was some type of agreement to attempt to pass the income tax increase bill in exchange for allowing a vote to be taken on this revenue source. Likely, holdouts on the income tax vote and the Democrat side of the aisle insisted that a vote for alternatives to the income tax increase be proposed and voted on before the vote on the income tax increase. That way, they could claim there was no other choice than raising the income tax since other revenue proposals failed.

Very few votes are ever taken when Speaker Madigan did not have a pretty good idea about the outcome. His rollcalls are always calculated and carried out meticulously. There are hard roll calls and there is the Madigan hard roll call. Considering the fact the number of seats he would control in the upcoming, 97th General Assembly, down by six, he needed to manipulate the vote count now. Currie was carrying the water on this one and the die was cast. It was designed to fail and, according to the plan, the tobacco tax increase failed to garner only 51 in favor and 66 against. It might have appeared to be perhaps a small victory. This was not a real win and nonconsequential when compared to the bill that was soon to be called for a vote.

The final version of the language containing the increase in the Illinois income tax would soon be voted on and came in the form of Amendment # 3 to SB2505. This amendment was filed and rushed to the House floor without a substantive committee hearing. The ultimate example of the sinister use of a shell bill- SB2505 became the vehicle for a brand new Amendment that took money out of the pockets of the people of Illinois. This was a glaring example of a non-transparent government at its worst.

The proposed bill would raise the state income tax on individuals from 3% to 5%.

It would also raise the corporate income tax from 4.8% to 7%. This was a 67% increase in individual rates. The Democrat majority's reckless fiscal policies from the last several years were coming home to roost. Yes, Blagojevich had been part of the problem, but the House of Representatives, with Madigan in control the entire time Blagojevich was governor, and also after that, had not done enough to stop him or try anything else. Blagojevich often warned people that Madigan had a plan to increase income taxes. It appeared he was correct.

I reminded Currie that under this proposal, a family of four with an income of $40,000 a year would be paying an additional $800 under this plan. The bill also reduced revenue the local municipalities and county governments would receive by reducing the amount of Local Government Distributive Fund (LGDF) which was, by law, returned to towns and cities all across Illinois. The LGDF distributes revenue back to local governments as a percentage of the sales taxes collected from within that city or county. The irresponsible, reckless budget behavior by the Democrats would be felt by towns, cities and counties who had nothing to do with creating the problem.

All the years of warning the Democrats about the irresponsible fiscal behavior was coming to a head. The worst part was that there was nothing in the plan that required any type of fiscal restraint. The Democrats claimed that it contained a 2% cap on increased spending but that is hardly fiscal restraint. They were not willing to freeze spending or listen to a host of other ideas about how the fiscal crisis could be addressed without such a drastic increase in the income tax. To them, raising taxes and more revenue is always the solution. Now their attitude was simply that they had the votes, boosted by the lame ducks, and they were going to push the tax increase through.

Under normal circumstances, this proposal would never have passed. But, remember, this was not a normal circumstance. This was a *lame-duck* legislature with around a dozen members who would not be returning and likely never be held accountable by an electorate for their vote.

After a long and **very** heated floor debate, SB2505 was called for a vote. **It passed with the bare minimum of 60 votes needed. The final vote was 60-57.** Several of the yes votes necessary to get to 60 votes came from the *lame ducks*.

The often stated prediction made by Rod Blagojevich turned out to be true. The Speaker did indeed lead the charge to raise the income tax on the people of Illinois once Blagojevich was gone. And, the Speaker accomplished that task in the lamest of ways.

At the time the income tax vote was passed, the federal criminal case against Blagojevich was underway. That did not stop him from pointing out that he had stopped this type of tax increase while he was governor. He then even implied that the reason for the impeachment and the criminal accusations against him was to be out of the way so Madigan could raise taxes. There was plenty of blame to go around regarding the fact that Illinois was in a fiscal crisis. When I look back, I sincerely believe that **both** Madigan and Blagojevich played a major part in the disastrous circumstances that led to the day the Democrats used a lame-duck majority to bail them out.

Of the sixty 'yes' votes, I counted at least 7 or 8 that came from *lame ducks*. Shamefully, but not to the surprise of anyone, several of the *lame ducks* were appointed to paid State boards or commissions or became Directors of state agencies. I won't mention names, they know who they are. One of the individuals recently aired commercials and ads during the November election that they would never vote for an income tax increase. Of course, there was never any absolute proof of a quid pro quo related to these appointments and their vote. But, in several cases the individual did not have any past experience in the areas of their new position.

After the Blagojevich years, this was no way to restore faith in the Illinois government.

I was somewhat surprised that Quinn participated in such a scheme. It was fairly obvious something happened to harvest the votes needed to pass the tax increase. It was a very sad day for Illinois and the taxpayers of the state. If there is ever to be true reform of Illinois government, lame-duck sessions, after the general election is held, must contain limits on what can be voted on. Perhaps the General Assembly should be limited to **only** voting on measures that had previously been introduced before the election and revenue bills should be off-limits unless there is a true emergency agreed upon by both parties. Something needs to be done to stop the *lame-duck ploys.*

After my fifth inauguration, in January of 2011, my office **space** was now even larger, and my seniority level had increased significantly. This was in part due to the election and partially due to the lame ducks leaving to occupy new positions in State government. My license plate number went from 70 to 53. After Inauguration, I worked diligently on my legislative agenda. There was some tension during 2011 that was not as evident in 2009-10. Any goodwill had been eroded by the shameless shenanigans associated with the lame-duck income tax increase. The vote to increase the income tax was mentioned plenty during a debate that spring. Democrats, despite the income tax increase, showed no signs of slowing government spending. Dozens of proposals to increase spending on existing programs or start new programs were introduced.

I also became friends with another Representative who I quickly came to respect.

Chad Hays replaced Bill Black as State Representative to the area north of my legislative district. As I mentioned, Bill's retirement left huge shoes to fill on the House floor. That was also true in Bill's legislative district. Chad was up to the challenge. He was a former hospital administrator and brought a wealth of knowledge to the General Assembly regarding medical issues.

One of the first days Chad was in the General Assembly, a debate began about some sort of hospital medical issue. I noticed that Chad had pushed his button which signaled that he wanted to speak about the proposal. Now starting my ninth year in the General Assembly, I was one of the Representatives who were supposed to keep an eye on new Members. As I recall, this might have been Chad's first day, or second day at the most. New Members were to be discouraged from speaking. I saw the light on his desk blinking, signaling his desire to speak and I said, I am sure rather indignantly something like, "WHAT ARE YOU DOING?!"

Chad assured me he had read the legislation and he was convinced he could add some expertise to the discussion and even perhaps influence the final vote. While the debate was carrying on in the background, I asked him to tell me exactly what he intended to say. After he explained his contribution to the oratory, I agreed that his expertise could indeed be helpful. My warning was that he needed to keep his remarks short, stick to what he had recited to me and then, for heaven's sake, sit down! That is exactly what he did. His contribution to the debate was great. From that day on, Chad proved to be a terrific and effective Member of the General Assembly.

As mentioned earlier, he was also a pretty good musician. As lead singer and guitar player, Chad was a big part of the Boat Drink Caucus I described earlier. While Bill Black would be missed, Chad was a welcome addition. Bill could likely sing but I am not sure he could play the guitar. Vermilion County sent the General Assembly another winner. He retired in 2018 after only 7 ½ years in the General Assembly. During that short time, he left a positive mark on this state. Chad was definitely one of the best. Toward the end of his tenure, Chad, along with about a dozen other GOP Representatives displayed great courage and helped to end a multi-year budget impasse that was crippling Illinois.

I continued in my role as floor leader that year as well. I gained experience and felt a real comfort level with the role. I had great support. We put together a pretty effective group of GOP legislators to share the load. Mike Bost, Chapin Rose, and Dennis Reboletti were always ready to jump in if the legislation fell into their area of expertise. Patti Bellock and Mike Tryon were our experts in health care issues with Mike leading the way on environmental issues. It was a real team effort and I counted on their knowledge. It took a team to replace Bill Black. Often, I was the one who handled the closing remarks or the caucus message.

In 2011, I was fortunate enough to pass another five bills into law.

One was HB190. It became P.A. 97-0624 and added five **public** charter schools to the limited number of **public** charter schools that were allowed in the Chicago Public School System.

Notice that the big difference is that these were *public charter schools.* My belief was charter schools were meant to be provided for a specific purpose.

Charter schools, when first introduced to the United States public education scene in the early 1990s were intended to be places where education improvement ideas, reforms and policies could be incubated and tested. Then successful reforms could be replicated if the innovation was reflecting positive outcomes. In the years that followed the original purpose and theory of the public charter schools was hijacked by those wishing to funnel public money to exclusive private schools. Those private charter (or voucher) schools often bragged about higher test scores or better learning environments. Most of the time, these private charter and voucher schools operated under special rules which excluded certain student populations, especially special education students. It became a dirty secret that to get into many of the schools, the student had to be politically connected. All of this is unfortunately true.

HB190 was intended to provide specific new public charters for students identified as either dropouts or at-risk of dropping out. Innovative educational programming was designed to motivate these students to support them on the road to high school graduation. The proposal was, ironically, opposed by many of the same people who had supported a private voucher bill that I had helped defeat a year earlier. I guess they weren't that interested in establishing other options for students? Hypocrisy is an interesting dynamic.

I understand those newly established charter schools worked well and filled up quickly.

I also introduced HB192 which strengthened laws regarding no-contact orders issued by courts to protect students from other students. It became P.A. 97-0294.

The final Public Act that I sponsored which was signed into law was P.A. 97-0284.

This measure was also simple as it addressed concerns regarding special education caseloads. The fact that the final bill was simple was appropriate. I was blessed to be part of some very important and positive legislative proposals during my tenure in the General Assembly. However, most of the work I did, on a day to day basis, was of the routine variety. Working hard every day, not just on the tough or more glitzy newsworthy issues, is what public service is all about.

When George Brett, a Hall of Fame baseball player for the Kansas City Royals was asked what he wanted to have happen in his last at-bat in the major leagues, many were shocked by his answer. Most thought that he might wish for a grand slam, on a full count, in game seven of the Worlds Series. That would be quite a way to end a career. Brett's answer was much more profound. He said he wanted to be called out by half a step at first base while running as hard as he could to beat out a slow rolling ground ball to the second baseman. Reporters were puzzled by the response. Being thrown out at first base or hitting a grand slam? Brett very simply explained, "Because, that is the game." The 'game' is not defined by the highlights; it is remembered by the day to day grind.

People ask me from time to time if I miss the General Assembly. My canned response is, "I don't miss the circus, but I do miss some of the clowns." I miss the *people* and working on solutions, even across the aisle, on the policy issues and problems that face our State. I miss the constituent work the most. People need assistance to maneuver through State Government and the abundance of red tape.

HB192 was the final bill I passed because after the end of the 2011 session and before the spring session of 2012 advanced to the point that legislation could be moved, I resigned from the Illinois House to accept the position of Executive Director with the Illinois Association of School Boards.

I truly enjoyed my time in the house but an opportunity to return to an education-related position full time was something I could not decline. I was always an educator at heart and, for many months I had been looking at various ways to return to education on a full-time basis if an opportunity arose. The Hutsonville School District would be in good hands. By now, Julie Kraemer had several years' experience as an 'acting Superintendent' and was well prepared to take over. The offer to become the Executive Director of the Illinois Association of School Boards (IASB) provided me with that opportunity. The selection process took over a year.

In March **of** 2012, I resigned from my seat in the Illinois House. It was indeed bittersweet. The day before, on March 11th, I walked over to the House floor and stood in an empty Chamber, at my desk, and closed my eyes, soaking in events of the past ten years. No tears, no regrets, simply a big smile on my face. I had indeed been blessed.

Unfortunately, my resignation came just weeks before the Primary election in which I was running for State Representative in a newly formed legislative district. The map creating the region that I ran in ten years earlier was being replaced by the same process that created it. I now resided in the 110th District. I announced my intention to run about a year earlier, long before some of the opportunities in education became known and there was never a guarantee that I would be chosen as the executive Director at IASB.

The campaign for that seat had already been an ugly one up until the point I accepted the position with the School Board Association. A non-resident of the new 110th had challenged me for the seat. Along with the support of others he waged a very negative, smear filled campaign against me. My opponent's campaign was funded by wealthy Chicago area interests who were still holding a grudge against me due to my lack of support for the aforementioned private voucher bill that went down to defeat. This was the threat of retribution he had long ago promised.

The only poll taken during the primary showed I held a huge margin over the field of three contenders. As I remember, I was ahead 52-9 in the only poll that was conducted. The poll was conducted by the Illinois Manufacturers Association a few weeks before the scheduled date of the primary. There is no doubt in my mind that I would have been easily elected in the new legislative district.

The timing was not great, in fact, it was terrible. But, I filed the proper paperwork with the Secretary of State to have my candidacy suspended. Any votes in my favor would not count. Signs were placed at polling places informing voters to not vote for me.

There was no doubt in my mind that the hateful dirty attacks against me would have continued in the future. The people that attacked me continued the negative attacks for several months after I accepted the position of Executive Director at IASB. Even after a couple of years, as a private citizen, there were cheap shots and articles written attacking me for, I guess, my success? I don't understand that type of hatred. Once in a while, even now, over ten years later, their hatred is stoked by something and one of the minions in this angry group will take a swipe at me.

Recently in the spring of 2020, I was asked to endorse a candidate for the State Senate. I got to know and like the candidate and agreed to endorse him and record a radio ad for him. I agreed to endorse him only if the ad was not a negative ad aimed at this opponent.

The Senate candidate I endorsed had no desire to run such a negative ad, so the endorsement ad ran. The response from the opponent and his supporters was to produce and run negative radio attack ads against me personally, even though I was obviously not on the ballot.

A political organization designed to allow candidates to hide campaign funds for use without directly associating their name with the negative ad paid for the negative ads. The Senate candidate who was opposing the candidate I endorsed helped to fund that organization with sizeable contributions. It was a cowardly move. As the old saying goes, follow the money. To many, it appears the haters are still concerned about the possibility of me having political success in the future.

I doubt the grudge over the voucher vote will ever end. I am mostly amused by it. My family and many of my friends get very upset by these attacks though. It is most unfair to them. I just remind them that, *"Haters Gonna Hate."* My advice is to not waste any time or emotion on these people. It is like the old saying goes- if you get in the mud with a pig, both get dirty, but the pig enjoys it.

The position of Executive Director allowed me to continue to work on statewide issues that would improve public education. The staff there was one of the best groups of people I have ever worked with. The Directors of the other Associations working and advocating for public education were great to work with. Dr. Brent Clark at the Illinois Association of School Administrators (IASA); Dr. Michael Jacoby at the Illinois Association of School Business Officials (IASBO); and Dr. Jason Leahy at the Illinois Principal's Association (IPA) are all hard-working champions for children and public education.

Together, after Dr. Clark initiated an attempt to highlight the direction public education should move in the future, the four Associations worked in unison to develop one of the most successful public education advocacy movements in the nation. Vision 2020 became the blueprint for the future direction of public education in Illinois. Instead of describing what our Associations and Members were opposed to, we developed a clear message as to what we were in favor of. Of course, we still pointed out that were opposed to unfunded mandates.

It also contained the initial recommendation about what eventually resulted in a new, more equitable funding formula in Illinois. The Evidence-Based Funding Formula was originally part of the Vision 2020 blueprint.

(Vision 2020 was used as a Blueprint to fulfill the promise of public education in Illinois)

The success of Vision 2020 and my time at IASB were certainly major highlights of my almost 38 years in public education. While leaving the General Assembly was difficult, returning to my roots and working in public education was the right decision.

I retired from IASB in July of 2018. That makes me a retired Superintendent, Representative, and Executive Director. Since retirement I have stayed busy with my wife and family. No big surprise that I especially enjoy being able to spend time with my grandchildren. Bella, Jenna, Presley, Lewis and Myah have brought so much joy and happiness to our lives. Plus, we just learned we will soon be blessed with grandchild number six in the fall of 2020. With five **married** children: Matt, Lisa, Brenda, Beth, and Jessica, it is difficult to estimate the final tally of grandchildren. Life is indeed good and I can guarantee you that no attempts to ruin my joy from, "The Haters", will ever cause me any concerns.

While I am enjoying retirement, the fact is some people fail at retirement or get a low grade. After a year off and not doing **much** but golf and yard work, I returned to do some work in public education. I resurrected a mentoring and induction program for new teachers at the request of a local Regional Superintendent, Monte Newlin. As a by-product, to better understand what the classroom of 2020 is like, I began to substitute teach. My return to the classroom has been enlightening for sure. The joy of teaching and seeing a student learn is still a thrill.

At this point, as a former teacher, I would give myself a solid C- in retirement. There is always another chapter to be written and I have always believed **the best is yet to come.**

Chapter Nineteen
Epilogue- He's Baaaaack!

This book was originally designed to end with a few lines about my retirement from the General Assembly, a couple of highlights about my time at IASB, retirement and the future. When I started writing this book, in January of 2020, it was at the urging of friends who thought that a story involving the Impeachment of Rod Blagojevich would be interesting, especially during the time that Donald Trump was being impeached. Many also were interested in how campaigns work and wanted some insights into how the General Assembly operates. That was the goal.

As I have already suggested, my opinion is **that** the two impeachments were not at all similar.

The impeachment of Blagojevich was bi-partisan. The evidence was overwhelming and rose to an enormous level of severity and displayed a continual pattern of repeated illicit behavior which met all standards necessary to impeach. The Trump impeachment, many suggested and believed, contained evidence of wrong-doing by the President. I am not convinced that a single quid pro quo ever took place concerning the most serious charges brought against Trump.

What is an **undeniable fact** is that the Trump impeachment was a completely partisan undertaking. There was ample evidence that the purely political impeachment scheme hatched against Trump started in the days after he was elected and even before he took office. Not one single Republican voted to impeach Trump while several Congressional Democrats voted against impeachment in the Trump case.

The vote against Blagojevich was nearly unanimous, except for the vote of Blagojevich's sister-in-law, Debbie Mell. The impeachment votes in the Illinois House were 114 yes and 1 present (Mell) in the 95th General Assembly and 117-1 (again a nay from Debbie Mell) in the 96th General Assembly.

The impeachment of Blagojevich was bi-partisan and not political in the sense of party politics. That fact is indisputable. Even so, I have heard some try to say that the Trump impeachment was not at all politically motivated. I am concerned about those who truly believe what they are saying.

There was no way to know that while I was writing this book that the very same Donald Trump who was being impeached was going to use his constitutional authority as President to commute the prison sentence of Blagojevich. But that is exactly what happened. First, let's make sure it is understood that Trump *commuted* the prison sentence of Rod Blagojevich. He did NOT pardon Rod Blagojevich. Those are two completely different things. I have, unfortunately, heard this misreported several times. As I previously mentioned, we live in a world of fake news.

This is just one example of very poor reporting regarding the Blagojevich early release.

A commutation is a form of clemency that reduces the punishment for a crime. In this case, it was a reduction in the prison sentence from 14 to around 8 years, which is the amount of time Blagojevich served. A *pardon,* on the other hand, is an action the President can take which would have completely set aside the conviction and sentence. If a pardon would have been granted, Blagojevich's federal prosecution and a felony conviction would have been completely removed. He is still a convicted felon. If a pardon would have been granted, he would not be considered a felon.

United States Presidents, throughout history, have used clemency powers as granted in the U.S. Constitution (*Article 2- Section 1*) to either pardon or reduce the sentences of thousands of people.

During his time in office, President Obama used **it** 1,937 times, including 1715 commutations and 212 pardons. When he left office, there were around 11,000 petitions for commutation still pending. Perhaps the most controversial commutation granted by Obama was of Chelsea Manning. Manning was the person convicted of providing confidential U.S. military secrets to Wikileaks. She was sentenced to 35 years in federal prison and President Obama reduced the sentence to time served, about 7 years, and she was released in May of 2017. The other commutation made by Obama which was well-publicized came during his last week as President when he commuted the sentence of Oscar Lopez Riviera. Riviera, a Cuban Nationalist, was convicted of playing a role in bombings in U.S. cities. He claimed to be a political prisoner. Obama decided to reduce his 55-year sentence to time served. By the way, Obama also commuted the sentence of one of my favorite baseball players, Willie McCovey. McCovey had been sentenced to two years of probation for failing to pay income he earned on the sale of sports memorabilia.

In my lifetime, perhaps the most controversial pardon that I can remember was the pardon of former President Richard Nixon. Nixon resigned the Presidency amid the likelihood of impeachment in 1974. Vice-president Gerald Ford replaced Nixon and about a month into his time as President, Ford pardoned Nixon. Nixon had not yet even been charged with a crime. The political fallout from this move was a contributing factor in Ford's loss in 1976 to Georgia peanut farmer Jimmy Carter.

Donald Trump had already created controversy as far as the use of his pardon and clemency powers shortly after he took office when he pardoned Lewis 'Scooter' Libby in 2018. Libby, once the Chief of Staff to former Vice-President Dick Chaney, was sentenced to 30 months in prison and fined $250K for perjury and obstruction of justice.

Toward the end of George Bush's term as President, Cheney reportedly asked Bush to pardon Libby. Bush, while refusing to grant a pardon did commute the prison sentence. He did not reduce the $250K fine even though he did have that authority. Trump completely pardoned Libby in 2018 claiming that while he did not know Libby, he felt he had been treated unfairly. The fine and the felony conviction **were** removed with the pardon.

In another controversial pardon, Trump pardoned Joe Arpaio. Arpaio was the nationally known, hard-line sheriff of Maricopa County, Arizona for 24 years.

He was famous for detaining prisoners in 'tent city jails' and forcing them to wear pink underwear. He was found in contempt of court in July of 2016 for refusing to follow the order of a federal judge to stop such practices that the court **deemed as** racial profiling. The Contempt of Court citation could carry up to a six-month prison sentence. He was due to be sentenced in October of 2016. Delays pushed the sentencing into the next year and Trump pardoned him in early 2017. It was Trump's first use of the power to pardon.

These cases remind us that throughout history, even recent history, Presidents have granted thousands of pardons. While historical events and other factors have affected the number of pardons individual

Presidents have granted. Here is a list of the number of **pardons, (does not include commutations)** that some past Presidents have granted:

Franklin Delano Roosevelt- 2,819
Harry S. Truman- 1,913
Dwight D. Eisenhower- 1,110
Woodrow Wilson- 1,087
Lyndon Johnson- 960
Richard Nixon- 863
Calvin Coolidge- 773
Herbert Hoover- 672
Theodore Roosevelt- 668
Jimmy Carter- 534
John F. Kennedy- 472
Wiliam Jefferson Clinton- 396
Ronald Reagan- 393
William H. Taft- 383
Gerald Ford- 382
Warren Harding- 386
William McKinley- 291
Barack Obama- 212

Keep in mind that these are only pardons granted and these numbers do not include commutations such as the one granted to Blagojevich. Very early in his Presidency, it became clear that Trump was not shy about using his Presidential powers related to pardoning and leniency. In a short time, with the actions he had taken related to 'Scooter' Libby and Sheriff Joe Arpaio, Trump had already made two of the more controversial moves ever made by a President regarding these powers.

Why did Trump decide to commute the sentence of Blagojevich? According to Trump, he had been considering the move since 2018. The request for leniency made by Blagojevich lawyers was left over from the Obama era. When the request was made, it was well known that Obama wasn't going to touch it. When Trump became President, the lobbying of Trump for leniency began.

But, how did it happen?

The effort was led by Blagojevich's wife, Patti and a Chicago-based political consultant named Mark Vargas. Vargas had actually once worked for Blagojevich's political opponents in Illinois during the time

Rod was Governor. It is odd where support sometimes comes from. Vargas was also once an intern for former U.S. Congressman and later Speaker of the United States Congress, Dennis Hastert. Vargas apparently first made contact with Patti Blagojevich via LinkedIn and offered his assistance. At the time, it is reported that Patti Blagojevich was skeptical that Vargas could do any good. But she decided there was no other momentum and agreed to work with Vargas.

In a March 18th, 2020 article published in the Wall Street Journal, Vargas is quoted as saying, "I told Patti that if this has any shot at working, it is going to take a Republican with Chicago roots." He then went on to say, that it needed to be someone, "Who can figure out a way to get on the President's radar. I told her. I think I'm that guy." In May of 2018, Vargas published an article in the *Washington Examiner* entitled, "How Robert Mueller and James Comey's Best Friend Sent Rod Blagojevich to Prison." Of course the title of the story referred to the, "best friend", and lead prosecutor in Blagojevich's federal court case, Patrick Fitzgerald.

The article in the *Washington Examiner*, along with other tactical measures got the attention of the White House. Trump does not like Comey or Mueller and since Fitzgerald was being tied to them, the link was critical. The effort to discredit Fitzgerald and the prosecution of Blagojevich was full throttle. After some nudging, the article also got the attention of folks at Fox News. Vargas was soon in direct communication with Jared Kushner, President Trump's son-in-law.

Vargas was also instrumental in getting Patti Blagojevich onto Fox News Channel shows.

Trump is known to tune in to Fox News regularly. The movement to free Blagojevich seemed to have some real momentum.

Then in June of 2018, Congressional Republicans from Illinois got wind that the President was considering some type of leniency and strongly objected to any thought of such a thing. The seven GOP Members of Congress signed a joint letter to the President stating their objection. Portions of the letter include these strong words, "The integrity of our democracy and the core of American values depend on our elected officials being honest…"

More from the letter, "It's important that we take a strong stand against pay-to-play politics, especially in Illinois, where four of our last eight governors have gone to federal prison for public corruption." All seven of the Illinois Congressional delegation signed the letter, including

Congressman Mike Bost. Congressman Bost and I had served on the Special Investigative Committee together in the Illinois House. Bost, now a Member of the U.S. Congress knew the details perhaps as well, or better than anyone.

It seemed for a while that the President cooled on the notion of any leniency after receiving this letter from the Illinois delegation to Congress.

However, Vargas continued to work the plea for leniency. According to media reports, he requested assistance from other political heavy hitters like Rudy Giuliani and Alan Dershowitz. Giuliani is Trump's personal lawyer and Dershowitz a legal advisor to Trump.

Dershowitz is a well-known Constitutional scholar, Harvard law professor, and self-proclaimed Democrat. He was instrumental as one member of the Counsel defending President Trump during the recent U.S. Senate trial after the impeachment of Trump. Dershowitz railed for days against the impeachment case and Trump was, as everyone knows, acquitted by the Senate.

There is also much more to the connection between Fitzgerald and the FBI's Washington DC upper echelon that likely caught Trump's attention. Fitzgerald is also referred to in emails between Peter Strzok and Lisa Page which were released by the federal government in January of 2020 after being declassified. Those emails seem to suggest that Fitzgerald is some sort of 'fixer.' Page and Strzok brought Fitzgerald up in one email dated March 18th, 2016 while the two were discussing how best to deal with a problem someone at the FBI was having.

The following is a portion of the released, redacted email transcript:

Inbox:	"Thought of the perfect person D can bounce this off of"
Outbox:	"Who?"
Inbox:	"Pat…you gotta give me credit if we go with him…and delay briefing him on until I can get back next week to do it. Late next week or later."
Outbox:	"We talked about him last night, not for this, but how great he is. He's in private practice though, right? Suppose you could still bring him back. And yes, I'll hold."
Inbox:	"Yes, he's at Skadden in Chicago. I haven't talked to him for a year or two. Don't forget that Dag Comey appointed

	him as special counsel in the Plame matter, and that he
	was there for Comey's investiture."
Inbox:	"I could work with him again...and damn we'd get sh*t
	DONE"
Outbox:	"I now. Like I said, we discussed boss and him
	yesterday."

Fitzgerald is still known and appreciated by the FBI. He certainly waited a long time to bring charges against Blagojevich, especially during the time Obama was a candidate for President. There is information still emerging which suggests that during the Blagojevich years Obama may have benefitted from the investigations of Blagojevich. The evidence is clear that Blagojevich was the target of federal investigations for a valid reason. It is interesting how there are so many overlapping pieces.

These types of connections were sure to get the attention of President Trump. This was all happening after the Mueller report and the investigation of Trump and the "Russia, Russia, Russia" allegations leading up to and including the time Trump was being impeached.

Many believe the connection between the Reverend Jesse Jackson and Trump helped.

Jackson, after reportedly being approached by Vargas, apparently encouraged Trump to look at the Blagojevich case again and consider leniency. Between all of the encouragement, the possible connection of Fitzgerald to Comey's FBI inner circle and other factors, Trump reconsidered his position on the Blagojevich matter. He eventually decided to look at the case one more time despite all objections and on February 18th, 2020, shortly after Trump was acquitted of the impeachment charges by the United States Senate on February 5th, Trump commuted the sentence of Blagojevich. Rod was a free man after serving eight years of his fourteen-year sentence.

The announcement was met with emotions ranging from disappointment to outrage among those who felt that Blagojevich was set free too soon. Interestingly, several public opinion polls were taken both nationally, and in Illinois revealed that almost half surveyed felt that Blagojevich had served enough time and the action by Trump was warranted. Many pointed to lighter sentences for more serious crimes and others believed from the beginning that the punishment did not fit the crime. Others began to question the connection to the Blagojevich federal case to Comey's FBI connection. And some simply thought the original sentence was too long. When I first heard of the fourteen-year sentence back in 2012, I do remember thinking something like, "Wow that is a long sentence." Did I think it was too long? Not really at the time. Of course, I had lived the Blagojevich years as a Member of the House and had been privy to lots of information about the entirety of the corruption charges due to the knowledge I gained during the time serving on the Special Investigative Committee. It was difficult for me to have a completely unbiased opinion.

Everyone has their own opinion about the commutation. Some still refer to Trump's action as a pardon when describing Blagojevich being set free. I wish people would get their facts straight. As stated earlier, that is not true, he is still a convicted felon and he is not eligible to hold state office in Illinois again based on the Illinois Senate Trial and conviction. Whether or not eight years in prison is enough punishment for the conviction is up for debate. What is not up for debate is the outcome or the authority Trump has to issue the action.

The President holds the Constitutional power to do exactly what he did, like it or not.

Was the reason Trump eventually commuted the sentence a jab at Comey and Mueller?

Maybe that was part of it, only Trump knows what part that played in the action. His personal experiences with both men did not give him much confidence in their capabilities. The Mueller report, in Trump's opinion, was full of political rhetoric and false accusations. Perhaps those appealing to Trump on Blagojevich's behalf struck that chord. Trump did mention the names of both Mueller and Comey in comments related to his decision. He also specifically mentioned Patrick Fitzgerald in his remarks. Fitzgerald was the lead prosecutor in the criminal case against Blagojevich. There is much more to be investigated and written about the entire episode.

I do believe that Trump was struck by the fact the Blagojevich family, including wife Patti and his two daughters, Amy and Annie also suffered. And, I think he took that into account when considering the totality of punishment. Amy graduated from Northwestern University in 2018 and now holds a Master's Degree in marketing from the University of Edinburgh. She was around 15 years of age when Blagojevich began serving his sentence. Annie is now 16 years old and has a driver's license. Blagojevich missed some important time with his family that he will never get back. As the father of five children, that strikes a chord with me.

What has been the tone taken by Blagojevich since his release? I could best describe it as defiant. No question his old style is still present. He continues to claim his innocence and lashes out at the, "corrupt legal system," that wrongly convicted him. Federal prosecutor Patrick Fitzgerald is the target of much of Rod's criticism of the justice system. Blagojevich vows to work hard now to reform that corrupt system. Perhaps his efforts will reveal even more about the investigation and his federal trial. One thing is for certain, he is likely to continue to discuss it all in a very public way.

Blagojevich also claims that what happened to him ten years ago has nothing to do with the continued fiscal problems facing Illinois today. Recently, he began to talk about how current Illinois Governor J.B. Pritzker spent millions to become governor and just before Election Day wrote a $7 million to the campaign fund of Michael Madigan. "Think about this, $7 million from J.B. to Mike Madigan's campaign coffers to get Madigan to support him for Governor, and frankly to pass his legislative agenda. Madigan is holding him up for that campaign money, similar to what he does, what he tried to do with me", said Blagojevich. He also claims Madigan asked him for $2.5 million in campaign money back in 2006. He claims the fact that he did not comply with this request resulted in the impeachment. Perhaps, but the handcuffs also convinced Madigan to finally take action.

Blagojevich also had several conversations with current Illinois Governor JB Pritzker in December of 2008 during the time in which he was contemplating who to appoint to the U.S. Senate seat left vacant when Obama was elected President. Pritzker is heard on tape discussing the Senate appointment with Blagojevich. He also discussed being named Attorney General if by some chance Lisa Madigan was named to the U.S. Senate. Based on Blagojevich's relationship with Lisa Madigan's father, Michael Madigan, her appointment was a long shot at best.

That fact did not stop Pritzker and Blagojevich from discussing the possibility. There might be more to conversations between Blagojevich and Pritzker. Blagojevich likes to talk so we might find out more.

It is somewhat concerning that Pritzker, another billionaire, spent $171 million of his own money to become Illinois' Governor. Bruce Rauner, who preceded Pritzker as Governor of Illinois, also spent over $100 million to get elected. When the two faced each other in 2018, all records were broken and over a quarter of a million dollars was spent. It almost seems like the Governor's mansion in Illinois will be occupied by the highest bidder in the future. How can anyone, short of being another billionaire, compete?

Since his release from prison, Blagojevich's comments aimed at Madigan continue to be harsh. Recently, he described Madigan this way: "He's the wizard of Oz.....He's a guy that once you move the curtain back, he ain't so tough. But, he's a sneaky little guy. And he's been there for 100 years. And he controls all the apparatus of government. And he's got a bunch of lemmings, Democrat state reps, who talk a big game when they're back home. And as soon as they get back to Springfield, they forget about all that and they take their marching orders from Madigan."

In a radio appearance after his release, he described the House Committee appointment system this way: "When I left for prison...virtually every one of those lawmakers were on a committee...and they all get paid extra money. You get an extra $10,000...and if you don't go along with Madigan, you're not on that committee. He controls them that way. He controls the ability to call a bill. And these lawmakers allow him to have control. They've abdicated to him." The $10K figure is not accurate by the way. Committee chairs do receive an additional stipend but it is considerably less than $10K. But, hey, this is Blagojevich talking and he has been known to be slightly off in his some of his comments.

I have described, in detail in this book the House Committee system flaws as well as many other House Rules that are definitely NOT democratic in nature. Changes are needed and any assistance from Blagojevich to expose the flaws is welcome. One man has way too much power.

In another public statement, Blagojevich was quoted by popular talk show host Mancow, as saying, "The heart of the question you should ask J.B. is if the feds applied the same standard used against me, and I got 14 years for a $25K campaign contribution. OK, that I didn't cross a line-how would he stay out of prison for giving Madigan $7 million to move his legislative agenda?"

The responses to reporters from Blagojevich and the comments are often rambling in nature and sometimes do not make complete sense. He did a nice job in his remarks at a press conference outside of his home the day after his release. His tone was not as caustic and he seemed thankful although never admitting that he had done anything wrong.

His post-prison comments and sentiment are crystal clear and he has nothing to lose. Do not be surprised at anything he says or does. The story of Rod Blagojevich, the man who now refers to himself as a, "Trumpocrat," rather than a Democrat, will likely have many more chapters. Someone might even decide to write a book about him and his story!

As I write these final words and finish this chronicle, the entire world is battling a raging and deadly pandemic. Travel restrictions are being enforced throughout the world and some states and cities in the United States are being locked down. It is ironic that the man who is finally free after eight years, still living in Chicago, has his newfound freedoms stifled.

My seat is no longer in the front row of a Special Investigative Committee of the Illinois House, nor from any House Committee, or on the House floor. I now watch from a different seat, as a private citizen, in front of my television. From this seat, I have had a chance to reflect on a very interesting time in the General Assembly, much of it spent with one of the more colorful and controversial Governors in the history of Illinois and the nation. One thing will be constant; the entertaining, interesting and ever-evolving saga of Rod Blagojevich. Stay tuned!

Bill Ollendorf was a professional artist for decades and passed away in 1996. These sketches, of the homes of the *Sons of Illinois*, were commissioned by former Illinois Governor James Thompson in the 1980's in honor of Ronald Reagan. Reagan was visiting his home State of Illinois while President of the United States. It is possible that if Ollendorf were still around today, there would also be a sketch of Barack Obama's Illinois home. The sketches were given to Jack Morris as a gift by Governor Thompson and reflect some of the great leaders that have come out of Illinois. Not all of our politicians were sent to prison and only one has been impeached!

Lincoln's Home- Built in 1839 and purchased by Lincoln in 1844. It is the only home Lincoln, our 16th President ever owned. It is a national historic site in Springfield, IL. Lincoln was born in Kentucky before moving to Illinois via Indiana.

Grant's Home- Built in 1857. This home was purchased by Grant, our 18th President, in 1865. He lived there until 1881 and the family owned the home until 1904 when it was given to the city of Galena. It is a national historic site.

Reagan's Home. Ronald Reagan, our 40th President, lived there from 1920-1924. The home, located in Dixon, IL is a national historic Site.

The Governor's mansion in Springfield, IL, built between the time period 1853-55 was the home of Governor Jim Thompson when these sketches were made.

About the Author

Roger Eddy is a retired school superintendent, former Executive Director of the Illinois Association of School Boards, and five-term State Representative. He resides in rural Hutsonville with his wife, Becca. They have five children and five grandchildren, with their six grandchild due to arrive in October of 2020. Since retiring in July of 2018, he has developed and facilitated a new teacher mentoring program and returned to the classroom as a substitute teacher.